HOW TO UNDERSTAND STATUTES AND BY-LAWS

by

DONALD J. GIFFORD
B.A. (Hons), LL.B. (Hons), Ph.D. (Cantab.)

KENNETH H. GIFFORD
Q.C., LL.B.

MICHAEL I. JEFFERY
B.A., LL.B., LL.M., Q.C.

CARSWELL
Thomson Professional Publishing

The publisher is not engaged in rendering legal, accounting or other professional advice. If legal advice or other expert assistance is required, the services of a competent professional should be sought. The analysis contained herein represents the opinions of the authors and should in no way be construed as being either official or unofficial policy of any governmental body.

Canadian Cataloguing in Publication Data

Gifford, D.J. (Donald James)
 How to understand statutes and by-laws

Includes bibliographical references and index.
ISBN 0-459-55321-6

1. Law – Canada – Interpretation and construction.
2. By-laws – Canada – Interpretation and
construction. I. Gifford, Kenneth H. (Kenneth
Harril), 1923- . II. Jeffery, Michael I.
(Michael Irwin), 1942- . II. Title.

KE482.S84G54 1995   349.71   C95-932169-1
KF425.G54 1995

The paper used in this publication meets the minimum requirements of American National Standard for Information Sciences –Permanence of Paper for Printed Library Materials, ANSI Z39.48-1984.

CARSWELL
Thomson Professional Publishing

One Corporate Plaza, 2075 Kennedy Road, Scarborough, Ontario M1T 3V4
Customer Service:
Toronto 1-416-609-3800
Elsewhere in Canada/U.S. 1-800-387-5164
Fax 1-416-298-5094

Preface

There is a very real need today for people to know how to approach an understanding of the numerous Acts of Parliament and other forms of legislation that affect so many aspects of their daily lives. The age in which we live is an age of governmental control. That control has extended into every walk of life. For all of us there is legislation of one type or another that affects the things we can do and controls how we can do them. From the breadcarter to the manufacturer, from the sales staff to the secretary of a corporation, there are Acts of Parliament, bylaws and regulations and other forms of subordinate legislation, that must be complied with if penalties are to be avoided.

There was a time when only the lawyer had to know how to understand an Act of Parliament. That time has long since passed. Today there are many walks of life in which the knowledge of how to understand an Act of Parliament is essential. In the professional field the accountant, the architect, the engineer, the appraiser, the chief executive of a hospital or a geriatric complex, and the townplanner must have a good working knowledge of the special rules that govern the reading of legislation; they must know how to understand legislation and how to use it. In the commercial field this knowledge is of growing importance for the landlord, the chief executive, the manager, the developer and the builder. In the field of government this knowledge is perhaps most important of all—and it is of importance not merely for those in the public service as such but for those also in government agencies and local authorities.

An Act of Parliament is not something that can be read like a book. That is not just because the Act of Parliament is heavier reading, as indeed it usually is, but because over the years the law has developed special rules that govern the reading of the Act of Parliament. Every Act of Parliament must be read in the light of those rules, and the person who attempts to read an Act of Parliament, without a working knowledge of the more important rules of interpretation, may fall into error. That error may be expensive.

These special rules are rules that have been laid down by the Supreme Court of Canada, the Federal Court of Canada, the Exchequer Court of Canada, the Supreme Courts and Courts of Appeal of the Provinces and the Northwest Territories, and Cour d'appel and Cour supérieure du Québec. In this book, therefore, we have drawn upon the decisions of the Supreme Court and Federal Court of Canada and the decisions of the courts of superior court status. In addition to the Canadian decisions, courts throughout Canada also have regard to decisions of the comparable courts in England and accordingly, in respect of the comparatively few points on which there is no Canadian decision, we have drawn upon the English decisions.

The rules which govern the reading and interpretation of an Act of Parliament also govern the reading and understanding of legislation in all the other forms that legislation takes today. They govern the reading and understanding of the maze of subordinate legislation, whether made by central or local government or by other statutory authorities. Such subordinate legislation is made today in growing profusion in the administration of an increasing number of statutes.

The object of this book is to explain the more important of the rules that govern the reading and understanding of legislation, and to do so as far as possible in ordinary, everyday language. The reader who studies and understands those rules will gain more from the reading of legislation, whether it is reading an Act of Parliament or any other form of legislation. The reader will not, however, become an expert in the science of interpreting legislation, and must therefore expect to have to turn to members of the legal profession for help in solving the many complications that arise in the course of modern legislation. The more legislation grows, the greater is the service which the legal profession can, and does, give to the community through its interpretation of the legislation and through its unravelling of the tangled legislative knot.

D.J. GIFFORD
KENNETH H. GIFFORD
M.I. JEFFERY

Table of Contents

Preface iii

Table of Cases xv

Chapter 1   HOW AN ACT OF PARLIAMENT IS MADE

What an Act of Parliament Is 1

How an Act of Parliament Begins 1

How the Act of Parliament is Prepared 4

How the Act is Considered in Parliament 5

How the Act of Parliament comes into force ... 6

Acts Obtained by Fraud 7

Chapter 2   THE SPECIAL RULES FOR UNDERSTANDING ACTS OF PARLIAMENT

Ambiguity in Acts of Parliament 9

Judges' criticisms of the drafting of Acts of Parliament 9

Legislation by reference 11

The Need for Special Rules for the Reading of Acts of Parliament 13

Chapter 3   THE ELEMENTS OF AN ACT OF PARLIAMENT

Introduction 15

The elements of an Act of Parliament 15

Chapter 4   THE REGNAL YEARS

The Regnal Year 17

Chapter 5   THE NUMBER OF THE ACT

The Nature of the Number 19

The form of the number 19

The effect of the number 20

Chapter 6   THE LONG TITLE OF THE ACT

The Form of the Long Title 23

The Long Title as Part of the Act 23

Using the Long Title to Find the Meaning of the Act 24

Chapter 7   THE ENACTING WORDS

The Use of Enacting Words 27

The Effect of the Enacting Words 27

Chapter 8   THE SHORT TITLE

The Nature of the Short Title 29

The Place Where the Short Title is to be Found ... 29

The Use of the Short Title 29

The Legal Effect of a Short Title 29

Chapter 9   WHEN AN ACT COMES INTO FORCE
The Date on the Act of Parliament 33
What the Date on the Act of Parliament Means ... .33
The Date on Which the Act Comes into Force 33
Bringing the Act into Force on a Later Day 35
Treating an Act as Having Been in Force from a
Day Before the Date on Which It Was Passed 36
The Effect of a General Revision of the Acts of
Parliament 36
Continuance in Force 36

Chapter 10   THE PREAMBLE
An Alternative Name 37
The Nature of the Preamble 37
The Form of a Preamble 37
The Preamble as Part of the Act of Parliament 38
The Preamble When the Meaning of the Act is
Clear 38
The Use of the Preamble to Find the Meaning of a
Section 39

Chapter 11   THE PURPOSES SECTION OF AN ACT
What the Purposes Section of an Act Is 41
The Purposes Section is Part of the Act 41
Where to Find the Purposes Section 42
How to Use the Purposes Section 42
Traps to Using the Purposes Section 42

Chapter 12   THE ANALYSIS
Other Names for the Analysis 45
The Nature of the Analysis 45
The Use of the Analysis 47
The Effect of the Analysis 47

Chapter 13   SECTIONS, SUBSECTIONS AND PARAGRAPHS
Sections 49
Subsections 49
Paragraphs 50
The effect of the setting out of the Act in
numbered sections, subsections, and
paragraphs 50
Conflicting Sections in the One Act 51
The Way in Which Sections, Subsections,
Paragraphs and Subparagraphs are Referred to 51

Chapter 14   PARTS AND DIVISIONS
The Nature of Parts and Divisions 53
The Effect of Dividing an Act into Parts and
Divisions 54

Chapter 15   HEADINGS
The Nature of Headings 55
The Form of Headings 55
The Use of Headings 55
The Effect of Headings When the Meaning
Is Clear 57
The Effect of Headings When the Meaning of a
Section Is Not Plain 57
The Effect of a Heading When there is only one
Section Under It 58

Chapter 16   MARGINAL NOTES
The Nature of Marginal Notes................... 59
The Form of a Marginal Note 59
Parliament and the Marginal Notes 60
The Dangers of Marginal Notes................. 60
The Problem as to Whether Marginal Notes can be
Used to Find the Meaning of an Act 60
The Value of Marginal Notes................... 61
An Alternative System 61
References to Former Enactments 62

Chapter 17   DEFINITIONS
The Need for Definitions 63
The Definitions Section 64
The Effect of Definitions in an Act of Parliament . 65
Definitions Which Use "Mean" or "Include" or
Both.. 66
    Definitions in other Acts 68
Dictionary Definitions and Technical Terms 69

Chapter 18   SCHEDULES
The Nature of a Schedule
Ascertaining the Status of a Schedule............ 73
Conflict Between a Section of an Act and a
Schedule to that Act........................... 73
Conflict Between a Preamble to an Act and a
Schedule Referred to in that Act 73
The Use of Scheduled Forms 74

Chapter 19   PROVISOS
The Nature of a Proviso 75
The Form of a Proviso 75
The Effect of a Proviso........................ 75
Proviso Inserted Unnecessarily 76

Chapter 20   PUNCTUATION
Acts of Parliament Passed Before 1850 77
Punctuation in Acts of Parliament Passed in 1850
or Later 77

Chapter 21   THE MEANING OF WORDS NOT DEFINED IN THE ACT
The Difficulty of Finding the Meaning
of Words 79
Where Possible, a Word Is to be Given
a Constant Meaning Throughout the Act 79
Words in an Act of Parliament have the Meaning
Which They Bore at the Date
When the Act was Passed 80
Dictionary Definitions 81
Technical Terms and Legal Terms............... 81

Chapter 22   THE DIFFERENCE BETWEEN THE GENERAL
RULES AND THE SPECIFIC RULES
The General Rules 83
Conflicts Between the General and the Specific
Rules 83

Chapter 23   THE PLAIN MEANING RULE
The Names by Which the Plain Meaning Rule
Is Known 85
The Effect of the Plain Meaning Rule 85
The Importance of the Plain Meaning Rule 87
The Plain Meaning Rule Cannot Apply if the
Meaning is not Plain 87

Chapter 24   MANIFEST ABSURDITY AND INJUSTICE ARE TO BE
AVOIDED
The Nature of the Rule 89
A Warning about the Rule 91

Chapter 25   THE MISCHIEF RULE
The Nature of the Rule 93
The State of the Law Before the Act
was Passed 94
The Mischief or Defect 94
Ascertaining the Mischief or Defect 95
The Remedy Parliament has Appointed 95
The Reason for the Remedy 95
Applying the Rule............................. 96
The Mischief Cannot Limit the Meaning
of Plain Words 96

Chapter 26   THE PURPOSE OF THE ACT OF PARLIAMENT
A Section Specifying the Purposes of the Act 97
The Act Is to be Interpreted According to Its
Object and Intent 97
The Parliamentary Intent Should Be Effectuated,
Not Defeated 98
The Meaning of ''Intention'' in this Context 99
When the Purposive Approach is Unavailable 100

Finding the Intention by Necessary Implication 102
Caution Must be Exercised in Interpreting by
Intention 103

Chapter 27   HANSARD
The Nature of Hansard 105
Can Hansard Be Used at Common Law in the
Interpretation of an Act? 105
Why the Common Law Limits the Use of Hansard
to Find the Meaning of an Act of Parliament 106
Common Law Does Not Use the History of a Bill
Before Parliament to Interpret the Act 107

Chapter 28   USING OTHER MATERIAL FROM OUTSIDE AN ACT TO
UNDERSTAND THE MEANING OF THAT ACT
The Use of Extrinsic Materials to Interpret an Act . 109
Surrounding Circumstances.................... 109
Reports by Law Reform Commissions 109
Reports by Royal Commissions and Boards or
Committees of Inquiry......................... 110
Parliamentary Committee Reports............... 111
Drafter's Reports 111
Miscellaneous Reports 111
Explanations by Government Departments 111
Subordinate legislation 112

Chapter 29   THE ACT MUST BE READ AS A WHOLE
Words Must Be Read in the Light of the
Section as a Whole........................... 113
A Section Must Be Read in the Light of the Act
as a Whole................................... 114
Limits to the Use of this Rule 116

Chapter 30   EFFECT MUST BE GIVEN TO THE WHOLE ACT
Words Should Not be Discarded 117
Sense Should Be Made of a Provision
if Possible................................... 117
Repetition and Surplusage..................... 118
A warning to be regarded 119

Chapter 31   OMISSIONS FROM THE ACT
The Rule as to Things Left Out of the Act........ 121
Implied Terms 122

Chapter 32   MISTAKES IN AN ACT OF PARLIAMENT
Common Causes of Mistakes in Acts of
Parliament 125
The Effect of a Mistake as to the Law 126
The Effect of a Mistake as to Policy 127
The Effect of a Drafter's Oversight 127
Misprints.................................... 128

The Extent to Which the Courts Will
Correct Mistakes in Acts of Parliament 129

Chapter 33   THE CLASS RULE
The Nature of the Class Rule 131
There Must Be a General Word 133
The General Word Must Follow After a Class of
Specific Words 133
There Must Be Two or More Specific Words
Before the General Word 134
A Court Will Not Necessarily Apply the Class
Rule 134
The Class Rule Does Not Give Guidance on the
Meaning of Specific Words within the Class 135
The Name Which Lawyers Give to the Class
Rule 135

Chapter 34   WORDS OF SIMILAR MEANING
The Nature of the Rule 137
The Meaning of Similar Words When They are
Associated with Each Other 137
The Rule Is to be Applied with Caution 138

Chapter 35   EXPRESS INCLUSIONS AND IMPLIED EXCLUSIONS
The Effect of the Rule 141
The Use of the Rule in Relation to
Definitions 142
The Rule Must Be Applied with Caution 142
The Name Lawyers Give the Rule 143

Chapter 36   INTERPRETING AN ACT IN THE LIGHT OF OTHER
ACTS
Acts Which Are Related to the Act Being
Considered 145
Incorporating One Act into Another 148
The Effect of Acts Which are Not Related to the
Act under Consideration 148

Chapter 37   ACTS INCONSISTENT WITH EACH OTHER
Conflicts Between Different Acts of Parliament 149
A Conflict Between a General Act and
a Specific Act 149
Other Conflicts Between Acts of Parliament 150
Implied Repeal 150
Which Act is the Later? 151

Chapter 38   EIGHT CLASSES OF ACTS OF PARLIAMENT
Amending Acts 153
Codes 153
Declaratory Acts 154
Enabling Acts 154

Explanatory Acts 155
Remedial Acts 155
Revised Acts 156
Validating Acts 158

Chapter 39   ACTS WHICH ARE READ NARROWLY
The Kinds of Acts That Are Read Narrowly 159
Acts Which Impose a Penalty 159
Acts Which Empower Arrest or Detention 161
Acts Which Create a Tax or Charge............. 161
Acts Imposing Pecuniary Obligations 163
Acts Which Affect Vested Rights 163
The Rights to be Protected Must Be
Vested Rights................................ 164
Expropriating Property 164
The Purposive Approach May Deprive a
Landowner of the Protection Afforded by Narrow
Interpretation of Expropriation Provisions 165
Legal rules as to court procedure or as to law
costs do not create "vested rights" 165
Acts Affecting a Fundamental Principle of the
Common Law 166
Acts That Apply from Before the Date on Which
They were Passed 167

Chapter 40   ACTS THAT APPLY FROM BEFORE THE DATE ON
WHICH THEY WERE PASSED
Retroactive or Retrospective?................... 169
The Power of Parliament to Make Acts
That Apply from a Date Before the Date
on Which They Were Passed 170
The Presumption that Statutes Are Not
Intended to be Retrospective 170
Clear Words Are Needed to Make an Act
Operate From Before the Date on Which
It was Passed................................ 171
Taking Away Existing Rights 172
Providing Penalties for Things Done
Before the Coming Into Force of the Act 172
Acts Declaring the Existing Law
are Retrospective............................ 174
Acts Relating to Procedure or Evidence
are Usually Retrospective 174

Chapter 41   THE AREA IN WHICH AN ACT OF PARLIAMENT
OPERATES
An Act Operates Within the Territory of the
Parliament That Made It....................... 177

Applying the Principle to Bodies
Under Parliament 178
Parliament Can Make the Act Operate
Beyond Its Territory............................ 178
Applying the Act to Foreigners Beyond the
Territory 179
Actions Outside the Territory Affecting Persons
Inside It 179

Chapter 42   HOW ACTS OF PARLIAMENT AFFECT THE CROWN
The Meaning of "The Crown" 181
When an Act of Parliament Binds the Crown 181
The Extent of "The Crown" 182

Chapter 43   HOW JUDICIAL DECISIONS AFFECT THE READING OF
AN ACT
Prior Judicial Decisions Can Be Taken into
Consideration.................................. 183
Judicial Decisions on Principles of the
Common Law 183
Judicial Decisions on the Meaning of Particular
Words and Phrases............................ 183
Existing Judicial Interpretation of a Statutory
Provision 184
Re-enactment After an Act Has Been
Interpreted by the Courts 184
Technical Legal Terms........................ 185

Chapter 44   SUBORDINATE LEGISLATION
Subordinate Legislation is Interpreted so as
To Be Within Power 187
Subordinate Legislation Cannot Normally
Be Used to Interpret a Statute 187
Subordinate Legislation is Interpreted by Using the
Same Rules as Apply to Interpretation of Acts 188
Terms Used in Both the Subordinate Legislation
and the Empowering Act...................... 188
Subordinate Legislation Needs Authorisation to be
Retrospective 188

Chapter 45   THE CANADIAN CHARTER OF RIGHTS AND FREEDOMS
The Purpose of This Chapter................... 189
The Nature of the Charter 189
The Basis for Interpreting the Charter 189
The Wide Approach to Interpretation of the
Charter 190
Applying the Purposive Approach to Interpreting
the Charter................................... 192
Interpretation Acts Do Not Apply to the Charter .. 192

Headings..................................... 192
Bilingual Versions Affecting Interpretation
of the Charter 192
Use of American Court Decisions to Interpret
the Charter................................. 193
Chapter 46   BILINGUAL ACTS AND SUBORDINATE LEGISLATION
The Nature of Bilingual Acts and Bilingual
Subordinate Legislation 195
The Form of a Bilingual Act or Bilingual
Subordinate Legislation 195
The Weight to be Accorded to the English and to
the French Versions 196
The Parliaments Which Use the Bilingual
System...................................... 197
The Status of a Bilingual Act or
Subordinate Legislation 197
Each Version, Whether English or French,
is Part of the Context in Which the Other Version
Is to be Read............................... 197
Conflicting Versions — The Importance of
Grammar 197
Conflicting Versions — The Advantage of
Clarity...................................... 198
Conflicting Versions — Objectionable and
Unobjectionable Provisions.................... 198
Conflicting Versions — Bringing the Two into
Accord 198
Conflicting Versions — Choosing the Wider
Rather Than the Narrower Version............. 198
Conflicting Versions — The Useful Version
will be Preferred to One Lacking in Utility........ 199
The Purposive Approach...................... 199
Penal Acts 199
The Difficulties Created by the Bilingual System ... 199
Chapter 47   NOW READ ON
Highlights and History 201
Further Reading on the Rules for Finding
the Meaning of Acts of Parliament.............. 201
Canadian Textbooks........................... 202
English Textbooks 202
Glossary 203
Index 205

Table of Cases

Abel v. Lee (1871), L.R. 6 C.P. 365 129

Aeric Inc. v. Canada Post Corp. (1985), 16 D.L.R. (4th) 686
(Fed. C.A.) 197

Air-India v. Wiggins, [1980] 1 W.L.R. 815 .... 178, 179

Alaska Trainship Corp. v. Pacific Pilotage Authority, [1981]
1 S.C.R. 261, 35 N.R. 271, 120 D.L.R. (3d) 577 96

Alberta v. Very, [1983] 6 W.W.R. 143, 27 Alta. L.R. (2d) 19,
29 R.P.R. 179, 149 D.L.R. (3d) 688, 47 A.R. 340 (Q.B.) .. 132

Alberta (Attorney General) v. Huggard Assets Ltd.,
[1953] A.C. 420 177

Alberta (Board of Directors of the Western Irrigation District)
v. Trobst (1990), 49 M.P.L.R. 93, 103 A.R. 65 (Q.B.) 145

Alexander v. McKenzie, [1947] J.C. 155 78

Alkali Lake Indian Band v. Westcoast Transmission Co.,
[1986] 1 W.W.R. 766 (B.C.C.A.) 165

Allen v. Emmerson, [1944] 1 K.B. 262 134

Alloway v. St. Andrews (Rural Municipality) (1905), 1 W.L.R.
407, 15 Man. R. 188 (K.B.) 37, 39

"Amalia" The, Re (1863), 1 Moore P.C. (N.S.) 471, 15 E.R.
778 179

Anderson v. Lacey, [1948] 2 W.W.R. 317, [1948] 4 D.L.R. 229
(Man. C.A.) 166

Andrews v. British Columbia (Law Society), [1989] 1 S.C.R. 143,
91 N.R. 255, 34 B.C.L.R. (2d) 273, 56 D.L.R. (4th) 1 191

Archibald v. Royer, [1924] 1 D.L.R. 897, 57 N.S.R. 12 (C.A.) ... 80

Argyle Motors (Birkenhead) Ltd. v. Birkenhead Corp. [1975] A.C.
99 60

Argyll (Duke) v. Inland Revenue Commissioners (1913), 109
L.T. 893 150

Ashmore v. Bank of British North America (1913), 13 D.L.R. 73,
4 W.W.R. 1014, 18 B.C.R. 257 (C.A.) 7

Assam Railways & Trading Co. v. Inland Revenue Commissioners,
[1935] A.C. 455 106

Assheton Smith v. Owen, [1906] 1 Ch. 179 81

Associated Newspapers Group Ltd. v. Fleming, [1973] A.C.
628 93

Attorney-General v. Great Eastern Railway (1879), 11 Ch. D.
449 60

Attorney-General v. Theobold (1890), 2 Q.B.D. 557 154

Auchterarder Presbytery v. Lord Kinnoull (1839), 6 Cl.
& F. 646, 7 E.R. 841 117
Auger v. St. Paul L'Érmite (Paroisse), [1942] Qué. K.B. 725
(C.A.) 57
Azar v. Sydney (City) (1958), 15 D.L.R. (2d) 124 (N.S.T.D.) ... 126

BBC Enterprises Ltd. v. Hi-Tech Xtravision Ltd., [1990]
Ch. 609 (Eng. C.A.); on appeal, [1991] 2 A.C. 327 123
BP Refinery (Westernport) Pty. Ltd. v. Shire of Hastings
(1977), 52 A.L.J.R. 20 (P.C.) 123, 124
Bains v. British Columbia (Superintendent of Insurance)
(1973), 38 D.L.R. (3d) 756 (B.C.C.A.) 134
Baker, Re (1907), 7 W.L.R. 69, 1 Sask. L.R. 7 (C.A.) 153
Baniuk v. Carpenter (1987), 85 N.B.R. (2d) 385, 21 A.P.R. 385
(C.A.) 165
Barrett v. Winnipeg (City) (1891), 19 S.C.R. 374 103
Bell v. North Vancouver School District 44 (1979), 16
B.C.L.R. 94 (S.C.) 135
Bell-Irving v. Vancouver (City) (1892), 4 B.C.R. 219 (S.C.) 123
Berton Dress Inc. v. R., [1953] Ex. C.R. 83 (Ex. Ct.) 163
Bills v. Sims (1922), 53 O.L.R. 57, [1923] 3 D.L.R. 726 (H.C.) .. 74
Bishop of Rochester v. Bridges (1831), 1 B. & Ad. 847, 109
E.R. 1001 (K.B.) 156
Black and Decker Manufacturing Co. v. R., [1975] 1 S.C.R.
411, 15 C.C.C. (2d) 193, 43 D.L.R. (3d) 393, 13
C.P.R. (2d) 97, 1 N.R. 299 199
Black-Clawson International Ltd. v. Papierwerke Waldhof-
Aschaffenburg AG, [1975] A.C. 591 95
Blouin c. Dumoulin, [1958] Qué. Q.B. 581 (C.A.) 197
Blyth v. Blyth (No. 2), [1966] A.C. 643 175
Boaler, Re, [1915] 1 K.B. 21 .... 30, 31, 32
Bombay Province v. Bombay Municipal Corp., [1974] A.C.
58 181
Boulanger v. Québec (Federation des producteurs d'oeufs
de consommation) (1982), 141 D.L.R. (3d) 72, leave to appeal
refused 141 D.L.R. (3d) 72 (note) (S.C.C.) 170
Bourke v. Murphy (1856), 1 P.E.I. 126 145
Boutilier v. Nova Scotia Trust Co., [1940] 2 D.L.R. 221,
14 M.P.R. 456 (N.S.C.A.) 156
Boykiw v. Calgary (City) Development Appeal Board
(1992), 9 M.P.L.R. (2d) 113, 2 Alta. L.R. (3d) 86, 90 D.L.R.
(4th) 558, 127 A.R. 380, 20 W.A.C. 380 (C.A.) 89, 90, 97
Bradbury, Re (1916), 30 D.L.R. 756, 50 N.S.R. 298 (C.A.)
.... 34, 98, 177
Bristol Airport plc v. Powdrill, [1990] 2 W.L.R. 1362 101

British Columbia (Attorney General) v. Bailey, [1919] 1 W.W.R.
191, 44 D.L.R. 338 (B.C.S.C.) 164
British Columbia (Attorney General) v. Canada (1889), 4 App.
Cas. 295 111
British Columbia (Attorney General) v. Canada (Attorney General),
[1936] S.C.R. 398, [1936] D.L.R. 622, 66 C.C.C. 180 54
British Columbia (Attorney General) v. R. (1922), 63 S.C.R. 622,
[1922] 3 W.W.R. 269, 68 D.L.R. 106 .... 133, 139
British Columbia (Law Society) v. Lawrie, [1988] 1 W.W.R. 351,
18 B.C.L.R. (2d) 247, 38 C.C.C. (3d) 525, 46 D.L.R. (4th)
456 (B.C.S.C.) 150
British Railways Board v. Pickin [1974] A.C. 765 7
Brittain Steel Fabricators v. New Westminster Bylaw 3869, Re
(1963), 39 D.L.R. (2d) 676, 42 W.W.R. 586 (B.C.C.A.) ... 188
Bromley London Borough Council v. Greater London Council,
[1983] 1 A.C. 768 167
Brook v. Brook (1861), 9 H.L.C. 193, 11 E.R. 703 178
Brophy v. Manitoba (Attorney General), [1895] A.C. 202 102
Buckman v. Button, [1943] K.B. 405, [1943] 2 All E.R. 82 173
Bulman v. Anderson, [1946] 4 D.L.R. 679 (B.C.S.C.) 76
Burnham v. Stratton (1908), 17 O.L.R. 612 (K.B.) 147

Campbell v. Dowdall (1992), 12 M.P.L.R. (2d) 27 (Ont. Gen.
Div.) 111
Canada (Attorney General) v. Jackson, [1946] S.C.R. 489, [1946]
2 D.L.R. 481 56
Canada (Attorney General) v. Reader's Digest Assoc., [1961]
S.C.R. 775, 30 D.L.R. (2d) 296 105
Canada (Attorney General) v. Saskatchewan Water Corp. (1990),
5 C.E.L.R. (N.S.) 252, [1991] 1 W.W.R. 426, 88 Sask. R.
13 (Q.B.) 115, 117
Canada (Deputy Minister of National Revenue) v. Film Technique
Ltd., [1973] F.C. 75 (T.D.) 198
Canada Life Assurance Co. v. Rieb, [1943] 1 W.W.R. 759 (Alta.
T.D.) 184
Canada Southern Railway Co. v. International Bridge Co. (1883),
8 App. Cas. 723 12
Canada Sugar Refining Co. v. R., [1898] A.C. 735 116
Canadian Acceptance Corp. v. Fisher, [1958] S.C.R. 546,
14 D.L.R. (2d) 225 184
Canadian Eagle Oil Co. v. R., [1946] A.C. 119 162
Canadian Indemnity Co. v. British Columbia (Attorney General)
(No. 3), [1975] 3 W.W.R. 224 (B.C.S.C.) 110
Canadian National Railway v. Ottawa (City), [1924] 4 D.L.R.
1217, 56 O.L.R. 153 80

Canadian Northern Railway, Re (1909), 42 S.C.R. 443 ...... 10, 124
Canadian Northern Railway v. Winnipeg (City) (1917), 54 S.C.R.
    589, [1917] 2 W.W.R. 100, 36 D.L.R. 222 86
Canadian Pacific Ltd. v. Canadian Transport Commission (1983),
    2 D.L.R. (4th) 630, 49 N.R. 354 (Fed. C.A.) 117
Canadian Pacific Railway v. James Bay Railway (1905), 36
    S.C.R. 42 .... 80, 89, 107, 109
Canadian Pacific Railway v. Northern Pacific & Manitoba Railway
    (1888), 5 Man. R. 301 (Q.B.) 122
Canadian Pacific Railway v. R. (1906), 38 S.C.R. 137 147
Canadian Performing Right Society Ltd. v. Famous Players
    Canada Corp., [1929] 2 D.L.R. 1 (P.C.) 85, 86
Canadian Railway v. R. (1922), 64 S.C.R. 264, [1923] 2
    W.W.R. 836, [1923] 2 D.L.R. 693 7
Canadian Westinghouse Co. v. Grant, [1927] S.C.R. 625, [1927]
    4 D.L.R. 484 151
Cape Brandy Syndicate v. Inland Revenue Commissioners, [1921]
    1 K.B. 64 162
Capital Grocers Ltd. v. Saskatchewan (Registrar of Land Titles)
    (1952), 7 W.W.R. (N.S.) 315 (Sask. C.A.) 145
Cardinal v. R. (1979), 97 D.L.R. (3d) 402, [1980] 1 F.C. 149,
    97 D.L.R. (3d) 402, [1979] 1 C.N.L.R. 32 (T.D.) 78, 198
Carrington v. Term-a-Stor Ltd., [1983] 1 W.L.R. 138 (C.A.) 96
Carter v. Sudbury (City), [1949] 3 D.L.R. 756, [1949] O.R. 455,
    64 C.R.T.C. 113, [1949] O.W.N. 411 (H.C.) 71
Casanova v. R. (1866), L.R. 1 P.C. 268 146
Cassell v. Minister of National Revenue, [1947] 1 D.L.R. 89
    (Ex. Ct.) 57
Cedar Rapids Saving Bank v. Dominion Purebred Stock Co.,
    [1923] 3 W.W.R. 1214, 19 Alta. L.R. 800, [1923] 4 D.L.R.
    1197 (C.A.) 157
Central Ontario Coalition Concerning Hydro Transmission Systems
    v. Ontario Hydro (1984), 10 D.L.R. (4th) 341, 27 M.P.L.R.
    165, 46 O.R. (2d) 715, 8 Admin. L.R. 81, 4 O.A.R. 249
    (Div. Ct.) 164
Century Aviation Services Ltd. v. British Columbia (Industrial
    Rela tions Board) (1976), 69 D.L.R. (3d) 176 (B.C.S.C.) ... 123
Chance v. Adams (1696), 1 Ld. Raym. 77, 91 E.R. 948 23
Chandler v. Vancouver (City), [1919] 1 W.L.R. 605, 45 D.L.R.
    121, 26 B.C.R. 465 (C.A.) 115
Chapman v. Purtell (1915), 22 D.L.R. 860, 7 W.W.R. 1155, 25
    Man. R. 76 (K.B.) 24
Cheyney v. Inuvik (Town) (1992), 11 M.P.L.R. (2d) 267, [1992]
    N.W.T.R. 383 (S.C.) 146, 163
Child Welfare Act, Re, [1945] 1 W.W.R. 252 (Alta. T.D.) 163

Churchill Falls (Labrador) Corp. v. Newfoundland (Attorney
General), [1984] 1 S.C.R. 297, 47 Nfld. & P.E.I.R. 125,
139 A.P.R. 125, 8 D.L.R. (4th) 1, 53 N.R. 268 112
City Tours Ltd. v. Toronto Transit Commission (1985), 51 O.R.
(2d) 696 (C.A.) 75
Clark v. Bradlaugh (1881), 8 Q.B.D. 63 12
Clark v. Docksteader (1905), 36 S.C.R. 622 146
Clearwater Election, Re (1913), 12 D.L.R. 598, 6 Alta. L.R. 343,
4 W.W.R. 1025 (C.A.) 39
Coleman (Town) v. Head Syndicate, [1917] 1 W.W.R. 1074, 11
Alta. L.R. 314 (C.A.) 145
Colonial Commodities Ltd. v. Siporex Trade SA, [1990] 2 All
E.R. 552 80
Colonial Sugar Refining Co. v. Melbourne Harbour Trust
Commissioners, [1927] A.C. 343 164
Colquhoun v. Brooks (1887), 19 Q.B.D. 400, affirmed (1888),
21 Q.B.D. 52 .... 142, 143
Commercial Credit Corp. v. Niagara Finance Co., [1940] S.C.R.
420, [1940] 3 D.L.R. 1 123
Commercial Taxi v. Alberta (Highway Traffic Board), [1950]
2 W.W.R. 289, [1951] 1 D.L.R. 342 (Alta. T.D.) 166
Commissioner of Police of the Metropolis v. Curran, [1976]
1 W.L.R. 87 86
Composers, Authors and Publishers Assoc. of Canada v. Western
Fair Assoc., [1951] S.C.R. 596 197
Conger v. Kennedy (1896), 26 S.C.R. 397 147
Connell v. Minister of National Revenue, [1947] 1 D.L.R. 89,
[1946] C.T.C. 306, [1946] Ex. C.R. 562 (Ex. Ct.) 56
Construction Equipment Co. v. Bilida's Transport Ltd. (1966),
57 W.W.R. 513, 58 D.L.R. (2d) 674 (Alta. T.D.) .. 157
Contrôleur du Revenu de la Province de Québec v. Boulet,
[1952] Qué. K.B. 598 24
Converse v. Michie (1865), 16 U.C.C.P. 167 34
Cope & Taylor v. Scottish Union & National Insurance Co. (1897),
5 B.C.R. 329 (C.A.) 126
Copeland, ex parte (1852), 22 L.J. Bcy. 17 145
Cosyns v. Canada (Attorney General) (1992), 7 O.R. (3d) 641,
88 D.L.R. (4th) 507, 53 O.A.C. 127 (Div. Ct.) 191
County of London Housing Order, Re, [1956] 1 W.L.R. 499 ... 126
Cowper-Essex v. Acton Local Board (1889), 14 App. Cas.
153, [1886-90] All E.R. Rep. 901 118
Cox v. Army Council, [1963] A.C. 48 178
Cox v. Hakes (1890), 15 App. Cas. 506 86
Crawford v. Spooner (1846), 6 Moore P.C. 1, 13 E.R. 582 121

Creighton v. United Oils Ltd., [1927] 3 D.L.R. 804, [1927]
2 W.W.R. 458 (Alta. T.D.) 188
Cronkhite Supply Ltd. v. British Columbia (Workers'
Compensation Board) (1978), 8 B.C.L.R. 54, 7 R.P.R. 121,
91 D.L.R. (3d) 423 (C.A.) 181
Cushing v. Dupuy (1880), 5 App. Cas. 409, C.R. [8] A.C. 355 .. 181

D. Moore Co., Re (1927), [1928] 1 D.L.R. 383, 8 C.B.R. 479,
61 O.L.R. 434 (C.A.) 69
D.R. Fraser & Co. v. Canada (Minister of National Revenue),
[1948] 4 D.L.R. 776, [1948] 2 W.W.R. 1119, [1949] A.C. 24,
[1951] Ex. Ct. 154 153
D'Avigdor-Goldsmid v. Inland Revenue Commissioners, [1953]
A.C. 347, [1953] 1 All E.R. 403 162
Dain v. Gossage (1873), 6 P.R. 103 (Ont. H.C.) 34
Dartmouth (Town) v. Roman Catholic Episcopal Corp. of Halifax,
[1940] 2 D.L.R. 309, 15 M.P.R. 47 (N.S.C.A.) 80, 162
Davidson v. Hill, [1901] 2 K.B. 606 179
Davis v. Edmondson (1803), 3 B. & P. 382, 127 E.R. 209 145
Davisville Investment Co. v. Toronto (City) (1977), 2 M.P.L.R.
81, 15 O.R. (2d) 553 (C.A.) 101
Dawson Creek (City) v. Lougheed (1959), 19 D.L.R. (2d)
249 (B.C.C.A.) 138
De Roussy v. Nesbitt (1920), 53 D.L.R. 514, [1920] 2 W.W.R.
892, 15 Alta. L.R. 522 (Alta. C.A.) 175
Dean v. Green (1882), 8 P.D. 79 73
Director of Public Prosecutions of Jamaica v. White, [1978]
A.C. 426 122
Director of Public Prosecutions v. Lamb, [1941] 2 K.B. 89,
[1941] 2 All E.R. 499 173
Director of Public Prosecutions v. Turner, [1974] A.C. 357 161
Dixie v. Royal Columbian Hospital, [1941] 2 D.L.R. 138, [1941]
1 W.W.R. 389, 56 B.C.R. 74 (C.A.) 175
Donly v. Holmwood (1880), 40 O.A.R. 555 56
Dow v. Parsons (1917), 36 D.L.R. 510, 51 N.S.R. 41 (S.C.) 73
Dublin Continuation School Board v. Seaforth District High
School Board, [1952] O.R. 229 (H.C.) 147
Dufferin Paving and Crushed Stone Ltd. v. Anger, [1940]
S.C.R. 174, [1940] 1 D.L.R. 1 87
Dullewe v. Dullewe, [1969] A.C. 313 95

Earl of Mountcashel v. Grover (1847), 4 U.C.Q.B. 23 154
East & West India Docks v. Shaw, Savill & Albion Co. (1888),
39 Ch. D. 524 31

Eastern Counties & London & Blackwell Railway v.
Marriage (1860), 9 H.L.C. 32, 11 E.R. 639 .... 55, 57
Edmonton (City) v. Forget (1990), 74 D.L.R. (4th) 547, 1
M.P.L.R. (2d) 214 (Alta. Q.B.) 190
Edmonton (City) v. Northwestern Utilities Ltd., [1961] S.C.R. 392,
34 W.W.R. 600, 82 C.R.T.C. 129, 28 D.L.R. (2d) 125 87
Ells v. Ells (1979), 99 D.L.R. (3d) 686, 32 N.S.R. (2d) 51, 54
A.P.R. 51, 9 R.F.L. (2d) 251 (C.A.) 151
Engineering Industry Training Board v. Samuel Talbot (Engineers)
Ltd., [1969] 2 Q.B. 270, [1969] 1 All E.R. 480 (C.A.) 163
Esquimalt & Nanaimo Railway v. McGregor (1905), 2 W.L.R.
530 (B.C.S.C.), restored after intermediate reversal, [1907]
A.C. 462 39
Excelsior Lumber Co. v. Ross (1914), 6 W.W.R. 367, 19 B.C.R.
289, 16 D.L.R. 593, [1976] 2 All E.R. 721, [1976] Q.B. 345
(C.A.) 98

Fagnan v. Ure, [1958] S.C.R. 377, 13 D.L.R. (2d) 273 184
"Fairview" Church Street Bromyard, Re, [1974] 1 W.L.R. 579 ... 68
Farrell v. Alexander, [1977] A.C. 59 .... 100, 157
Fawcett Properties Ltd. v. Buckingham County Council, [1961]
A.C. 636, [1960] 3 All E.R. 503 13
Fenton v. J. Thorley & Co. [1903] A.C. 443 31
First National Bank of Idaho Springs v. Curry (1910), 16
W.L.R. 102, 20 Man. R. 247 (C.A.) 143
First National Securities Ltd. v. Chiltern District Council, [1975]
1 W.L.R. 1075 126
Flood v. Monargo Mines Ltd., [1938] 2 D.L.R. 460, [1938] O.R.
282 (C.A.) 119
Food Machinery Corp. v. Canada (Registrar of Trade Marks),
[1946] 2 D.L.R. 258, [1946] Ex. C.R. 266, 5 Fox Pat. C. 150,
5 C.P.R. 76 (Ex. Ct.) 198
Forster v. Mornington (Shire), [1949] V.L.R. 150 63
Fort Garry (Rural Municipality) v. Fort Garry School
District (1958), 26 W.W.R. 443 (Man. Q.B.) 91
Foxcroft v. London (City), [1928] 1 D.L.R. 849, 61 O.L.R.
553 (C.A.) 150
Francouer v. Prince Albert Community Clinic (1986), 52 Sask. R.
221 (Q.B.) 132
Freedman v. Howard, [1935] 2 D.L.R. 285, [1935] 2 W.W.R. 267,
49 B.C.R. 417 (C.A.) 51
Friends of Oak Hammock Marsh Inc. v. Ducks Unlimited
(Canada) (1991), 9 C.E.L.R. (N.S.) 52, 84 D.L.R. (4th) 371,
74 Man. R. (2d) 284 (Q.B.) 187

Friends of the Oldman River Society v. Canada (Minister
   of Transport), [1992] 1 S.C.R. 3, [1992] 2 W.W.R. 193,
   84 Alta. L.R. (2d) 129, 7 C.E.L.R. (N.S.) 1, 132 N.R. 321,
   88 D.L.R. (4th) 1, 3 Admin. L.R. (2d) 1, 48 F.T.R. 160
   (note) 109, 114, 181
Frontenac (District) License Commissioners v. Frontenac
   (County) (1887), 14 O.R. 741 (Ch.) 156
Fullum v. Waldie Brothers (1909), 13 O.W.R. 236 (Ex. Ct.) .. 59, 61

G.T. Campbell & Associates Ltd. v. Hugh Carson Co. (1979),
   99 D.L.R. (3d) 529, 7 B.L.R. 84, 24 O.R. (2d) 758, 11
   C.P.C. 1 (C.A.) 153
Gardner v. Lucas (1878), 3 App. Cas. 582 .... 166, 171
Gaudet v. Brown; Cargo ex "Argos" (1873), L.R. 5 P.C. 134 .. 118
Gauthier v. McRae (1977), 82 D.L.R. (3d) 671, 18 Nfld. &
   P.E.I.R. 484, 47 A.P.R. 484 (P.E.I.S.C.) 172
Geisha Garden Ltd., Re (1960), 30 W.W.R. 617, 32 C.R.
   246 (B.C.S.C.) 188
Giffels and Vallet of Canada Ltd. v. R., [1952] 1 D.L.R. 620,
   [1952] O.W.N. 196, [1951] O.R. 652 (H.C.) 79
Gilbert v. Gilbert and Boucher, [1928] P. 1 156
Gladysz v. Gross, [1945] 3 D.L.R. 208, [1945] 2 W.W.R.
   266 (B.C.C.A.) 50, 150
Glenn v. Schofield, [1928] S.C.R. 208, [1928] 2 D.L.R. 319 93
Goguen v. Shannon (1989), 50 C.C.C. (3d) 45 (N.B.C.A.) 192
Gordon Mackay & Co. v. Laroque Co. (1926), 7 C.B.R. 384,
   59 O.L.R. 293, [1926] 3 D.L.R. 864 (C.A.) 104
Gosselin v. R. (1903), 33 S.C.R. 255, 7 C.C.C. 139 106
Gossner v. Ontario Regional Assessment Commissioner (1983),
   22 M.P.L.R. 281, 42 O.R. (2d) 119, 28 R.P.R. 92, 148
   D.L.R. (3d) 643 (Div. Ct.) 162
Gough v. Gough, [1891] 2 Q.B. 665 68
Goulbourn (Township) v. Ottawa-Carleton (Regional Municipality)
   (1979), 101 D.L.R. (3d) 1, [1980] 1 S.C.R. 496, 101 D.L.R.
   (3d) 1, 29 N.R. 267 .... 13, 110, 147
Grand Trunk Pacific Railway v. Dearborn, [1919] 1 W.W.R.
   1005, 58 S.C.R. 315, 47 D.L.R. 27 123
Grand Trunk Railway v. Hepworth Silica Pressed Brick Co.
   (1915), 51 S.C.R. 81, 19 C.R.C. 365, 21 D.L.R. 480 103
Gravestock v. Parkin (1943), [1944] O.R. 49, [1944] 1 D.L.R.
   417 (C.A.) 135
Gray v. Ingersoll (Town) (1888), 16 O.R. 194 (Ch.) 167
Greater Niagara Transit Commission v. Matson (1977), 16 O.R.
   (2d) 351, 78 D.L.R. (3d) 265 (H.C.) 163

Green Meadows Estate Ltd. v. Nova Scotia (Director of
    Assessment) (1982), 17 M.P.L.R. 296, 50 N.S.R. (2d) 602,
    98 A.P.R. 602, 132 D.L.R. (3d) 722 (C.A.) 162
Greene v. D.R. Sutherland Ltd. (1982), 40 N.B.R. (2d) 27
    105 A.P.R. 27 (Q.B.) 198
Greenwood (City) v. Board of School Trustees, School District No.
    18 (1965), 55 D.L.R. (2d) 663, 54 W.W.R. 432 (B.C.C.A.) .. 99
Grinnell v. R. (1888), 16 S.C.R. 119 162
Gundy v. Johnston (1912), 28 O.L.R. 121, 12 D.L.R. 71
    (C.A.) 89, 164
Hadden v. R., [1983] 3 W.W.R. 661, 21 M.P.L.R. 343, 23 Sask.
    R. 303 (Q.B.) 55, 59
Haddock v. Ontario (Attorney General) (1990), 70 D.L.R. (4th)
    644, 12 R.P.R. (2d) 98, 73 O.R. (2d) 545 (H.C.) 191
Haigh v. Charles W. Ireland Ltd., [1974] 1 W.L.R. 43 81
Haldimand-Norfolk (Regional Municipality) v. Copland (1992), 12
    M.P.L.R. (2d) 85, 96 D.L.R. (4th) 443 (Ont. Gen. Div.) ... 164
Halifax Branch of Navy League of Canada, Re (1927), 59
    N.S.R. 212, [1927] 2 D.L.R. 184 (C.A.) 121
Halifax Pilot Commissioners v. Farquhar (1894), 26 N.S.R.
    333 (C.A.) 184
Hamilton (City) v. Hamilton Harbour Commissioners (1984),
    28 M.P.L.R. 1, 48 O.R. (2d) 757, 14 D.L.R. (4th) 338 (H.C.) ..
    116, 162
Hamilton Harbour Commissioners v. Hamilton (City) (1976),
    1 M.P.L.R. 133, 21 O.R. (2d) 459, 91 D.L.R. (3d) 353
    (H.C.) 116
Hammersmith & City Railway v. Brand (1869), L.R. 4 H.L.
    171, [1869] All E.R. 199 57
Hammond v. Bank of Ottawa (1910), 22 O.L.R. 73 (C.A.) ... 37, 38
Hanlon v. Law Society, [1981] A.C. 124, [1980] 2 All E.R.
    199 .... 78, 188
Happy Investments Management Ltd. v. Dorio (1987), 46
    D.L.R. (4th) 381, 20 B.C.L.R. (2d) 300 (S.C.) 169
Hare v. Gocher, [1962] 2 Q.B. 641 86
Harley v. Harley, [1960] O.W.N. 357, 24 D.L.R. (2d) 438
    (C.A.) 99, 101
Harrison Brothers Ltd. v. St. Jean (Municipality) (1936), 62
    Qué. K.B. 357 (C.A.) 12
Hartnell v. Minister of Housing and Local Government, [1963]
    1 W.L.R. 1141, affirmed on appeal, [1965] A.C. 1134 164
Harvie v. Calgary (City) Regional Planning Commission (1978),
    8 M.P.L.R. 227, 12 A.R. 505, 8 Alta. L.R. (2d) 166, 94
    D.L.R. (3d) 49 143
Hassard v. Toronto (City) (1908), 16 O.L.R. 500 (C.A.) 93

Hayduk v. Pidoborozny, [1972] S.C.R. 879, [1972] 4 W.W.R.
522, 29 D.L.R. (3d) 8 67
Hayes, Re (1931), 12 C.B.R. 225, [1931] 1 W.W.R. 301, 25
Sask. L.R. 257 (K.B.) 103
Heinze, Re (1914), 29 W.L.R. 131 (B.C.C.A.) 37
Henry Morgan & Co. v. Guérin, [1942] Qué. S.C. 444 98
Hereford and Worcester County Council v. Craske (1976), 75
L.G.R. 174 106
Herron v. Rathmines and Rathgar Improvement Commissioners,
[1892] A.C. 498 107
Heydon's Case (1584), 3 Co. Rep 7, 76 E.R. 637............... 93
Hibbert v. Acton (1889), 5 T.L.R. 274 63
Hickey v. Stalker (1923), 53 O.L.R. 414, [1924] 1 D.L.R. 440
(C.A.) 103
Him, Re (1910), 15 B.C.R. 163, 16 C.C.C. 383 (S.C.) 118
Hirsch v. Montreal Protestant School Board, [1926] S.C.R.
246, [1926] 2 D.L.R. 8 99
Hirsch v. Montreal Protestant School Board, [1928] A.C. 200,
[1928] 1 D.L.R. 1041 39
Hirshman v. Beal (1916), 38 O.L.R. 40, 28 C.C.C. 319, 32
D.L.R. 680 (C.A.) 61
Hobrecker v. Sanders (1909), 44 N.S.R. 14 (N.S.C.A.) 7
Holmes v. Bradfield (Rural District Council), [1949] 2 K.B. 1,
[1949] 1 All E.R. 381 91
Holton, Re, [1952] O.W.N. 741 (H.C.) 147
Home Oil Distributors Ltd. v. British Columbia (Attorney
General), [1939] 1 W.W.R. 49 (B.C.C.A.) 110
Hough v. Windus (1884), 12 Q.B.D. 224 163
Houghton's Case, Re (1877), 1 B.C.R. (Pt. 1) 89 (S.C.) 73
Houston v. Burns, [1918] A.C. 337 77
Huber v. Regina (City) (1956), 19 W.W.R. 657 (Sask. Q.B.) .. 67, 68
Hughes v. Moncton (City) (1991), 6 M.P.L.R. (2d) 203, 39
C.C.E.L. 309, 118 N.B.R. (2d) 306, 296 A.P.R. 306
(C.A.) 114
Hull Dock Co. v. Browne (1831), 2 B. & Ad. 43, 109 E.R.
1059 162
Hy Whittle Ltd. v. Stalybridge Corp. (1967), 65 L.G.R. 344 132

I.A.F.F., Local 209 v. Edmonton (City) (1979), 9 Alta. L.R.
(2d) 119, 15 A.R. 594, 99 D.L.R. (3d) 109 (C.A.) 67, 68
I.A.F.F., Locals 913, 953, 1399, 1746 v. Okanagan Mainline
Municipal Labour Relations Assn. (1988), 30 B.C.L.R. (2d)
320 (S.C.) 166
Income Tax Commissioners v. Pemsel, [1891] A.C. 531, [1891-94]
All E.R. Rep. 28 .... 118, 129, 185

Ingle v. Farrand, [1927] A.C. 417 173
Inland Revenue Commissioners v. Hinchy, [1960] A.C. 748,
    [1960] 1 All E.R. 505 77
Insurance Corp. of British Columbia v. Canada (Registrar of
    Trade Marks), [1980] 1 F.C. 669, 44 C.P.R. (2d) 1
    (T.D.) 24, 59, 78

Jackson v. Hall, [1980] A.C. 854, [1980] 2 W.L.R. 118, [1980]
    1 All E.R. 177 187
James v. Inland Revenue Commissioners, [1977] 1 W.L.R. 835 .. 173
Johnson v. Upham (1859), 2 E. & E. 250, 121 E.R. 95 31
Johnston v. Canadian Credit Men's Trust Assoc., [1932] S.C.R.
    219, [1932] 2 D.L.R. 462, 58 C.C.C. 1 24
Joint Properties Ltd. v. Williamson, [1945] S.C. 68 10
Jones v. Wrotham Park Settled Estates, [1980] A.C. 74 123

Kadishewitz v. Laurentian Insurance Co., [1931] O.R. 529, [1931]
    4 D.L.R. 401 (C.A.) 141
Kanerva v. Ontario Assoc. of Architects (1986), 56 O.R. (2d) 518,
    32 D.L.R. (4th) 150, 17 O.A.C. 374 (Div. Ct.) 165
Karch, Re (1921), 50 O.L.R. 509, 64 D.L.R. 541 (C.A.) 155
Kariapper v. Wijesinha, [1968] A.C. 716 150
Kent v. R., [1924] S.C.R. 388, [1924] 4 D.L.R. 77 171
Kilgour v. London Street Railway Co. (1914), 30 O.L.R. 603,
    19 D.L.R. 827 (C.A.) 12
King (Township) v. Marylake Agricultural School & Farm
    Settlement Assoc., [1939] O.R. 13, [1939] 1 D.L.R. 263
    (C.A.) 80, 134
Kirby v. Portugal Cove (Municipality) (1989), 41 M.P.L.R. 142,
    41 L.C.R. 104, 2 R.P.R. (2d) 146, 74 Nfld. & P.E.I.R. 142,
    231 A.P.R. 142 (Nfld. C.A.) 164
Klippert v. R., [1967] S.C.R. 822, 2 C.R.N.S. 319, 61 W.W.R.
    727, [1968] 2 C.C.C. 129, 65 D.L.R. (2d) 698 199
Knill v. Towse (1889), 24 Q.B.D. 186 12
Knowles & Sons v. Lancashire & Yorkshire Railway Co. (1889),
    14 App. Cas. 248 148

Labrador Co. v. R., [1893] A.C. 104 126
Lake v. Bennett, [1970] 1 Q.B. 663 148
Lambert v. Anglo-Scottish General Commercial Insurance Co.,
    [1930] 1 D.L.R. 284, 64 O.L.R. 439 170
Landex Investments Ltd. v. Red Deer (City) (1991), 6 M.P.L.R.
    (2d) 36, [1991] 6 W.W.R. 275, 81 Alta. L.R. (2d) 381, 45
    L.C.R. 241, 117 A.R. 123, 2 W.A.C. 123 (C.A.) 110
Lanston Monotype Machine Co. v. Northern Publishing Co. (1922),
    63 S.C.R. 482, [1922] 2 W.W.R. 529, 67 D.L.R. 140 68

Larence v. Larence (1911), 17 W.L.R. 197, 21 Man. R. 145
(K.B.) 129
Lauri v. Renad, [1892] 3 Ch. 402 173
Laursen v. McKinnon (1913), 9 D.L.R. 758, 3 W.W.R. 717,
18 B.C.R. 10 (C.A.) 184
Lawrie v. Rathbun (1876), 38 U.C.Q.B. 255 (Ont.) 61
Lawson v. Fox, [1974] A.C. 803 .... 177, 187
LeBlanc Estate v. Bank of Montreal, [1989] 1 W.W.R. 49
(Sask. C.A.) 141
Lee v. Showmen's Guild of Great Britain, [1952] 2 Q.B. 329,
[1952] 1 All E.R. 1175 (C.A.) 81
Lee-Verhulst (Investments) Ltd. v. Harwood Trust, [1973] 1 Q.B.
204 79
Leiriao c. Val-Bélair (Ville), [1991] 3 S.C.R. 349, 7 M.P.L.R.
(2d) 1 .... 165, 166
Lessard v. R. (1939), 67 Qué. K.B. 448, 73 C.C.C. 52, [1940]
1 D.L.R. 128 (C.A.) 36
Lethbridge (City) v. Northern Trusts Co., [1925] 4 D.L.R. 422
(Alta. C.A.) 123
Lions v. Meaford (Town) (1977), 2 M.P.L.R. 121 (Ont. Div. Ct.) ...
162
London (City) v. Wood (1701), 12 Mod. Rep. 669, 88 E.R.
1592 103
London (County) v. Pearce, [1892] 2 Q.B. 109 63
London County Council v. Central Land Board, [1959] Ch.
386 112
Lonhro, Re (No. 2), [1990] Ch. 695 100
Lor-West Contracting Ltd. v. R., [1986] 1 F.C. 346
(T.D.) 105, 106
Lord Advocate v. Dumbarton District Council, [1989] 3
W.L.R. 1346 181
Lumsden v. Inland Revenue Commissioners, [1914] A.C.
877 .... 106, 107

M. v. Law Society (Alberta), [1940] 3 W.W.R. 600, [1941] 1
D.L.R. 213 (Alta. C.A.) 122
MacMillan v. Brownlee, [1937] S.C.R. 318, 68 C.C.C. 7 184
Maguire v. Hinton (Municipality) Commissioners of Police (1980),
14 Alta. L.R. (2d) 199, 116 D.L.R. (3d) 268, 25 A.R. 1
(Q.B.) 115
Main v. Stark (1890), 15 App. Cas. 384 171
Mainwaring v. Mainwaring, [1942] 2 D.L.R. 377, [1942] 1
W.W.R. 728, 57 B.C.R. 390 (C.A.) 10, 12
Mangano v. Moscoe (1991), 6 M.P.L.R. (2d) 29, 4 O.R. (3d)
469 (Gen. Div.) 160

Mangin v. Inland Revenue Commissioners, [1971] A.C. 739 91
Manitoba v. Forest, [1979] 2 S.C.R. 1032 197
Marr, Re, [1990] 2 All E.R. 880 .... 51, 150
Marshall v. Cottingham, [1982] 1 Ch. 82 78
Martin v. Saskatchewan (Beef Stabilization Appeal Committee)
    (1986), 48 Sask. R. 89 (Q.B.) 188
Maxwell v. Callbeck, [1939] S.C.R. 400, [1939] 3 D.L.R.
    580 .... 170, 171
Mayfair Property Co., Re, [1898] 2 Ch. 28 93
McArthur v. R., [1943] Ex. C.R. 77, [1943] 3 D.L.R. 225
    (Ex. Ct.) 82
McBratney v. McBratney, [1919] 3 W.W.R. 1000, 59 S.C.R.
    550, 50 D.L.R. 132 102
McCaffry v. Law Society (Alberta), [1941] 1 D.L.R. 213
    (S.C.C.) 90, 91
McCallum v. Hurry (1911), 17 W.L.R. 533, 3 Alta. L.R. 342
    (C.A.) 124
McGowan v. Hudson's Bay Co. (1901), 5 Terr. L.R.
    147 (N.W.T.C.A.) 114
McIntyre Porcupine Mines Ltd. v. Morgan (1921), 62 D.L.R. 619,
    49 O.L.R. 214 (C.A.) 81
McIntyre Ranching Co. v. Cardston No. 6 (Municipality), [1982]
    20 M.P.L.R. 49, [1983] 1 W.W.R. 345, 23 Alta. L.R. (2d)
    63 (Q.B.) 164
McKenzie v. Jackson (1898), 31 N.S.R. 70 (C.A.) 12
McKittrick v. Byers (1925), 58 O.L.R. 158, [1926] 1 D.L.R.
    342 (C.A.) 34, 163
McPherson v. Giles (1919), 45 O.L.R. 441 (H.C.) 77
Medicine Hat (City) v. Howson (1920), 53 D.L.R. 264, [1920]
    2 W.W.R. 810, 15 Alta. L.R. 508 (C.A.) 77
Meldrum v. Black (1916), 27 D.L.R. 193, 10 W.W.R. 519, 22
    B.C.R. 574 (C.A.) 51, 151
Mennonite Collegiate Institute v. Gretna (Village) (1990), 2 M.P.L.R.
    (2d) 209, 76 D.L.R. (4th) 528, 69 Man. R. (2d) 33 (Q.B.) .. 162
Mersey Docks & Harbour Board v. Henderson Brothers (1888),
    13 App. Cas. 595 121
Meux v. Jacobs (1875), L.R. 7 H.L. 481 66
Middlesex Justices v. R. (1884), 9 App. Cas. 757 31
Midland Railway v. Young (1893), 22 S.C.R. 190 122
Millar v. Taylor (1769), 4 Burr. 2303, 98 E.R. 201 106
Ministry of Housing and Local Government v. Sharp, [1970] 2
    Q.B. 223, [1970] 1 All E.R. 1009 (C.A.) 148
Minneapolis-Honeywell Regulator Co. v. Irvine & Reeves Ltd.
    (1954), 13 W.W.R. 449, [1954] 4 D.L.R. 800
    (B.C.C.A.) 25, 103

Minor v. R. (1920), 52 D.L.R. 158, 53 N.S.R. 551 (C.A.) ... 97, 133
Mischeff v. Springett, [1942] 2 K.B. 331 173
Moir v. Williams, [1892] 1 Q.B. 264 63
Montreal (City) v. Civic Parking Centre Ltd. (1981), 18
    M.P.L.R. 239 (S.C.C.) 163
Moose Jaw (City) v. British American Oil Co., [1937] 2 W.W.R.
    309 (Sask. C.A.) 109, 162
Morgan v. Winnipeg (City) Assessor (1990), 2 M.P.L.R. (2d) 169,
    70 Man. R. (2d) 22 (Q.B.) 162
Morguard Properties Ltd. v. Winnipeg (City) (1983), 24 M.P.L.R.
    219, [1984] 2 W.W.R. 97, 25 Man. R. (2d) 302, 3 D.L.R.
    (4th) 1, 50 N.R. 264, [1983] 2 S.C.R. 493, 6 Admin. L.R.
    206 162
Morley v. Story Mountain Institution (1981), 8 Man. R. (2d) 258,
    59 C.C.C. (2d) 361 (Q.B.) 150
Morris v. Beardmore, [1981] A.C. 446, [1980] 2 All E.R. 753, 71
    Cr. App. R. 256 166
Morris v. Structural Steel Co. (1917), 35 D.L.R. 739, [1917]
    2 W.W.R. 749, 24 B.C.R. 59 (C.A.) 91, 128
Morrison v. Canada (Minister of National Revenue), [1928] 2
    D.L.R. 759, [1928] Ex. C.R. 759 (Ex. Ct.) 99, 113, 114
Mortgage Corp. of Nova Scotia v. Walsh (1925), 57 N.S.R. 547,
    [1925] 1 D.L.R. 665 (C.A.) 154
Mountain Park Coals Ltd. v. Minister of National Revenue,
    [1952] Ex. C.R. 560, [1951] C.T.C. 392, [1952] D.T.C. 1221
    (Ex. Ct.) 107
Muirhead v. Lawson (1884), 1 B.C.R. (Pt. 2) 113 (S.C.) 167
Mullins v. Surrey (Treasurer) (1880), 5 Q.B.D. 170 75
Murphy v. Canadian Pacific Railway (1955), 17 W.W.R. 593,
    1 D.L.R. (2d) 197, 73 C.R.T.C. 90 (Man. Q.B.), affirmed
    (1956), 19 W.W.R. 57, 4 D.L.R. (2d) 443, 74 C.R.T.C. 166
    (Man. C.A.) 147

Nairn v. University of St. Andrews [1909] A.C. 147 13
National Farmers Union v. Prince Edward Island (Potato
    Marketing Council) (1989), 56 D.L.R. (4th) 753 102
National Telephone Co. v. Postmaster-General, [1913] A.C. 546
    30
Neuhaus Estate, Re, [1923] 3 W.W.R. 873, [1923] 4 D.L.R.
    1190 (Man. K.B.) 150
New Brunswick Broadcasting Co. v. Canada (Canadian Radio-
    Television & Telecommunications Commission), [1985] 2
    F.C. 410 (T.D.) 110
New Brunswick Liquor Corp. v. C.U.P.E., Local 963 (1978),
    21 N.B.R. (2d) 441, 37 A.P.R. 441 (C.A.) 117

New Brunswick (Minister of Social Services) v. L. (M.) (1984),
    56 N.B.R. (2d) 343, 146 A.P.R. 343 (Q.B.) 38
Newcorp Properties Ltd. v. West Vancouver (District) (1989),
    45 M.P.L.R. 297, 58 D.L.R. (4th) 362 (B.C.S.C.) 85
Newman v. Grand Trunk Railway (1910), 20 O.L.R. 285
    (C.P.) 118
Northern Crown Bank v. International Electric Co. (1911), 24
    O.L.R. 57 (C.A.) 154
Northman v. Barnet London Borough Council, [1979] 1 W.L.R.
    67 123
Northumberland and Durham (United Counties) v. Board of
    Public School Trustees Union School Sections 16 and 18 of
    Murray and Brighton (Northumberland County), [1941]
    S.C.R. 204 13
Norton v. Spooner (1854), 9 Moore P.C. 103, 14 E.R. 237 127
Nova Scotia (Minister of Environment) v. Cacchione (1987),
    1 C.E.L.R. (N.S.) 177, 35 D.L.R. (4th) 196, 77 N.S.R. (2d)
    372, 191 A.P.R. 372 (T.D.) 96
Nova Scotia (Public Utilities Board) v. Nova Scotia Power Corp.
    (1976), 75 D.L.R. (3d) 72, 18 N.S.R. (2d) 692 (C.A.) 171

O'Connor v. Nova Scotia Telephone Co. (1893), 22 S.C.R.
    276 24
Old Kildonan (Municipality) v. Winnipeg (City), [1943] 2
    W.W.R. 268 (Man. K.B.) 151
Ontario (Attorney General) v. Canada Temperance Foundation,
    [1946] A.C. 193 36
Ontario (Attorney General) v. Perry, [1934] 3 W.W.R. 35, [1934]
    4 D.L.R. 65, [1934] A.C. 477 .... 146, 147
Ontario (Joint Board under Consolidated Hearings Act) v. Ontario
    Hydro (1993), 1 C.E.L.R. (N.S.) 135 (Ont. Div. Ct.) 115
Ottawa (City) v. Canada Atlantic Railway Co. (1903), 33 S.C.R. 376
    42, 98
Ottawa (City) v. Eastview (Town), [1941] S.C.R. 448, [1941]
    4 D.L.R. 65 150
Ottawa (City) v. Hunter (1900), 31 S.C.R. 7 .... 147, 151
Ottawa-Carleton v. Goulbourn (Township) (1978), 5 M.P.L.R.
    195 117
Ouellette v. Canadian Pacific Railway, [1925] 2 D.L.R. 677,
    [1925] 2 W.W.R. 494, [1925] A.C. 569, 39 Que. K.B. 208,
    30 C.R.C. 207 .... 146, 147

Palmer's Case (1784), 1 Leach C.C. 355 145
Partridge v. Aylwin, [1924] 3 D.L.R. 324, [1924] 2 W.W.R.
    671 (C.A.) 113

Pasmore v. Oswaldtwistle Urban District Council, [1898] A.C.
  387 156
Peart v. Stewart, [1983] 2 A.C. 109 81
Peel (Regional Municipality) v. Great Atlantic & Pacific Co.
  of Canada (1991), 4 M.P.L.R. (2d) 113, 91 C.L.L.C. 14,013,
  2 O.R. (3d) 65, 78 D.L.R. (4th) 333, 44 O.A.C. 179, 5
  C.R.R. (2d) 204 (C.A.) 192
Pepper v. Hart, [1993] A.C. 593, [1992] 3 W.L.R. 1032 107
Peterson v. Bitulithic Co. (1913), 4 W.W.R. 223, 23 Man. R. 136,
  12 D.L.R. 444 (C.A.) 155
Pfizer Co. v. Canada (Deputy Minister of National Revenue
  (Customs and Excise)) (1975), [1977] 1 S.C.R. 456, 6 N.R.
  440, 24 C.P.R. (2d) 195, 68 D.L.R. (3d) 9 82
Pic-N-Save Ltd., Re (1972), 32 D.L.R. (3d) 431, [1973] 1 O.R.
  809 (S.C.) 146
Pickles v. Barr, [1947] 2 W.W.R. 272 (B.C.S.C.) 121
Point Grey By-law No. 15, Re (1911), 16 B.C.R. 374, 19 W.L.R.
  638 (C.A.) 150
Post Office v. Union of Communication Workers, [1990] 1
  W.L.R. 981 101
Powell v. Kempton Park Racecourse Co., [1899] A.C. 143 38

Québec (Contrôleur du Revenu) v. Boulet, [1952] Qué. Q.B. 598,
  33 C.B.R. 106 24
Quong-Wing v. R. (1914), 49 S.C.R. 440 91
Québec (Attorney General) v. Blaikie, [1979] 2 S.C.R. 1016,
  49 C.C.C. (2d) 359, 101 D.L.R. (3d) 394, 30 N.R. 225 197
Québec (Attorney General) v. Blaikie, [1981] 1 S.C.R. 312, 36
  N.R. 120, 123 D.L.R. (3d) 15, 60 C.C.C. (2d) 524 197
Québec (Attorney General) v. Eastmain Band (1992), 9
  C.E.L.R. (N.S.) 257 (Fed. C.A.) 160

R. v. Alberta Railway & Irrigation Co. [1912] A.C. 827 145
R. v. American News Co. [1957] O.R. 145, 25 C.R. 374, 118
  C.C.C. 152 (C.A.) 147
R. v. B.C. Fir & Cedar Lumber Co., [1932] 2 D.L.R. 241, [1932]
  2 W.W.R. 253, [1932] A.C. 441 67
R. v. Baines (1840), 12 A. & E. 210, 113 E.R. 792 73
R. v. Barber Asphalt Paving Co. (1911), 23 O.L.R. 372, 18
  C.C.C. 261 (C.P.) 135
R. v. Bata Industries Ltd. (1993), 11 C.E.L.R. (N.S.) 208, 14
  O.R. (3d) 354 (Gen. Div.) 111
R. v. Batista (1912), 9 D.L.R. 138 (Qué. C.A.) 60
R. v. Berkshire Justices (1879), 4 Q.B.D. 469 113
R. v. Beru, [1936] 4 D.L.R. 805, [1936] 2 W.W.R. 574, 50 B.C.R.
  444, 66 C.C.C. 295 (S.C.) 67, 68

R. v. Big M Drug Mart Ltd., [1985] 1 S.C.R. 295 191
R. v. Boudreau, [1924] 3 D.L.R. 75, 51 N.B.R. 234, 42 C.C.C.
    169 (C.A.) 142
R. v. Broughton, [1951] O.R. 263, 11 C.R. 346, 99 C.C.C.
    225 (C.A.) 151
R. v. Budget Car Rentals (Toronto) Ltd. (1981), 15 M.P.L.R.
    172, 31 O.R. (2d) 161, 9 M.V.R. 52, 20 C.R. (3d) 66, 121
    D.L.R. (3d) 111, 57 C.C.C. (2d) 201 (C.A.) 160, 162
R. v. Chambers, [1948] 2 W.W.R. 246, 92 C.C.C. 113, 6 C.R.
    360 (C.A.) 167
R. v. Chief Metropolitan Stipendiary Magistrate, [1990] 3
    W.L.R. 986 90
R. v. Cie Immobilière BCN Ltée, [1979] 1 S.C.R. 865, 25 N.R.
    361, 97 D.L.R. (3d) 238 199
R. v. Cohen (1984), 15 C.C.C. (3d) 231, [1984] C.A. 408 (Qué.
    C.A.) 199
R. v. Collins, [1987] 1 S.C.R. 265, [1987] 3 W.W.R. 699, 56
    C.R. (3d) 193, 74 N.R. 276, 13 B.C.L.R. (2d) 1, 33 C.C.C.
    (3d) 1, 38 D.L.R. (4th) 508, 28 C.R.R. 122 199
R. v. Consolidated Maybrun Mines Ltd. (1993), 12 C.E.L.R.
    (N.S.) 171, 86 C.C.C. (3d) 317 (Ont. Gen. Div.) 97
R. v. Crown Zellerbach Canada Ltd. (1954), 14 W.W.R. 433,
    21 C.R. 94, 111 C.C.C. 54, 25 C.P.R. 13 (B.C.S.C.) 162
R. v. Cummings, [1925] 1 W.W.R. 325, 21 Alta. L.R. 117,
    43 C.C.C. 254, [1925] 1 D.L.R. 1126 (C.A.) 143
R. v. Cuthbertson [1960] Ex. C.R. 83 (Ex. Ct.) 113
R. v. Dagley (1979), 32 N.S.R. (2d) 421, 54 A.P.R. 421
    (C.A.) 118
R. v. Dojacek (1919), 49 D.L.R. 36, [1919] 2 W.W.R. 667, 30
    Man. R. 1, 31 C.C.C. 224 (C.A.) 146
R. v. Donald B. Allen Ltd. (1975), 11 O.R. (2d) 271, 65 D.L.R.
    (3d) 599 (Div. Ct.) 129
R. v. Doreen Rungay Ltd. (1974), 51 D.L.R. (3d) 240, 19
    C.C.C. (2d) 150 (Man. C.A.) 161
R. v. Dowsey (1866), 6 N.S.R. 93 (C.A.) 86
R. v. Dubois, [1935] S.C.R. 378, [1935] 3 D.L.R. 209 99
R. v. Durnion (1887), 14 O.R. 672 (Q.B.) 156
R. v. Dursley (Inhabitants) (1832), 3 B. & Ad. 465, 110 E.R.
    168 155
R. v. Eaton (1881), 8 Q.B.D. 158 12
R. v. Enso Forest Products Ltd. (1992), 8 C.E.L.R. (N.S.) 253,
    70 B.C.L.R. (2d) 135 (S.C.) 99, 114
R. v. Flaman (1978), 43 C.C.C. (2d) 241 (Sask. C.A.) 128
R. v. Fraser Companies Ltd., [1931] S.C.R. 490 115
R. v. Giftcraft Ltd. (1984), 13 C.C.C. (3d) 192 (Ont. H.C.) 111

R. v. Girone (1953), 17 C.R. 60, 9 W.W.R. (N.S.) 255,
106 C.C.C. 33 (B.C.C.A.) 67

R. v. Goulis (1981), 125 D.L.R. (3d) 137, 33 O.R. (2d) 55, 20
C.R. (3d) 360, 37 C.B.R. (N.S.) 290, 60 C.C.C. (2d) 347
(C.A.) 137, 138, 161

R. v. Govedarov (1974), 3 O.R. (2d) 23, 25 C.R.N.S. 1, 16
C.C.C. (2d) 238 (C.A.) 57, 59, 61, 161

R. v. Grant (1898), 30 N.S.R. 368 (C.A.) 74

R. v. Graves (1910), 21 O.L.R. 329, 16 C.C.C. 318 (C.A.) 143

R. v. Houghton (Inhabitants) (1853), 1 E. & B. 501, 118 E.R.
523 125

R. v. Howe (1890), 2 B.C.R. 36 (S.C.) 50

R. v. Inland Revenue Commissioners, [1990] 1 W.L.R. 1400 101

R. v. Irwin, [1926] Ex. C.R. 127 (Ex. Ct.) 129

R. v. Jasperson, [1958] O.W.N. 360 (H.C.) 155

R. v. Jeanotte, [1932] 2 W.W.R. 283 (Sask. C.A.) 111

R. v. Johnston (1979), 52 C.C.C. (2d) 57, 20 A.R. 524 (Q.B.) ... 160

R. v. Kelt, [1977] 1 W.L.R. 1365 61

R. v. Kostynk, [1945] 1 D.L.R. 103, 52 Man. R. 305, [1944]
3 W.W.R. 545, 82 C.C.C. 358 (C.A.) 37

R. v. Kynaston (1926), 19 Cr. App. R. 180 35

R. v. L. (1922), 69 D.L.R. 618, 51 O.L.R. 575, 38 C.C.C. 242
(S.C.) 80

R. v. L. (M.J.) (1986), 46 M.V.R. 301, 77 N.B.R. (2d) 212,
195 A.P.R. 212 (Q.B.) 150

R. v. Lane, [1937] 1 D.L.R. 212, 11 M.P.R. 232, 67 C.C.C.
273 (N.B.C.A.) 24

R. v. Lee Sha Fong, [1940] 3 D.L.R. 317, [1940] 2 W.W.R. 160,
55 B.C.R. 129, 73 C.C.C. 375 (C.A.) 90

R. v. Loxdale (1758), 1 Burr. 445, 97 E.R. 394 145

R. v. MacKay (1918), 40 D.L.R. 37, [1918] 1 W.W.R. 945, 14
Alta. L.R. 182, 29 C.C.C. 194 (C.A.) 61

R. v. Marchioness of Donegal (1923), 51 N.B.R. 309, [1924]
2 D.L.R. 1191 (C.A.) 115

R. v. McEachern, [1935] 3 D.L.R. 298, 9 M.P.R. 366, 63 C.C.C.
335 (N.S.C.A.) 86

R. v. Morgentaler, [1988] 1 S.C.R. 30, 82 N.R. 1, 63 O.R. (2d)
281(n), 62 C.R. (3d) 1, 28 O.A.C. 1, 44 D.L.R. (4th) 385,
31 C.R.R. 1, 37 C.C.C. (3d) 449 191

R. v. Murray (Nicholas), [1990] 1 W.L.R. 1360 179

R. v. New Brunswick (Public Utilities Commission) (1926), 54
N.B.R. 138 (C.A.) 115

R. v. O'Donnel, [1979] 1 W.W.R. 385 198

R. v. Oberlander (1910), 13 W.L.R. 643, 15 B.C.R. 134, 16
C.C.C. 244 (S.C.) 51

R. v. Oliver, [1944] K.B. 68, 29 Cr. App. Rep. 137, [1943] 2
All E.R. 800 (C.A.) 173
R. v. Paré, [1987] 2 S.C.R. 618, 60 C.R. (3d) 346, 80 N.R. 272,
11 Q.A.C. 1, 38 C.C.C. (3d) 97, 45 D.L.R. (4th) 546 114
R. v. Popovic, [1976] 2 S.C.R. 308, 25 C.C.C. (2d) 161, 7 N.R.
231, 62 D.L.R. (3d) 56 199
R. v. Quon, [1948] S.C.R. 508, 6 C.R. 160, 92 C.C.C. 1, [1949]
1 D.L.R. 135 91
R. v. Raiche, 24 C.C.C. (2d) 16 (Sask. Q.B.) 34
R. v. Rao (1984), 9 D.L.R. (4th) 542, 46 O.R. (2d) 80, 40 C.R.
(3d) 1, 12 C.C.C. (3d) 97, 4 O.A.C. 162, 10 C.R.R. 275
(C.A.) 193
R. v. Richards, [1974] 3 All E.R. 696 122
R. v. Rivet, [1944] 3 D.L.R. 353, [1944] 2 W.W.R. 132, 81
C.C.C. 377 (Alta. C.A.) 165, 166
R. v. Robb (1925), 57 O.L.R. 23 (S.C.) 164
R. v. Robinson, [1939] O.R. 235, 20 C.B.R. 476, [1939] 2
D.L.R. 801 (S.C.) 164
R. v. Robinson, [1951] S.C.R. 522, 12 C.R. 101, 100 C.C.C. 1 .. 13
R. v. Royal Bank (1912), 2 D.L.R. 762, 1 W.W.R. 1159, 4
Alta. L.R. 249 (C.A.) 37, 38
R. v. Ruddick (1928), 62 O.L.R. 248, [1928] 3 D.L.R. 208,
49 C.C.C. 323 (H.C.) 36, 91, 151
R. v. Sayward Trading and Ranching Co., [1924] Ex. C.R. 15
(Ex. Ct.) 34
R. v. Scory (1965), 51 W.W.R. 447 (Sask. Q.B.) 66
R. v. Security Storage Co. (1957), 22 W.W.R. 216, 26 C.R. 241,
118 C.C.C. 227, 65 Man. R. 170, 76 C.R.T.C. 109, 11
D.L.R. (2d) 150 (C.A.) 178
R. v. Seilke, [1930] 3 D.L.R. 630, [1930] 1 W.W.R. 653, 38 Man.
R. 549, 53 C.C.C. 237 (C.A.) 68
R. v. Sommerville, [1974] S.C.R. 387, [1973] 2 W.W.R. 65,
32 D.L.R. (3d) 207 102
R. v. Soon, [1919] 1 W.W.R. 486, 26 B.C.R. 450, 31 C.C.C. 78,
45 D.L.R. 78 (C.A.) 122
R. v. St. John, Westgate, Burial Board (1862), 2 B. & S. 703,
121 E.R. 1232 118
R. v. Stevenson (1980), 57 C.C.C. (2d) 526, 19 C.R. (3d) 74
(Ont. C.A.) 107
R. v. Surrey Assessment Committee, [1948] 1 K.B. 29 57
R. v. Swan (1952), 7 W.W.R. (N.S.) 1, 15 C.R. 239, 104 C.C.C.
153 (Sask. C.A.) 90
R. v. Thompson (1913), 5 W.W.R. 157, 7 Alta. L.R. 40, 22
C.C.C. 78, 14 D.L.R. 175 (C.A.) 124
R. v. Titterton, [1895] 2 Q.B. 61 146

R. v. Voisine (1984), 57 N.B.R. (2d) 38, 148 A.P.R. 38 (Q.B.) .. 199

R. v. Washington (1881), 46 U.C.Q.B. 221 (Ont. C.A.) 24

R. v. Wesley, [1932] 4 D.L.R. 774, [1932] 2 W.W.R. 337, 26
    Alta. L.R. 433, 58 C.C.C. 269 (C.A.) 75

R. v. Westendorp (1982), 17 M.P.L.R. 178, [1982] 2 W.W.R. 728,
    18 Alta. L.R. (2d) 204, 26 C.R. (3d) 374, 65 C.C.C. (2d) 417,
    134 D.L.R.(3d) 338, 35 A.R. 228 (C.A.) reversed (1983),
    20 M.P.L.R. 267, [1983] 2 W.W.R. 385, [1983] 1 S.C.R. 43,
    23 Alta. L.R. (2d)289, 32 C.R. (3d) 97. 2 C.C.C. (3d) 330,
    46 N.R. 30, 41 A.R. 306 188

R. v. Western Canada Liquor Co., [1920] 3 W.W.R. 352
    (B.C.C.A.) 166

R. v. Wilcock (1845), 115 E.R. 509, 7 Q.B. 317 129

R. v. Wolfe, [1928] 2 W.W.R. 689, 50 C.C.C. 189, [1928] 4
    D.L.R. 941 (Alta. T.D.) 129

Rance v. Mid-Downs Health Authority, [1991] 2 W.L.R. 159 96

Redpath v. Allan (1872), L.R. 4 C.P. 518 145

Reese v. Alberta (1992), 7 C.E.L.R. (N.S.) 89, 87 D.L.R. (4th) 1,
    85 Alta. L.R. (2d) 153, 123 A.R. 241 (Q.B.) 117

Reference re Liquor Licence Act (Manitoba) (1913), 4 W.W.R.
    551 (Man. C.A.) 147

Reference re Medical Act (Ontario) (1906), 13 O.L.R. 501
    (C.A.)... 24, 85

Reference re s. 189 of Railway Act, 1919, Canada, [1926]
    S.C.R. 163, 32 C.R.C. 83, [1926] 1 D.L.R. 161 184

Reference re Temperance Act (Canada), [1939] O.R. 570, 72
    C.C.C. 145, [1939] 4 D.L.R. 14 (C.A.), affirmed [1946] A.C.
    193, [1946] 2 D.L.R. 1, [1946] 2 W.W.R. 1, 85 C.C.C. 225 . 36

Rempel-Trail Transportation Ltd. v. Neilsen (1978), 93 D.L.R.
    (3d) 595, 8 C.E.L.R. 91 (B.C.S.C.) 169

Ricard v. Lord (1939), [1941] S.C.R. 1, [1941] 1 D.L.R. 536 67

Richard Brothers Co. Estate, Re, [1917] 2 W.W.R. 722, 11
    Alta. L.R. 495 (T.D.) 167

Rippon Housing Order, Re, [1939] 2 K.B. 838 81

Robinson v. Lumsden (1986), 32 D.L.R. (4th) 154, 57 O.R. (2d)
    47, 17 O.A.C. 281 (Div. Ct.) 77

Robitaille v. Beauprés (1937), 75 Qué. S.C. 502 111

Rolls-Royce Co., Re, [1976] 1 W.L.R. 1584 157

Rome v. Punjab National Bank (No. 2), [1989] 1 W.L.R. 1211 ... 75

Rosseter v. Cahlmann (1853), 155 E.R. 1586, 8 Ex. 361 178

Royal Bank v. Acadia School Division No. 8, [1943] 1 W.W.R.
    256 (Alta. T.D.) 104

Rumbolt v. Schmidt (1882), 8 Q.B.D. 603 160

Ryley Hotel Co., Re (1910), 15 W.L.R. 229, 3 Alta. L.R. 281
    (C.A.) 56

"SS Magnhild" (The) v. McIntyre Brothers & Co., [1920] 3 K.B.
321 134
Sage v. Eicholtz, [1919] 2 K.B. 171 24
Salmon v. Duncombe (1886), 11 App. Cas. 627 .... 127, 130
Saltspring Island Sewer Alternatives Committee v. Capital
    Regional District (1982), 134 D.L.R. (3d) 751 (B.C.S.C.) ... 158
Sam Richman Investments (London) Ltd. v. Riedel (1974),
    6 O.R. (2d) 335, 52 D.L.R. (3d) 655 (Div. Ct.) 57
Sandhu v. Mann (1986), 34 D.L.R. (4th) 717, 9 B.C.L.R.
    (2d) 254 (S.C.) 169
Saskatchewan (Human Rights Commission) v. Engineering Students'
    Society, University of Saskatchewan (1989), 56 D.L.R. (4th)
    604, 72 Sask. R. 161 (C.A.) 10, 57, 114, 131, 132, 137
Saskatoon (Episcopal Corp.) v. Saskatoon (City), [1936] 2
    W.W.R. 91 (Sask. C.A.) 162
Sawczuk v. Padgett, [1927] 1 D.L.R. 849, 59 O.L.R. 638, 47
    C.C.C. 78 (C.A.) 89
Scales v. Pickering (1828), 4 Bing. 448, 130 E.R. 840 138
Schiell v. Morrison, [1930] 4 D.L.R. 664, [1930] 2 W.W.R. 737,
    25 Sask. L.R. 18 (C.A.) 25, 167
Seale, Re, [1961] Ch. 574, [1961] 3 All E.R. 136 179
Selangor United Rubber Estates Ltd. v. Craddock (No. 2), [1968]
    1 W.L.R. 319 165
Seward v. "Vera Cruz" The (1884), 10 App. Cas. 59, [1881] All
    E.R. Rep. 216 149
Sewell v. British Columbia Towing and Transportation Co. (1884),
    9 S.C.R. 527 39
Sharp v. McGregor (1988), 50 D.L.R. (4th) 183, 38 M.P.L.R. 315,
    64 O.R. (2d) 449 (Div. Ct.) 160
Shuniah (Township) v. Richard (1982), 37 O.R. (2d) 471,
    19 M.P.L.R. 71, 136 D.L.R. (3d) 638 (H.C.) 169
Silliker v. Newcastle (Town) (1974), 10 N.B.R. (2d) 118
    (Q.B.) 164
Simms v. Registrar of Probates, [1990] A.C. 323 91
Singh v. Winnipeg (City) (1992), 80 Man. R. (2d) 132, 11
    M.P.L.R. (2d) 236 (Q.B.) 129
Skapinker v. Law Society of Upper Canada, [1984] 1 S.C.R. 357,
    9 D.L.R. (4th) 161, 8 C.R.R. 193, 53 N.R. 169, 3 O.A.C.
    321, 11 C.C.C. (3d) 481, 20 Admin. L.R. 1 .... 56, 58, 189,
                                                    190, 191, 192
Slaney v. Kean, [1970] 1 Ch. 243 77
Smart Hardware Co. v. Melfort (Town) (1917), 32 D.L.R.
    552, [1917] 1 W.W.R. 1184, 10 Sask. L.R. 40 (C.A.) 77
Smiles v. Belford (1877), 1 O.A.R. 436 (C.A.) 106
Smith v. Callader, [1901] A.C. 297 173

Smith v. Canada (Attorney General), [1924] Ex. C.R. 193
    (Ex. Ct.) 93
Smith v. Hughes, [1960] 1 W.L.R. 830, [1960] 2 All E.R. 859 ... 95
Smith v. London (City) (1909), 20 O.R. 133 (Div. Ct.) 171
Smith v. National Trust Co. (1912), 1 W.W.R. 1122, 45 S.C.R.
    618, 1 D.L.R. 698 145
Smith v. Richmond, [1899] A.C. 448 63
Smith v. Schofield, [1990] 1 W.L.R. 1447 98
South Eastern Railway Co. v. Railway Commissioners (1881),
    50 L.J.K.B. 201 106
Southam, Re (1991), 19 Ch. D. 169 113
"Spray" (The) v. St. Clair, [1928] Ex. C.R. 56 (Ex. Ct.) 24
Spruce Creek Power Co. v. Muirhead (1904), 11 B.C.R. 68 184
Spruce Grove (Town) v. Yellow Head Regional Library Board
    (1982), 18 M.P.L.R. 278, 19 Alta. L.R. (2d) 122, 134
    D.L.R. (3d) 378 (Q.B.) 141
St. Peters Estates Ltd. v. Prince Edward Island (Land
    Use Commission) (1990), 2 M.P.L.R. (2d) 58, 86 Nfld. &
    P.E.I.R. 271, 268 A.P.R. 271 (P.E.I.S.C.) 41, 102, 104
St. Peter's Evangelical Lutheran Church (Trustees) v. Ottawa
    (City) (1980), 12 M.P.L.R. 241, 27 O.R. (2d) 264 (S.C.),
    reversed (1982), 20 M.P.L.R. 121, [1982] 2 S.C.R. 616, 14
    O.M.B.R. 257, 140 D.L.R. (3d) 577, 45 N.R. 271 165
Stadnick v. Bifrost (Rural Municipality), [1929] 2 D.L.R. 703,
    [1929] 1 W.W.R. 785, 38 Man. R. 180 (C.A.) 121
Stamford (Township) v. Welland (County) (1916), 31 D.L.R. 206,
    37 O.L.R. 155 (C.A.) 80, 85
Statutes of the Province of Manitoba Relating to Education,
    Re (1894), 22 S.C.R. 577 151
Stephenson v. Parkdale Motors, [1924] 3 D.L.R. 663, 55 O.L.R.
    680 (H.C.) 56
Stock v. Frank Jones (Tipton) Ltd., [1978] 1 W.L.R. 231 ... 100, 103
Strachan v. Lamont (1906), 3 W.L.R. 571 (N.W.T.S.C.) 79
Stratton v. Trans-Canada Air Lines (1962), 37 W.W.R.
    577, 32 D.L.R. (2d) 736, 83 C.R.T.C. 15 (B.C.C.A.) 171
Street v. Ottawa Valley Power Corp., [1940] S.C.R. 40, [1939]
    4 D.L.R. 574 184
Sun Alliance Insurance Co. v. Angus, [1988] 2 S.C.R. 256,
    52 D.L.R. (4th) 193, 9 M.V.R. (2d) 245, 87 N.R. 200,
    65 O.R. (2d) 638n, 30 O.A.C. 210 .... 170, 174, 175
Sussex Peerage Case (1844), 8 E.R. 1034, 11 Cl. & Fin. 85 87

T. G. Bright & Co. v. Institut National des Appellations
    d'Origine des vins et eaux-de-vie (1981), 130 D.L.R. (3d)
    12, [1981] C.A. 557, 63 C.P.R. (2d) 99 (Qué.) 170

Theberge v. Laudry (1876), 2 App. Cas. 102 181
Thompson v. Goold & Co., [1910] A.C. 409 123
Thomson v. Halifax Power Co. (1914), 47 N.S.R. 536, 44
    D.L.R. 424 (C.A.) 164
Three Bills Passed by the Legislative Assembly of the Province
    of Alberta, Re; Reference re Alberta Legislation [1938]
    S.C.R. 100 .... 39, 95, 118, 183
Tiedmann v. Basiuk (1977), 4 Alta. L.R. (2d) 12, 7 C.P.C. 192,
    5 A.R. 435 (T.D.) 134
Toronto & Niagara Power Co. v. North Toronto (Town),
    [1912] A.C. 834 104
Toronto (City) v. Presswood Brothers, [1944] 1 D.L.R. 569
    (Ont. C.A.) 172
Toronto (City) v. Toronto & York Radial Railway (1918), 42
    O.L.R. 545, 23 C.R.C. 218, 43 D.L.R. 49 (C.A.) 143
Toronto College Street Centre Ltd. v. Toronto (City) (1986),
    31 D.L.R. (4th) 402, 34 M.P.L.R. 138, 17 O.A.C. 113, 56
    O.R. (2d) 522 (C.A.) 165
Toronto General Trusts Corp v. Shaw, [1942] 2 D.L.R. 439,
    [1942] 1 W.W.R. 818 (Sask. C.A.) 166
Toronto Transit Commission v. Toronto, [1971] S.C.R. 746,
    18 D.L.R. (3d) 68 102
Town Investments Ltd. v. Department of the Environment,
    [1976] 1 W.L.R. 1126 182
Tritt v. United States (1989), 68 O.R. (2d) 284, 33 C.P.C. (2d)
    154 (H.C.) 165
Trizec Equities Ltd. v. Area Assessor Burnaby—New
    Westminster (1983), 22 M.P.L.R. 318, 45 B.C.L.R. 258,
    147 D.L.R. (3d) 637 (S.C.) 162
Turgeon v. Dominion Bank, [1930] S.C.R. 67, 11 C.B.R. 205,
    [1929] 4 D.L.R. 1028 142
Turner v. Insurance Corp of British Columbia (1982), 137
    D.L.R. (3d) 188 (B.C.S.C.) 184

Union Gas Ltd. v. Dawn (Township) (1977), 2 M.P.L.R. 23, 15
    O.R. (2d) 722, 76 D.L.R. (3d) 613 (Div. Ct.) 149, 150
United Brotherhood of Carpenters and Joiners of America,
    Local 1976 v. National Labor Relations Board, 2 L. ed.
    (2d) 1194 13
United Buildings Corp. v. Vancouver (City) (1914), 19 D.L.R. 97,
    6 W.W.R. 1335, [1915] A.C. 345 56
United States v. Aluminium Co. of America, 148 F.2d 416
    (1945) 179
United Towns Electric Co. v. Newfoundland (Attorney
    General), [1939] 1 All E.R. 423 (P.C.) 133

University Hospital Board v. Boros (1985), 24 D.L.R. (4th)
628, [1986] 2 W.W.R. 587, 44 Sask. R. 231 (C.A.) 85
Upper Canada College v. Smith (1920), 61 S.C.R. 413
.... 163, 170, 171, 174

Vacher & Sons Ltd. v. London Society of Compositors, [1913]
A.C. 107 .... 25, 30, 31, 90, 127
Valley View Heritage Assoc. Inc. v. Estevan (City) (No. 2) (1989),
47 M.P.L.R. 24, 81 Sask. R. 84 (Q.B.) 149
Van Allen, Re, [1953] O.R. 569, [1953] 3 D.L.R. 751 (C.A.) 66
Van Schyndel v. Harrell (1991), 7 M.P.L.R. (2d) 97, 6 O.R. (3d)
335, 53 O.A.C. 172 (Div. Ct.) 160
Vancouver (City) v. Grant (1993), 17 M.P.L.R. (2d) 204 at
209 (B.C.S.C.) 115
Victoria (City) v. Bishop of Vancouver Island (1921), 59 D.L.R.
399, [1921] 3 W.W.R. 214, [1921] 2 A.C. 384 50
Victoria and Grey Trust Co. v. Crawford (1986), 57 O.R. (2d)
484 (H.C.) 57
Villeneuve v. Pageau, [1956] Qué. Q.B. 847 (C.A.) 151
Viscountess Rhondda's Claim, [1922] 2 A.C. 339 107

West York (District), Re (1907), 15 O.L.R. 303 (C.A.) 147
Waddington v. Miah, [1974] 1 W.L.R. 683 172
Wall v. Dyke, [1949] 2 W.W.R. 1185 (Man. K.B.) 93
Walsh v. Trebilcock (1894), 23 S.C.R. 695 .... 90, 123
War Amputations of Canada v. Canada (Pension Review
Board), [1980] 2 F.C. 421, 108 D.L.R. (3d) 711 (C.A.) 102
Warburton v. Loveland (1831), 2 D. & Cl. 489, 6 E.R. 809 116
Warner v. Metropolitan Police Com'r, [1969] 2 A.C. 256 107
Warren v. Chapman (1985), 17 D.L.R. (4th) 261 (Man. C.A.) ... 137
Washington v. Grand Trunk Railway (1897), 28 S.C.R.
184 .... 49, 50, 76, 85, 91
Waugh v. Pedneault (Nos. 2 and 3), [1949] 1 W.W.R. 14
(B.C.C.A.) 91,
Way v. St. Thomas (City) (1906), 12 O.L.R. 240 (Div. Ct.) .. 89, 150
West Derby Union Guardians v. Metropolitan Life Assurance
Co., [1897] A.C. 647 76
West Midland Baptist (Trust) Assoc. Inc. v. Birmingham
Corp., [1970] A.C. 874 127
West York (District), Re (1907), 15 O.L.R. 303 (C.A.) 147
West v. Gwynne, [1911] 2 Ch. 1 164
Western Bank Ltd. v. Schindler, [1977] Ch. 1, [1976] 3 W.L.R.
341 121
Westfall v. Eedy (1991), 7 M.P.L.R. (2d) 226, 6 O.R. (3d) 422
(Ont. Gen. Div.) 132, 160

Westminster Bank Ltd. v. Minister of Housing and
  Local Government, [1971] A.C. 508 164
Whiteman v. Sadler, [1910] A.C. 514 141
Whitney v. Inland Revenue Commissioners, [1926] A.C. 37 117
Wildman v. R. (1984), 14 C.C.C. (3d) 321, [1984] 2 S.C.R. 311,
  5 O.A.C. 241, 12 D.L.R. (4th) 641, 55 N.R. 27 ...... 174, 175
Williams v. Box (1910), 44 S.C.R. 1 .... 97, 118
Williams v. Canadian National Railway (1976), 75 D.L.R. (3d)
  87 163
Wilson v. Albert, [1943] 3 D.L.R. 129, [1943] 2 W.W.R. 151
  (Alta. C.A.)
  12
Wilson v. Dagnall, [1972] 1 Q.B. 509 35
Winding Up Act, Re, [1923] 3 D.L.R. 1052, [1923] 3 W.W.R.
  171, 32 B.C.R. 360 (C.A.) 77
Windsor (City) Board of Education v. Ford Motor Co., [1939]
  S.C.R. 412, [1939] 4 D.L.R. 289 146
Winnipeg (City) v. Winnipeg Electric Railway, [1921] 2 W.W.R.
  282, 59 D.L.R. 251, 31 Man. R. 131 (C.A.) 73
Wood's Estate, Re (1886), 31 Ch. D. 607 12
Worthington v. Robbins, [1925] 2 D.L.R. 80, 56 O.L.R. 285
  (S.C.) 94
Would v. Herrington, [1932] 4 D.L.R. 308, [1932] 2 W.W.R.
  385, 40 Man. R. 365 (C.A.) 134

Yorkshire & Pacific Securities Ltd. v. Fiorenza (1938), 52
  B.C.R. 509, [1938] 1 W.W.R. 390 (S.C.) 50, 113

Zainal bin Hashim v. Malaysia (Government), [1980] A.C.
  734, [1979] 3 All E.R. 241 172
Zarezynska v. Levy, [1979] 1 W.L.R. 125 9
861168 Ontario Inc. v. Lindsay (Town) Chief Building Official
  (1991), 6 M.P.L.R. (2d) 84, 3 O.R. (3d) 721 (H.C.) 97

1

HOW AN ACT OF PARLIAMENT IS MADE

WHAT AN ACT OF PARLIAMENT IS

An Act of Parliament (or, to give it its other name, a "statute") is part of the law of the land. It is in fact law made by Parliament. If Parliament wants to make a law on some matter on which there is no law, or if Parliament wants to alter the existing law, it does so by making an Act of Parliament. Acts of Parliament are the way in which Parliament sets out its decisions on what the law is to be.

If heads of business or heads of departments wish to lay down some rule for their staff, they can set it out in a written notice or they can tell the staff by word of mouth. Parliament, however, consists of a large number of elected representatives who are known as Members of Parliament. Members of Parliament as such cannot make law on their own as individuals. Parliament is a body which consists of a large number of Members but which can only act as a body. What Parliament decides is to be found in the Acts passed by it.

HOW AN ACT OF PARLIAMENT BEGINS

The first Act of Parliament was what is known today as the *Statute of Merton*. It took its name from the Surrey village in the priory of which Parliament met to pass the Act. It became part of the law of England in 1235, and some of it is still part of the law in England today.[1]

The King of England at the time when the *Statute of Merton* was passed was Henry III. In those early days, and for some hundreds of years afterwards, many of the Acts of Parliament came into being because they were suggested by the reigning king himself. For example, when King Henry VIII wanted to divorce Katherine of Aragon in order to marry Anne Boleyn, a special Act of Parliament was passed to let him do so. As Parliament said, that Act was passed so that

---

[1] See *Jowitt's Dictionary of English Law* (2nd ed., Sweet & Maxwell, 1977), p. 1178. For other Acts of Parliament passed in the 13th century and still part of the law of England in the 20th century see Fay, *Discoveries in the Statute Book* (Sweet & Maxwell, 1939), p. 9.

"the lawful matrimony had and solemnized between your Highness and your most dear and entirely beloved Queen Anne shall be established and taken for undoubtful true sincere and perfect ever hereafter." [2]

Two years later King Henry VIII persuaded Parliament to pass another Act to say that

"the same marriage between your Highness and the late Queen Anne shall be taken deemed reputed and judged to be of no force strength virtue or effect"[3]

because, as Parliament said,

"the lady Anne, inflamed with pride and carnal desires of her body, putting apart the Dread of God and the excellent benefits received of your Highness . . . most traitorously committed and perpetrated divers detestable and abominable treasons." [4]

One of the most notorious of the Acts of Parliament that came into being because it was suggested by the king was another of the Acts suggested by King Henry VIII. It was passed in 1531. In that year the Bishop of Rochester's cook put poison in a large quantity of porridge that was cooked for the bishop's household and for the poor of the parish. Many people became ill after eating the porridge and one person died. Henry VIII, who was very fond of his food, was no doubt alarmed at this risk of poisoning, and a special Act was rushed through Parliament. It provided that a poisoner must be boiled to death. It was even applied to poisoning that was carried out before the Act had come into force, and so the bishop's cook was the first poisoner boiled to death.

Another poisoner known to have been boiled to death was a servant girl who poisoned her husband in 1531,[5] and there seems to have been at least one other.[6] The Act has since been repealed.

Although for a long time the king was supreme, the day came when Parliament itself gained the greatest power. From that day the number of Acts of Parliament that came into being because the king suggested them became less and less; and today it must be seldom, if at all, that an Act of Parliament comes into being because the reigning king or queen suggests it.

The person in the street might think that most Acts of Parliament come into being because some Member of Parliament suggests them. That is far from being the case. Of course there are cases in which a Member of Parliament sees the need for a new Act of Parliament and persuades Parliament that that new Act should be made. That Member of Parliament may not even be a member of the party that is in power in Parliament at the time. The way in which Parliament works, however, makes

---

[2] *Act of Succession* 1534 (England), quoted in Fay, *Discoveries in the Statute Book*, p. 64.
[3] *Act of Succession* 1536 (England), quoted in Fay, *Discoveries in the Statute Book*, p. 64.
[4] Quoted in Fay, *Discoveries in the Statute Book*, p. 65.
[5] See Fay, *Discoveries in the Statute Book*, pp. 77-78 (the Act was repealed in 1547).
[6] See Megarry, *Miscellany-at-Law* (3rd imp., Stevens & Sons, 1958), pp. 334-335.

it more difficult for a proposal for an Act of Parliament to be brought forward by a member of the opposition than it is for the same proposal to be brought forward by a member of the party that is in power, and especially by a member of Cabinet. Indeed, the pressure of government business has become such that a Member of Parliament who is not a Minister may have great difficulty in having a Bill that is proposed by him or her (known as a "Private Member's Bill") even considered by Parliament.

Parliament works through a government and an opposition.[7] The government consists of a large number of Members of Parliament who are known as backbenchers, and a smaller number who comprise the executive, or, as it is called, the Cabinet. Various Acts of Parliament begin when Cabinet decides that Parliament must take action to meet some need in the community. For example, the Federal and Provincial Cabinets have been concerned at the need to protect the environment and have caused Acts of Parliament to be brought forward creating special environmental protection legislation.

Another way in which an Act of Parliament can begin is by a decision made by a political party. Some political party may adopt a policy which can be put into effect by the making of an Act of Parliament. The decision to adopt that policy may be made by the executive of a political party, or by Members of Parliament belonging to that party and meeting at a party meeting in the party room, or it may be made at a conference attended by a large number of the members of that party. In such a case that decision may result in an Act of Parliament being made. Of course, not every policy adopted by a political party is necessarily enacted into law immediately that party gains office — if at all.

It is not only a political party that may make decisions that result in Parliament passing an Act. Pressure for the making of Acts of Parliament to alter the law can come from the business community. There are, of course, other groups, too, which can persuade Parliament to change the law. The councils which have to give effect to local government law naturally come to know the defects in it. When some defects in the law affecting local government become known to a council that council may seek the change in the law that it needs to overcome the defect.

There is a strong tendency today for the Cabinet to decide to appoint what is most commonly known as a royal commission or a board of inquiry to inquire into a particular matter. Other commissions may be appointed on a continuing basis, law reform commissions being a well-known example. Such boards and commissions produce reports. Those reports

---

[7] There may, of course, be other parties and independent Members of Parliament (who are not members of any party) who have not committed themselves to support either the government or the opposition.

in many instances are pigeonholed but in some instances form the basis for the enactment of new legislation or subordinate legislation.

The most important sources of new Acts of Parliament today are government departments. Senior members of the public service play an important part in the starting of new Acts of Parliament. The department which has to enforce an Act of Parliament of course becomes aware of the defects in the Act. The senior officers of the department are therefore in a position to suggest what new Act of Parliament should be made in order to cure the defects, and they also know what new powers should be given to the department in order to gain full effect for the Act. Indeed, the advice which the head of a government department may offer to Cabinet may go even further, and it may include suggestions for the making of completely new Acts of Parliament to cover new situations. Unfortunately, it is possible for this position of influence to be abused — as followers of the *Yes, Minister* and *Yes Prime Minister* series will be aware. The department may obtain legislation which benefits it, or benefits some pressure group, without necessarily benefiting the public.

HOW THE ACT OF PARLIAMENT IS PREPARED

Although there are many ways in which an Act of Parliament can get its start, the actual writing (or, as it is called, the "drafting") of the Act of Parliament is almost always carried out by a public servant in office for that purpose. The drafter has a difficult task. The number of Acts and regulations that the drafter is called upon to draft is increasing rapidly, and the Acts, bylaws, regulations and other subordinate legislation are becoming more and more technical in their nature. It is not easy to do this sort of work in a hurry, and it is never easy to prepare Acts or subordinate legislation dealing with technical matters. It is not surprising, therefore, that the Acts of Parliament and the subordinate legislation have phrases that can be interpreted in two or more different ways, and it is not surprising that there is often room for real doubt about the true meaning to be given to some particular portion of an Act of Parliament.[8]

One of the difficulties in drafting the modern Act of Parliament is that often the Act deals with something of a technical nature that is beyond the ordinary, everyday experience of the person who is writing the Act. The departmental officer concerned may think that the drafter has been made fully aware of the problems with which the Act is intended to deal, and the drafter may think that he or she is fully aware of those problems. When the Act comes to be enforced, however, it often becomes apparent either that there has been a misunderstanding or that there is some aspect

---

[8] This room for doubt is not limited to Acts of Parliament, and it is certainly not limited to laws prepared by a public servant in office for that purpose.

of the matter which has not been thought of by the departmental officer or by the drafter. It is easy to criticize, but it is hard to draft. The fact that something has been overlooked may cause comment, but it is much easier to see the omission after it has been discovered in practice than it is to guard against that omission when drafting the Act of Parliament itself. The fact that these omissions do occur, however, adds to the difficulty of reading the finished Act of Parliament, which all too often has to be made to work in circumstances of which the drafter was unaware.

HOW THE ACT IS CONSIDERED IN PARLIAMENT

The fact that an Act of Parliament has been drafted does not make it part of the law. There is still much to be done before it becomes law. At that stage, therefore, it is not called an Act; it is called a "Bill".

The Federal Parliament, like Parliament in England, is comprised of two Houses of Parliament. Some of the Provincial legislatures have only one House. When a Bill is brought before Parliament itself it is considered three times by each House of Parliament[9] — or, to use the phrase which Parliament uses, it is given three "readings". In addition to those three readings Parliament may refer the Bill to a Parliamentary committee to examine it and report back to Parliament before the Bill progresses further, and the right to refer a Bill to such a committee is not confined to one House of Parliament: in those Parliaments which consist of two Houses, either House may refer the Bill to a committee for examination.

The fact that a Bill is brought before Parliament does not mean that it must become part of the law. Even if the Bill is brought before Parliament by the party which is in power in Parliament, Parliament as a whole may decide not to make that Bill part of the law.

It is said that at one time the English Parliament had to consider a Bill which provided that

> "all women of whatever age, rank or profession, whether maid or widow, who shall after this Act impose upon and seduce into matrimony any of His Majesty's subjects by means of scents, paints, cosmetics, artificial teeth, false hair, bolstered hips, high-heeled shoes, or iron stays, shall incur the penalties against witchcraft, and the marriage be declared null and void." [10]

Parliament did not make that Bill part of the law of the land!

Even if Parliament accepts the idea that the Bill should become part of the law of the land, it may decide to make changes in the Bill. The usual time at which these changes are made is when the Bill is receiving its second reading. The changes made at that stage may be quite extensive

---

[9] If the Parliament consists of one House only, the three readings are, of course, confined to that one House.

[10] Quoted in Fay, *Discoveries in the Statute Book*, pp. 196-197.

ones. Sometimes changes may be made because the pressure of public opinion forces the Cabinet to change its policy. Other changes may be made because the department or other body which will have to put the Act into force discovers defects in it, and so puts forward amendments to the Bill. Changes may also be made because the Members of Parliament themselves are not prepared to accept the Bill in the form in which it is brought before them. Of course there are many Bills that are passed as Acts of Parliament without any changes, but there is always the possibility of changes being made when any Bill is brought before Parliament.

If a Bill is brought before a Parliament which consists of two Houses, the Bill will ordinarily have to be passed by both Houses before it becomes an Act of Parliament. In practice it receives all three readings in one House before it is sent to the other. Of course, the House which receives the Bill after it has already been considered by the other House of Parliament is not bound to accept the Bill in the form in which the other House of Parliament has accepted it. The second House of Parliament may decide that changes should be made. If that happens, the Bill must be sent back to the first House of Parliament for further consideration. If the two Houses of Parliament cannot agree upon the changes which should be made to the Bill, there is a special system to try to overcome the difference of opinion between the two Houses of Parliament. In that case each House of Parliament appoints a small number of its Members to represent it. These Members are known as "managers". The managers of the two Houses then meet together to see if they can agree upon the changes that should be made in the Bill. As a result, the Bill, if it finally becomes an Act of Parliament, may be in a form that is very different to the form that was intended by the Member of Parliament who first brought it before Parliament.

How the Act of Parliament comes into force

When the Bill has been passed by Parliament it has still to be approved by the reigning Monarch (in practice, the Monarch's representative) before it can come into force. Some Acts of Parliament come into force as soon as they have been approved, but others come into force at some later date. The actual date on which an Act of Parliament comes into force is considered in chapter 9.

Once an Act of Parliament has come into force it will ordinarily continue to be in force indefinitely: "A law is not repealed by becoming obsolete: there is no doctrine of desuetude in English law."[11] However, Parliament may insert an express provision into the Act providing for that Act to cease to have effect after a specified period or on the happening

---

[11] *Maxwell on The Interpretation of Statutes*, 12th edition, by Langan, P. St. J. (NM Tripathi Private Ltd., 1976).

of a specified event. Such a provision cannot preclude Parliament from subsequently changing its mind and providing by an amending Act or other later Act, that the earlier Act is to continue in force either for a longer period or a shorter period, or perpetually.

ACTS OBTAINED BY FRAUD

Once the Act comes into force, the way in which it was obtained becomes irrelevant. An Act passed as a result of a request by a department, a professional body, or even an individual is interpreted in just the same way as an Act passed because the ruling party in Parliament decided that it should be enacted. Even if Parliament were misled by fraudulent misrepresentations or otherwise, to pass an Act which it would not have passed if it had known the true position, the Act has full force and effect unless and until Parliament repeals it; in this regard "the court will not inquire into what passed in the course of the passage of the Bill through Parliament."[12] This is because speculations as to the relative weight of possible motives which may be conceived as prompting such legislative action would carry us far beyond the strict limits of the judicial function.[13]

---

[12] *British Railways Board v. Pickin*, [1974] A.C. 765, Lord Cross of Chelsea at 802.
[13] *Canadian Railway Co. v. R.* (1922), 64 S.C.R. 264, Duff J. (later Duff C.J.C.) at 271. See also *Ashmore v. Bank of British North America* (1913), 13 D.L.R. 73, Irving J.A. at 74 (B.C.C.A.); *Hobrecker v. Sanders* (1909), 44 N.S.R. 14 (C.A.).

2

THE SPECIAL RULES FOR UNDERSTANDING ACTS OF PARLIAMENT

AMBIGUITY IN ACTS OF PARLIAMENT

Difficulties can arise in understanding an Act of Parliament because of a drafter's oversight, a misprint, or even a mistake as to the law as it existed when the Act was made by Parliament — difficulties which are considered in chapters 31 and 32. However, the difficulties in understanding an Act of Parliament are not limited to difficulties such as those. Parliament is passing an ever increasing number of Acts, and government departments are finding a need for an ever increasing number of regulations. The more Acts and bylaws that are required, the greater the pressure upon the drafter. The greater, therefore, is the risk of lack of clarity in the wording of the Acts of Parliament. It is the ambiguity and frequent lack of clarity in statutory provisions which create the need for special rules for understanding Acts of Parliament.

Judges' criticisms of the drafting of Acts of Parliament

Because of the pressure under which the drafting of Acts of Parliament has to be carried out, the task of the parliamentary drafter is a hard one. Indeed, as one leading writer has pointed out:

"in a sense, the scales are heavily weighted against the draftsman: if he has made himself plain, there is likely to be no litigation and so none to praise him, whereas if he has fallen into confusion or obscurity, the reports will probably record the results of the fierce and critical intellects of both bar and bench being brought to bear on his work."[1]

Certainly the meaning of words used in the Acts of Parliament has often been difficult to find, and the judges have frequently criticised the drafting of Acts of Parliament. For example, a judge has complained that "it has taken us a long period of acute concentration to disentangle the conceivably relevant passages from an accumulation of complicated terminology".[2]

---

[1] Megarry, *Miscellany-at-Law* (3rd imp.), p. 349.
[2] *Zarezynska v. Levy*, [1979] 1 W.L.R. 125, Kilner Brown J. at 128.

In the Supreme Court of Canada, Davies J. has observed that "The language of the section is unfortunately somewhat obscure and ambiguous";[3] also in that court, Idington J. has said: "I cannot assign legislative power to the phrase without leading to possible absurdities or at least inconsistencies when we consider its use elsewhere";[4] and at the level of Supreme Courts of Provinces, McDonald, the Chief Justice of British Columbia, said: "I find it no small task to discover its meaning. Though it has been copied by several Provincial legislatures, it would be hard to find a more embarrassing piece of legislation".[5]

At the Court of Appeal level, Cameron J. has complained that

"Tensions may . . . arise between the general purpose of the enactment and the specific language of its various sections, making it difficult, even impossible at times, to fulfill the purpose and at the same time respect the intention of the legislator. That is so in relation to some of the provisions of this Act, a fact which renders the task of interpreting and applying it considerably more burdensome."[6]

The English Acts of Parliament dealing with the position of landlords and tenants have been the subject of a great deal of criticism by judges. They have been called "a byword for confused draftsmanship".[7] One writer has collected some of that criticism:

"In this 'extraordinary and unique legislation', 'the Acts were passed in a hurry, the language used was often extremely vague', and the language 'resembles that of popular journalism rather than the terms of the art of conveyancing'. 'It is a patchwork legislation, has not been framed with any scientific accuracy of language, and presents great difficulties of interpretation to the courts that have to give practical effect to it.' As MacKinnon L.J. observed, 'anybody may be forgiven for making a mistake' about 'the hasty and ill-considered language' of 'this chaotic series of Acts', that 'welter of chaotic verbiage which may be cited together as the *Rent and Mortgage (Interest) Restrictions Acts* 1920 to 1939'. In one case Scrutton L.J. said: 'I regret that I cannot order the costs to be paid by the draftsman of the *Rent Restrictions Acts,* and the members of the legislature who passed them, and are responsible for the obscurity of the Acts.' 'If the judges now had anything to do with the language of Acts they are to administer, it is inconceivable that they would have to face the horrors of the *Rent and Mortgage (Interest) Restrictions Act* — horrors that are hastening many of them to a premature grave.' "[8]

As an example of drafting that is hard to understand, a textbook writer has quoted the following order:

"The Control of Tins, Cans, Kegs, Drums and Packaging Pails (No. 5) Order, 1942 (a), as varied by the Control of Tins, Cans, Kegs, Drums and Packaging Pails (No. 6) Order, 1942 (b), the Control of Tins, Cans, Kegs, Drums and Packaging Pails (No. 7)

---

[3] *Canadian Northern Railway, Re* (1909), 42 S.C.R. 443 at 454.
[4] *Canadian Northern Railway, Re,* Idington J. at 460.
[5] *Mainwaring v. Mainwaring,* [1942] 2 D.L.R. 377 at 378.
[6] *Saskatchewan Human Rights Commission v. Engineering Students' Society, University of Saskatchewan* (1989), 56 D.L.R. (4th) 604 at 614-615 (Sask. C.A.).
[7] *Joint Properties Ltd. v. Williamson,* [1945] S.C. 68, Lord Normand, Lord President at 74.
[8] Megarray, *Miscellany-at-Law* (3rd imp.), p. 352.

Order, 1942 (c), the *Control of Tins, Cans, Kegs, Drums and Packaging Pails (No. 8) Order,* 1942 (d), and the *Control of Tins, Cans, Kegs, Drums and Packaging Pails (No. 9) Order,* 1942 (e), is hereby further varied in the Third Schedule thereto . . . by substituting for the reference 2A therein the reference '2A (1)' and by deleting therefrom the reference 2B.

This Order shall come into force on the 25th day of August 1943, and may be cited as the *'Control of Tins, Cans, Kegs, Drums and Packaging Pails (No. 10) Order,* 1943*',* and this Order and the *'Control of Tins, Cans, Kegs, Drums and Packaging Pails (No. 5-9) Orders* may be cited as the *'Control of Tins, Cans, Kegs, Drums and Packaging Pails (No. 5-10) Orders,* 1942-43' "[9]

As the textbook writer added: "An explanatory note mercifully informs us: 'The above Order enables tin plate to be used for tobacco and snuff tins other than cutter lid tobacco tins.' "[10]

Unfortunately, the fact that a statute has to be read and obeyed by persons without any knowledge of law and without the benefit of a higher education does nothing to ensure that it will be in plain language.

The importance of the legislation to the community as a whole does not guarantee clarity. The provisions of environmental protection legislation are often inept in drafting and contain many ambiguities and a considerable degree of incoherence of language. Town planning legislation has been criticised repeatedly by judges. The very importance of environmental and town planning impacts on the community leads to numerous amendments to the statutes and therefore causes them to be more difficult to interpret.

Legislation by reference

There is one short cut that drafters of Acts of Parliament have taken from time to time. Instead of setting out in full, in the new Act of Parliament, everything that is to apply to the particular matter, the drafter takes the short cut of incorporating in the new Act of Parliament various provisions contained in other Acts of Parliament. Of course, since a short cut is being used, the drafter does not set out those provisions in full in the new Act, but merely refers to the provisions in the other Acts as being incorporated in the new Act. This is known as "legislation by reference", which raises difficulties of its own.[11] Often there is difficulty in applying to the new Act the provisions of the older Acts which were written for a different purpose.

Again, when Parliament says that two Acts are to be read as one (a common form of legislation by reference) the two Acts must be read together as if all the provisions of both Acts were really contained in

---

[9] Quoted in Allen, Professor Sir Carlton Kemp, *Law and Orders* (3rd ed.), p. 176.

[10] Allen, *Law and Orders* (3rd ed.), p. 177.

[11] Côté, P-E, *The Interpretation of Legislation in Canada* (Les Éditions Yvon Blais Inc., Cowansville, 1984) pp. 56-58.

one single Act of Parliament — the whole of the provisions must be read

"as if [they] had been contained in one Act unless there is some manifest discrepancy making it necessary to hold that the later Act has, to some extent, modified something found in the earlier Act".[12]

The two Acts are treated as if they were in fact only one Act and as if all the provisions in that one Act had been passed by Parliament at one and the same time.[13] "It seems to me that [the later order] . . . is in exactly the same position if instead of incorporating by reference s. 1 of [the earlier order], it had simply repeated the definition contained in that section."[14]

In a unanimous decision the Alberta Court of Appeal held that

"In *Clark v. Bradlaugh* (1881), 8 Q.B.D. 63 at 69, Brett L.J. said: 'There is a rule of construction that, where a statute is incorporated by reference into a second statute, the repeal of the first statute by a third does not affect the second.'
This rule seems quite logical. If a new statute incorporates a section from a former statute then that section becomes a part of the new statute and is not affected by the repeal or alteration of the former statute."[15]

If an Act which has been incorporated by reference into a second Act is subsequently amended, that amendment is not automatically incorporated into the other Act.[16]

As long ago as 1875, a select committee of the British Parliament described legislation by reference as making an Act so ambiguous, so obscure, and so difficult that the judges themselves could hardly assign a meaning to it, and the ordinary citizen could not understand it without legal advice.[17] Legislation by reference has been repeatedly criticised by judges for more than a century.[18] Judges of the Supreme Court of Canada have been prominent in their criticisms of legislation by reference. In 1941, Davis J. observed that "This appeal involves the interpretation of . . .

---

[12] *Canada Southern Railway Co. v. International Bridge Co.* (1883), 8 App. Cas. 723, Earl of Selborne L.C. at 727. See also *Kilgour v. London Street Railway Co.* (1914), 30 O.L.R. 603, 19 D.L.R. 827, Meredith C.J.O. at 828 (C.A.); *Harrison Brothers Ltd. v. St. Jean (Municipality)* (1936), 62 Qué. K.B. 357 (C.A.).

[13] *Wood's Estate, Re* (1886), 31 Ch. D. 607.

[14] *Wilson v. Albert*, [1943] 3 D.L.R. 129, unanimous decision at 133 (Alta. C.A.).

[15] *Wilson v. Albert*, [1943] 3 D.L.R. 129, unanimous decision at 133 (Alta. C.A.).

[16] *Mainwaring v. Mainwaring*, [1942] 2 D.L.R. 377, McDonald C.J.B.C. at 380 (B.C.C.A.), and *Harrison Brothers Ltd. v. St. Jean (Municipality)* (1936), 62 Qué. K.B. 357 (C.A.); *McKenzie v. Jackson* (1898), 31 N.S.R. 70 (C.A.). However, Parliament can change this as for example by section 32 of the British Columbia *Interpretation Act*, R.S.B.C. 1979, c. 206: "In an enactment reference to another enactment . . . is a reference to the other enactment as amended whether amended before or after the commencement of the enactment in which the reference occurs."

[17] See *Craies on Statute Law*, Sweet & Maxwell, London, 7th ed. by Edgar, S.G.G. (1971), p. 29.

[18] See, for example, *R. v. Eaton* (1881), 8 Q.B.D. 158 at 160; *Knill v. Towse* (1889), 24 Q.B.D. 186 at 195.

legislation by reference . . . and presents, as such legislation usually does, vexatious and quite unnecessary difficulties".[19] Nearly 40 years later, Estey J. complained that "The incorporation by reference of a segment of another statute is always fraught with danger and difficulty".[20]

THE NEED FOR SPECIAL RULES FOR THE READING OF ACTS OF PARLIAMENT

The difficulties that can arise in trying to find the true meaning of an Act of Parliament are numerous indeed. An Act of Parliament by its very nature is not something that can be read like a novel. It is something in which each word must be carefully examined. The rights of the private individual may depend upon which of two or more possible meanings are given to the words of the Act. Even the question whether or not a person is to be sent to prison can depend upon what meaning the court gives to ambiguous words used in an Act of Parliament.[21] It is important, therefore, to do whatever can be done to see that courts adopt as uniform an approach as possible to the reading of ambiguous Acts of Parliament. To try to achieve that uniformity, the courts have developed a series of rules which they have applied over the years:

"From early times courts of law have been continuously obliged, in endeavouring loyally to carry out the intentions of Parliament, to observe a series of familiar precautions for interpreting statutes so imperfect and obscure as they often are."[22]

It is those rules with which this book is concerned. The use of the rules helps readers of an Act of Parliament to find what the Act really means. Readers must, however, always bear in mind that what they are trying to do is not to carry out some school exercise but to find the real meaning of the Act. As a very distinguished American judge has said:

"Construing legislation is nothing like a mechanical endeavour. It could not be accomplished by the subtlest modern 'brain' machines. Because of the infirmities of language and the limited scope of science in legislative drafting, inevitably there enters into the construction of statutes the play of judicial judgment within the limits of the relevant legislative materials."[23]

---

[19] *Northumberland and Durham (United Counties) v. Board of Public School Trustees Union School Sections 16 and 18 of Murray and Brighton (Northumberland County)*, [1941] S.C.R. 204 at 209.

[20] *Goulbourn (Township) v. Ottawa-Carleton (Regional Municipality)* (1979), 101 D.L.R. (3d) 1 at 10 (S.C.C.).

[21] *Fawcett Properties Ltd. v. Buckingham County Council*, [1961] A.C. 636 at 671, *R. v. Robinson*, [1951] S.C.R. 522.

[22] *Nairn v. University of St. Andrews* [1909] A.C. 147, Lord Loreburn L.C. at 161.

[23] *United Brotherhood of Carpenters and Joiners of America, Local 1976 v. National Labor Relations Board*, 2 L. ed. (2d) 1194.

3

THE ELEMENTS OF AN ACT OF PARLIAMENT

INTRODUCTION

Before considering the special rules that are used in reading an Act of Parliament, it is necessary to know the various elements that make up the Act of Parliament and the particular rules that apply to each of those elements.

The elements of an Act of Parliament

The following are the more important elements that may be found in an Act of Parliament:

the regnal year
number of the Act
long title of the Act
enacting words
short title of the Act
date on which the Act comes into force
preamble (sometimes described as recitals)
purposes section
analysis (sometimes described as contents or a table of contents and
    sometimes as a table of provisions, and in Québec as sommaire)
sections, subsections and paragraphs
parts and divisions
headings
marginal notes (sometimes called sidenotes)
definitions (sometimes described as interpretation)
schedules
provisos
punctuation

4

THE REGNAL YEAR

THE REGNAL YEAR

The Federal Parliament follows the practice of setting out, at the beginning of the Act of Parliament, the regnal year(s) of the particular session of Parliament in which the Act was passed by Parliament. The regnal year is, of course, not the calendar year: it is the year of the reign of the particular king or queen. An example of this printing of the regnal year is:

40 ELIZABETH II, 1991
CHAPTER 45

The actual form of the regnal year depends upon the decision of the individual legislature. Thus the Legislative Assembly of the Province of British Columbia shows the regnal year as 44 Elizabeth II, 1995.

The printing of the regnal year has no legal effect; indeed, various Provinces do not use the regnal year. The Act is just as much an Act of Parliament and is just as much part of the law of the land if the regnal year is not printed on it.

5

THE NUMBER OF THE ACT

THE NATURE OF THE NUMBER

Every Act of Parliament receives a number. Each Parliament has its own numbering, and the system of numbering varies from Parliament to Parliament. For example, the system formerly used by the British Parliament was to start the numbering again at the beginning of each session of the sittings of Parliament, and is now to start it again at the beginning of each calendar year.

The Form of the Number

Because of the different systems of numbering that are in use, the form of the number differs according to the system in the particular Parliament.

When the British Parliament started the numbering of its Acts anew with the beginning of each new session of Parliament, its number referred to the regnal year. For example, the number of the *Slaughter of Animals Act* 1958 was printed as follows:

(7 ELIZ. 2 CH. 8)

However, the sessions of Parliament do not always coincide with the regnal year. It often happens that the session of Parliament starts towards the end of one year of the reign and extends into the next year of the reign. When that happened the number of the Act under the former British parliamentary system referred to both years of the reign. Thus for example, the number of the *Local Government Act* 1958 is:

(6 & 7 ELIZ. 2 CH. 55)[1]

The English system in use today is different. The number of the English *Finance Act* 1981 is printed as follows:

---

[1] In the example given, "ELIZ." is short for Elizabeth and "CH." is short for chapter. "6 & 7 ELIZ. 2 CH. 55" there means the 55th Act (or "chapter") in the parliamentary session in the sixth and seventh years of the reign of Queen Elizabeth II. In more recent Acts instead of "CH." the abbreviation used is c.

1981 Chapter 35

In the Federal Parliament every Act is progressively numbered in respect of that part of the relevant Session of Parliament in the regnal year in which the Act was passed, for example:

40 ELIZABETH II, 1991
CHAPTER 45

Examples of Provincial Acts are the *International Sale of Goods Act*, 1990 of British Columbia

CHAPTER 20

and of Ontario
An Act to amend the Ontario Lottery Corporation Act, 1992.

CHAPTER 29

In Ontario, private Acts of Parliament are numbered separately. For example, *An Act respecting FaithWay Baptist College of Canada*, 1992 is numbered

CHAPTER PR1[2]

From time to time a Parliament may decide to revise and consolidate its statutes. For example, the *Interpretation Act* of British Columbia (Chapter 206 of 1979) is numbered

R.S.[3] Chap. 206

The *Interpretation Act* of Ontario as set out in its revised statutes of 1980 is simply numbered

Chap. 219

The effect of the number

The number given to an Act of Parliament has no legal effect. It does not affect the meaning of the Act of Parliament in any way. It is merely an easy way of finding the Act of Parliament: when the Acts are bound into a volume, they are usually printed in their numerical order.

---

[2] "PR" means that this is a private Act.
[3] "R.S." refers to the Revised Statutes of that Parliament.

It is not essential when citing an Act to refer to its number. For example in British Columbia

> "An Act may be cited by reference to its chapter number in the Revised Statutes, reference to its chapter number in the Acts for the year or regnal year in which it was enacted, or by reference to its long or short title with or without reference to its chapter number."[4]

---

[4] *Interpretation Act*, R.S.B.C., c. 206, s. 44.

6

THE LONG TITLE OF THE ACT

THE FORM OF THE LONG TITLE

An example of an Act which has a long title is the Canadian statute, the short title of which is the *Trust and Loan Companies Act*, 40 Eliz. II, 1991, Ch. 45. Its long title is,

"An Act to revise and amend the law governing federal and trust and loan companies and to provide for related and consequential matters".

Another example of a long title is that of the Canadian *Miscellaneous Statute Law Amendment Act*, S.C. 1991:

"An Act to correct certain anomalies, inconsistencies, archaisms and errors in the Statutes of Canada, to deal with other matters of a non-controversial and uncomplicated nature therein and to repeal certain provisions thereof that have expired or lapsed or otherwise ceased to have effect."

The Ontario *Substitute Decisions Act*, S.O. 1992 has the long title:

"An Act to provide for the making of Decisions on behalf of Adults concerning the Management of their Property and concerning their Personal Care."

Not all Acts of Parliament, however, have long titles as lengthy as the examples set out above. For example, the *Ontario Lottery Corporation Amendment Act,* S.O. 1992 has the long title:

"An Act to Amend the Ontario Lottery Corporation Act".

THE LONG TITLE AS PART OF THE ACT

The first Acts of Parliament did not have titles. The first time that an Act of Parliament was given a title was about 1495.[1] Even when the long title came to be added to each Act of Parliament as a matter of course, as it did from about 1513,[2] the long title was not regarded as

---

[1] *Chance v. Adams* (1696), 1 Ld. Raym. 77 at 78, 91 E.R. 948. *Words and Phrases Judicially Defined* (1st ed. Butterworths, 1943), vol. 1, p. 50, gives the date as 1496. *Maxwell on The Interpretation of Statutes* (11th ed., Sweet & Maxwell, 1962), p. 40, gives the year as "about the 11th year of Henry VII" (that is, 1496). *Craies on Statute Law* (Sweet & Maxwell, London, 7th ed., Edgar, S.G.G. (1971)) , p. 190, quotes the date as 1495 but refers in a footnote to an Act passed eight years earlier.

[2] *Craies on Statute Law* (Sweet & Maxwell, London, 7th ed., Edgar, S.G.G. (1971)), p. 190.

part of the Act of Parliament itself. Today, however, whether the long title is part of the Act of Parliament depends upon the decision of the Parliament concerned. The contrast between the original rejection of long titles as part of an Act and the present acceptance of them in New Brunswick has been well put by Baxter C.J.:

> "The title is now a part of an Act. Originally it was not so . . . originally it appears a title was not enacted by the royal assent. It was simply a descriptive sentence added to the Bill after the latter had become law by the expression of the King's will."[3]

That also is the position in Ontario.[4] In British Columbia the Parliament has provided expressly that "the Title . . . of an enactment [is] part of it intended to assist in explaining its meaning and object".[5]

USING THE LONG TITLE TO FIND THE MEANING OF THE ACT

The long title is the first of the elements of an Act of Parliament that can be used to find the meaning of the Act, in particular to ascertain the general scope of the Act[6] and the objects of the legislature.[7] However, the court is not "slavishly bound by the title" in construing the statute.[8] Thus, the statute may be wider in scope than the title, and in that case the wider interpretation is to be given.[9]

Generally, the long title is not used to find the meaning of the Act unless the particular section of the Act that is being read is one which could have two or more different meanings. If the meaning of the section is clear, it should not be altered by reading the long title.[10] Thus it has been said that "I do not think that such . . . title can, according to any sound canon of construction, be called in aid to control the meaning of words in themselves clear and unambiguous."[11]

As Martin J.A. has held,

> "The conclusion to be drawn from the authorities I think is that . . . where the language

---

[3] *R. v. Lane, ex. p. Gould*, [1937] 1 D.L.R. 212, Baxter C.J. at 213 (N.B.C.A.).

[4] *Reference re Medical Act (Ontario)* (1906), 13 O.L.R. 501, Moss C.J.O. at 504 (C.A.). See also *Insurance Corp. of British Columbia v. Canada (Registrar of Trade Marks)*, [1980] 1 F.C. 669 (T.D.).

[5] *Interpretation Act*, R.S.B.C., c. 206, s. 9.

[6] *Chapman v. Purtell* (1915), 22 D.L.R. 860 (Man. K.B.).

[7] *O'Connor v. Nova Scotia Telephone Co.* (1893), 22 S.C.R. 276, Sedgewick J. at 292; *R. v. Washington* (1881), 46 U.C.Q.B. 221 (Ont. C.A.).

[8] Côté, P-E, *The Interpretation of Legislation in Canada* (Les Éditions Yvon Blais Inc., Cowansville, 1984) p. 37. Côté is there quoting from a County Court decision but it is his adoption of the principle that is important and clearly correct.

[9] *Contrôleur du Revenu de la Province de Québec v. Boulet*, [1952] Qué. K.B. 598; *Johnston v. Canadian Credit Men's Trust Association*, [1932] 2 D.L.R. 462 (S.C.C.).

[10] *Sage v. Eicholtz*, [1919] 2 K.B. 171.

[11] *"Spray" (The) v. St. Clair*, [1928] Ex. C.R. 56 (Ex. Ct.).

of the statute is plain, it must be given effect to notwithstanding the fact that it goes beyond the matters mentioned in the title."[12]

If any section of the Act contains words which have two or more meanings, the reader of the Act may use the long title to help choose between those meanings, for "it is legitimate to use it for the purpose of interpreting the Act as a whole and ascertaining its scope".[13]

A case decided by the British Columbia Court of Appeal gives an example of the way in which the long title is used to remove doubt as to the meaning of a section. It was held that

"The nature of the *Mechanics' Lien Act*, [R.S.B.C., 1948, Ch. 205] indicates in no uncertain way that s. 19 can apply only where a lien is in existence. The very commencement of the statute describes it as 'An Act respecting Liens of Mechanics, Wage-earners and Others.' That plainly refers only to situations where liens are in existence".[14]

---

[12] *Schiell v. Morrison*, [1930] 4 D.L.R. 664 at 668 (Sask. C.A.).

[13] *Vacher & Sons Ltd. v. London Society of Compositors*, [1913] A.C. 107, Lord Moulton at 128.

[14] *Minneapolis — Honeywell Regulator Co. v. Irvine & Reeves Ltd.* (1954), 13 W.W.R. 449, O'Halloran J.A. at 453-454 (B.C.C.A.).

7

THE ENACTING WORDS

THE USE OF ENACTING WORDS

Not all Acts of Parliament have enacting words. There was a period when Acts of the British Parliament did not use them. Many Canadian Acts, however, do have them.

If enacting words are used they are usually set out below the long title of the Act.

By statute, enacting words in legislation made by the Federal Parliament are required to "follow the preamble, if any".[1] In such case the enacting words are

> "Her Majesty, by and with the advice and consent of the Senate and House of Commons of Canada, enacts as follows".[2]

The Provinces of Ontario and British Columbia use the form of words:

> "HER MAJESTY, by and with the advice and consent of the Legislative Assembly of the Province of . . . , enacts as follows:"

However, the revised statutes of both those Provinces do not include enacting words.

THE EFFECT OF THE ENACTING WORDS

The enacting words do not affect the meaning of the Act in any way. Different words could be used, or no enacting words at all, without affecting the meaning or the binding effect of the Act.

---

[1] *Interpretation Act*, R.S.C. 1985, c. I-23, s. 4(2)
[2] *Interpretation Act*, R.S.C. 1985, c. I-23, s. 4(1)

8

THE SHORT TITLE

THE NATURE OF THE SHORT TITLE

As its name indicates, the short title is normally a brief one. For example, the short title of an Act made by the Federal Parliament is expressed as follows: "This Act may be cited as the *Trust and Loan Companies Act, 40 Eliz. II Ch. 45, 1991*".

The short title of *An Act respecting the Provision of Advocacy Services to Vulnerable Persons* (Ont.), 1992 Chap. 26 is the "*Advocacy Act, 1992.*"

THE PLACE WHERE THE SHORT TITLE IS TO BE FOUND

The practice of the British Parliament is to place the short title at the end of the Act of Parliament immediately before the schedules. Thus the short title of the *Housing Act*, 1957 appears in section 193(1) of that Act. This practice is also adopted in Ontario Acts. The practice elsewhere in Canada is to place the short title in the first section of the Act.

In British Columbia, there is no short title as such but a title appears at the head of the Act prior to the chapter number, for example the *International Sale of Goods Act, 1990* Chap. 20.

THE USE OF THE SHORT TITLE

The short title is the most convenient way of referring to an Act of Parliament. There is much less chance of a mistake if an Act of Parliament is referred to by its short title than there is if it is referred to by its number, since the possibility of an error in the printing or misrecollection can more readily arise in the case of a number than in the case of a title.

THE LEGAL EFFECT OF A SHORT TITLE

Justice is not a coin in the slot machine. Indeed, if the courts were worked upon a coin in the slot basis, they would not be able to give justice. One result of the legal system we have, however, is that judges can hold differing views upon those parts of the law in which there is as yet no clear rule. The use that is to be made of the short title in finding the meaning of an Act is one of those as yet uncertain parts of the law.

While it is clear that the long title can be used to find the meaning of a section which is capable of two or more meanings,[1] there is no clear rule with regard to the use of the short title.

Judges of high standing have said that the short title cannot be used to find the meaning of a section which could have two or more meanings. Lord Moulton said:

> "The [long] title of an Act is undoubtedly part of the Act itself, and it is legitimate to use it for the purpose of interpreting the Act as a whole and ascertaining its scope. This is not the case with the short title, which in this instance is '*The Trade Disputes Act* 1906'. That is a title given to the Act solely for the purpose of facility of reference. If I may use the phrase, it is a statutory nickname to obviate the necessity of always referring to the Act under its full and descriptive title. It is not legitimate, in my opinion, to use it for the purpose of ascertaining the scope of the Act. Its object is identification and not description."[2]

In a case decided shortly afterwards Lord Moulton repeated this view:

> "Attention was called to the short title of the Act, namely the '*Telegraph (Arbitration) Act* 1909', and it was urged that this gave countenance to the contention that the reference was merely an arbitration. With regard to this I adhere to the opinion which I expressed in my judgment in the case of *Vacher & Sons Ltd. v. London Society of Compositors*, namely, that, while it is admissible to use the full title of an Act to throw light upon its purport and scope, it is not legitimate to give any weight in this respect to the short title which is chosen merely for convenience of reference and whose object is identification and not description."[3]

Lord Justice Kennedy has expressed the same view:

> "I lay no stress upon the language of s. 2(2): 'This Act may be cited as the *Vexatious Actions Act.*' In the first place, although the use of the word 'actions' except in reference to civil proceedings is now obsolete, it is just possible that the parliamentary draftsman may have had in mind the fact that in a passage of *Bacon's Abridgement*, which was cited to us by counsel, is to be found the statement that 'actions are divided into criminal and civil'. In the second place, in two recent cases in the House of Lords there have been expressions of opinion on the part of the Lord Chancellor and Lord Moulton against the use of its short title as an aid to the interpretation of the statute."[4]

Lord Justice Buckley (later Lord Wrenbury) was of the same opinion:

> "As to title, the matter is governed by the title placed at the head of the Act, and that is 'An Act to prevent abuse of the process of the High Court or other courts by the institution of vexatious legal proceedings.' That is the governing title. The fact that for the purpose of identification only, and not of enactment also, authority is given to identify the statute by a particular name, in which the word 'action' occurs, is, I think, immaterial. The words 'This Act may be cited as the *Vexatious Actions*

---

[1] See chapter 6.
[2] *Vacher & Sons Ltd. v. London Society of Compositors*, [1913] A.C. 107, at 128-129.
[3] *National Telephone Co. v. Postmaster-General*, [1913] A.C. 546 at 560.
[4] *Boaler, Re*, [1915] 1 K.B. 21 at 35.

Act 1896' effect nothing by way of enactment. They do no more than create a name and whether it is as a matter of description accurate or not is immaterial. In support of this view I refer to that which Lord Haldane LC said in *Vacher & Sons Ltd. v. London Society of Compositors* as regards the title *'Trade Disputes Act 1906'*, and that which Lord Moulton said in the same case, and to that which the latter said further in *National Telephone Co. v. Postmaster General*".[5]

The reference made by the two Lords Justice to the view of the Lord Chancellor is to his statement that

> "it is true that it is provided that the Act may be cited by the short title of the *Trade Disputes Act* 1906. But the governing title is that which introduces the statute as an Act to provide for the regulation of trade unions and trade disputes."[6]

The opposite view, namely that the short title can be used to clarify the meaning of a section, the effect of which is uncertain, has been expressed by judges of equally high standing. Lord Selborne said:

> "I cannot but say that the mere fact that the Act of Parliament . . . is called *'The Superannuation Act* 1859', and is referred to here by that title, goes a long way to repel the narrow and technical interpretation which the argument of the appellants seeks to put upon that word 'superannuation'. The legislature thought that all the cases of pensions provided for by the Act came within the sense of the word 'superannuation', as conveniently and popularly used, sufficiently to make that short title a good general description of all that was done by the Act."[7]

Mr. Justice Scrutton[8] said:

> "Section 2 of the Act contains a subsection: 'This Act may be cited as the *Vexatious Actions Act 1896*.' This has certainly, in my mind, supported the conclusion to which I have come. I am aware that two members of the House of Lords have as dicta said that no attention should be paid to the short title of an Act. There are similar dicta with regard to the full title, but I think that the law is correctly stated by Lord Macnaghten in *Fenton v. Thorley & Co. Ltd.*[9]:
>
> > 'It has been held that you cannot resort to the title of an Act for the purpose of construing its provisions. Still, as was said by a very sound and careful judge: "The title of an Act of Parliament is no part of the law, but it may tend to show the object of the legislature." Those were the words of Wightman J. in *Johnson v. Upham*,[10] and Chitty J.[11] observed in *East & West India Docks v. Shaw, Savill & Albion Co.*,[12] that the title of an Act may be referred to for the purpose of ascertaining generally the scope of the Act. Surely, if such a reference is ever permitted, it must be permissible in a case like this.'
>
> Maxwell, *The Interpretation of Statutes* (5th ed.), p. 67, summarises the authority thus: 'It is now settled law that the title of a statute may be referred to for the purpose of

[5] *Boaler, Re*, [1915] 1 K.B. 21 at 27.
[6] *Vacher & Sons Ltd. v. London Society of Compositors*, [1913] A.C. 107 at 114.
[7] *Middlesex Justices v. R.* (1884), 9 App. Cas. 757, Earl of Selborne L.C. at 772.
[8] Later Scrutton L.J.
[9] [1903] A.C. 443 at 447.
[10] (1859), 2 E. & E. 250, 121 E.R. 95.
[11] Later Chitty L.J.
[12] (1888), 39 Ch. D. 524.

ascertaining its general scope.' I agree that the court should give less importance to the title than to the enacting part, and less to the short title than to the full title, for the short title being a label, accuracy may be sacrificed to brevity, but I do not understand on what principle of construction I am not to look at the words of the Act itself to help me to understand its scope in order to interpret the words Parliament has used by the circumstances in respect of which they were legislating. It is by no means conclusive, but it is striking . . .''[13]

When judges differ, it is not easy to say what rule the courts will finally adopt. All the judges quoted are agreed — as the fact undoubtedly is — that the short title is part of the Act. It is set out in a section of the Act itself. On the other hand, the fact that the short title is designed to be brief must obviously affect its value as a means of finding the meaning of the Act. Perhaps the true view is to be found in the last of the quotations set out above, namely that the short title can be used to find the meaning of a section that is not clear but that it has far less value for that purpose than has the long title. Côté suggests that "The question is really one of weight, and this will vary according to the situation."[14]

Particular care must be taken if an Act has both a long title and a short title. It cannot be assumed that the two will always be compatible; and, if they are not, it is the long title that should be used if help is needed to interpret the Act.

---

[13] *Boaler, Re*, [1915] 1 K.B. 21 at 40-41.
[14] Côté, P-E, *The Interpretation of Legislation in Canada* (Les Éditions Yvon Blais Inc., Cowansville, 1984) pp. 56-58.

9

WHEN AN ACT COMES INTO FORCE

THE DATE ON THE ACT OF PARLIAMENT

After the long title, where there is one, or after the number of the Act, each Act of Parliament has a date. The following example is from a Federal statute:

[Assented to 13th December 1991].

The next example is from a Provincial statute:

Assented to July 6, 1990.

WHAT THE DATE ON THE ACT OF PARLIAMENT MEANS

After a Bill has been passed by Parliament, it must be submitted for approval or rejection by the Queen (in practice by her representative). This approval to the Act is known as the "royal assent". The date shown on the Act of Parliament is the date upon which the Act received the assent.

THE DATE ON WHICH THE ACT COMES INTO FORCE

If the Act does not set out any date on which it is to come into force, the ordinary rule is that it comes into force on the day on which it receives the assent. Federal Acts are expressed to come into force on the day of receiving the assent, unless the particular Act specifies otherwise.[1] That provision accords with the common law principle that no regard is to be had to parts of a day. In consequence, whether an Act is subject to a statutory requirement such as the Federal one, or is to be controlled by the common law principle, the Act will inevitably come into force prior to receiving the assent because, as is rightly expressed in the relevant British Columbia statute

"An enactment shall be construed as commencing at the beginning of the day on which it comes into force."[2]

---

[1] *Interpretation Act*, R.S.C. 1985, c. 1-23, s. 5(2).

[2] *Interpretation Act*, R.S.B.C. 1979, c. 206, s. 41.

a principle which means that the Act comes into force at midnight preceding the hour on which it receives the assent.[3]

Parliament has power to set out in the Act that the Act will come into force on some day other than the day on which it receives the royal assent. Parliament can say that the Act is to come into force on some day later than the day on which it receives the royal assent, and Parliament also has power to say the Act is to be read as if it had come into force even before it has been passed by Parliament.

Whereas the "ordinary rule" is that all the provisions of an Act come into force at the one time,[4] the postponement of the coming into force of a statute or some provisions in it is common:

> "We are frequently passing Acts which come into force when the Lieutenant-Governor signifies his assent or the date fixed transpires, and in those Acts there are provisions which are by the terms of the legislative provisions suspended in effect until some preliminary provisions are worked out."[5]

Such provisions are within the legislative power of Parliament.[6]

If Parliament chooses to provide for the Act to come into force on some day after the day on which it receives the royal assent, it may either specify a particular date, or it may empower some person or body to decide on the date on which the Act is to come into force or on the various days on which various parts of the Act are to come into force. Commonly, this is done by empowering the Executive Council to decide the date or dates. In British Columbia:

> "Where an Act contains a provision that the Act or a portion of it is to come into force on a day other than the date of assent to the Act or on proclamation, that provision and the title of the Act are deemed to have come into force on the date of assent to the Act."[7]

The reader should be warned that, whereas the date of assent appears near the start of an Act, the sections setting out the date of commencement may appear at or near the end of a statute — so that it is dangerous simply to take the date of assent as the date at which the Act comes into operation. It is dangerous, too, because an Act or some of its sections, although duly enacted, may not be in force. For example, the Canadian *Grains Act*, which was passed in 1970, has some sections that are still not in force.

---

[3] *R. v. Sayward Trading and Ranching Co*, [1924] Ex. C.R. 15 (Ex. Ct.).

[4] *McKittrick v. Byers* (1925), 58 O.L.R. 158, unanimous decision at 161 (C.A.). See also *Converse v. Michie* (1865), 16 U.C.C.P. 167.

[5] *Bradbury, Re* (1916), 30 D.L.R. 756, Graham C.J. at 759. See also *R. v. Raiche*, 24 C.C.C. (2d) 16 (Sask. Q.B.).

[6] *Dain v. Gossage* (1873), 6 P.R. 103, Richards C.J.O. (Ont. H.C.)

[7] *Interpretation Act*, R.S.B.C. 1979, c. 206, s. 3(2).

BRINGING THE ACT INTO FORCE ON A LATER DAY

Parliament quite often uses the idea of bringing an Act into force on some day later than the day on which the Act receives the assent. When Parliament decides that an Act is to come into force on some day later than the date on which the Act receives the assent, it does so by setting that fact out in the Act itself. For example,

"This Act . . . shall come into force on the first day of January, nineteen hundred and twenty-nine."

The idea of delaying the coming into force of an Act of Parliament is one that can be used for various reasons. One reason is that the Act may be quite a long one, and it would take some time to print copies for members of the public to buy. Another reason may be that the Act of Parliament leaves something to be dealt with by regulations to be made under the Act, and Parliament thinks it wise to delay the coming into force of the Act until such time as the regulations have been made. Another reason may be that the new Act replaces an old one and makes some major changes that people must learn of before the new Act can be successfully brought into force. Whatever the motive may be in the particular case, Parliament never has to give a reason for delaying the coming into force of the Act. All it has to do is to set out in the Act that the date on which it starts to operate is a date after the date on which it receives the assent. If it does so, the Act cannot be applied until that date is reached, and, if something is done before that date which would have been an offence had the Act been in force, the Act cannot operate in respect of it.[8]

Parliament can also decide that some parts of the Act are to come into force on one date and other parts are to come into force on another date. Indeed, it could even decide that particular sections of an Act are to come into force on one date and the remainder of the Act is to come into force on another date.

If an Act is one that is to come into force on a date to be proclaimed, the person reading the Act must inquire to find out whether or not it has been proclaimed. In one case, it was sought to prosecute someone under an Act that had not been proclaimed. The court described the prosecution as resembling "nothing so much as pulling a bell-handle without a bell at the end".[9] Of course, the prosecution failed.

---

[8] This is so even if the question arises on the hearing of an appeal and the date of the hearing of that appeal is after the Act has come into force: *Wilson v. Dagnall*, [1972] 1 Q.B. 509.

[9] *R. v. Kynaston* (1926), 19 Cr. App. R. 180, Lord Hewart C.J. at 181.

TREATING AN ACT AS HAVING BEEN IN FORCE FROM A DAY BEFORE THE DATE ON WHICH IT WAS PASSED

Parliament has power to treat an Act as having been in force from a date before the day on which it came into force. The way in which to read such retrospective Acts is a topic of its own and is dealt with in chapter 40 of this book.

THE EFFECT OF A GENERAL REVISION OF THE ACTS OF PARLIAMENT

From time to time, a Parliament may constitute a body to revise the existing statutes. This is a desirable course to pursue, as it saves the reader from the problem of reading what may well be a substantial number of amendments, and from the risk of overlooking amendments. Generally, the effect in terms of when an Act comes into force is a formal one in the case of a general revision. The enactment of the general revision does not substitute a new date for the coming into force of any of the revised statutes. The effect is that "for all practical purposes, the prior statute remains in force, as if it had not been repealed. In other words, a repeal operated by the revised Statutes does not produce a legal hiatus between the old text and the new one".[10]

CONTINUANCE IN FORCE

Unless it is expressed to cease to operate after a specified date or event, or it is expressly or impliedly repealed by a later Act, a statute continues in force indefinitely: "where no time is limited for the operation of a statute it is deemed to continue in force until repealed".[11]

---

[10] Côté, P-E, *The Interpretation of Legislation in Canada* (Les Éditions Yvon Blais Inc., Cowansville, 1984) p. 34.

[11] *R. v. Ruddick* (1928), 52 O.L.R. 248, Wright J. at 253-4, [1928] 3 D.L.R. 208 (H.C.). See also *Reference re Temperance Act (Canada)*, [1939] O.R. 570, affirmed under the name of *Ontario (Attorney General) v. Canada Temperance Foundation*, [1946] A.C. 193, [1946] 2 D.L.R. 1; *Lessard v. R.* (1939), 67 Qué. K.B. 448 (C.A.).

10

THE PREAMBLE

AN ALTERNATIVE NAME

Although it is generally known as the preamble to an Act, there are cases in which the term used is not "preamble" but "recitals".[1] For greater clarity we use the word "preamble" and not "recitals" throughout this chapter.

THE NATURE OF THE PREAMBLE

The preamble is a preliminary statement. The preamble precedes the words of enactment, and is in the nature of a recital of the facts operative on the mind of the law-giver in proceeding to enact.

> "It is clear from the preamble that the regulations and all orders made by the Wartime Prices and Trade Board under the powers given to the Board are essential war measures. They are subject to special rules of construction."[2]

This is well illustrated in a British Columbia statute, the short title of which is the *Constitutional Amendment Approval Act, 1991*:

> "WHEREAS Canadians are involved in reassessing the Constitution of Canada; AND WHEREAS the Constitution of Canada is the Supreme Law of Canada; AND WHEREAS constitutional amendment has an impact on all British Columbians; AND WHEREAS it is essential that the Constitution of Canada reflect the values of British Columbians and that British Columbians have an opportunity to indicate their views on any proposed constitutional amendment"

THE FORM OF A PREAMBLE

An example of a preamble in a Federal statute is

> "Whereas the use of certain substitutes for butter heretofore manufactured and exposed for sale in Canada is injurious to health; and it is expedient to prohibit the manufacture and sale thereof."[3]

---

[1] *Heinze, Re* (1914), 29 W.L.R. 131 (B.C.C.A.); *R. v. Royal Bank* (1912), 2 D.L.R. 762 (Alta. C.A.); *Hammond v. Bank of Ottawa* (1910), 22 O.L.R. 73 (C.A.); *Alloway v. St. Andrews (Rural Municipality)* (1905), 1 W.L.R. 407 (Man. K.B.).

[2] *R. v. Kostynk*, [1945] 1 D.L.R. 103, Bergman J.A. at 120, 52 Man. R. 305 (C.A.).

[3] Chapter 42 of 49 Victoria 1885 (Canada).

An example from a statute of a Province is

"FaithWay Baptist Church has applied for special legislation providing for the incorporation and administration of a college with the power to grant degrees in the field of religious study. The applicant represents that it has maintained, since 1983, an institution of higher learning in theology, religious education, sacred music and related fields. It is appropriate to grant the application."[4]

Preambles are not confined to statutes. They may, of course, be found in any document. An example of a preamble in subordinate legislation is:

"Whereas by Order in Council . . . the *Wartime Prices and Trade Board Regulations* were made and established to provide safeguards under war conditions against any undue enhancement in the prices of food, fuel and other necessaries of life, and to ensure an adequate supply and equitable distribution of such commodities."[5]

THE PREAMBLE AS PART OF THE ACT OF PARLIAMENT

If Parliament does include a preamble in an Act, the preamble is treated as part of the Act itself.[6] It is somewhat similar in its effect to the long title.

THE PREAMBLE WHEN THE MEANING OF THE ACT IS CLEAR

There is an understandable reluctance to refer to the preamble as an aid to interpretation of an Act if the provision in the Act that is being considered is one with a plain meaning. Generally speaking, therefore, if the meaning of the section is plain, it will not be altered by the preamble: "If an enactment is itself clear and unambiguous, no preamble can qualify or cut down the enactment."[7]

The preamble will not have the effect of extending the meaning to be given to the substantive sections of the Act, if their plain meaning is narrower than the words of the preamble itself[8] or if "it has no relation to the actual transaction aimed at."[9]

---

[4] *FaithWay Baptist College of Canada Act*, S.O. 1992, Chapter Pr 1.

[5] *Wartime Prices and Trade Regulation Order* 308 (Canada), (1943), 3 C.W.O.R. 663.

[6] *New Brunswick (Minister of Social Services) v. L. (M.)* (1984), 56 N.B.R. (2d) 343 (Q.B.). In respect of Federal statutes it is expressly provided that the preamble is part of the statute in which it appears (*Interpretation Act*, R.S.C. 1985, c. I-23, s. 13) and this is also so in Ontario (*Interpretation Act*, S.O. 1980, s. 8).

[7] *Powell v. Kempton Park Racecourse Co.*, [1899] A.C. 143, the Earl of Halsbury L.C. at 157.

[8] *R. v. Royal Bank* (1912), 2 D.L.R. 762 (Alta. C.A.).

[9] *Hammond v. Bank of Ottawa* (1910), 22 O.L.R. 73, Moss C.J.O. at 80 (C.A.).

THE USE OF THE PREAMBLE TO FIND THE MEANING OF A SECTION

If an Act contains a preamble and some section in that Act could bear two different meanings, the preamble can be used to find the true meaning of that section. It "shows the scope of the Act",[10] and may provide "a key to [the] true intent and meaning" of the Act.[11] The Federal Parliament has provided this expressly for the interpretation of its statutes.[12]

---

[10] *Sewell v. British Columbia Towing and Transportation Co.* (1884), 9 S.C.R. 527, Strong J. See also *Hirsch v. Montreal Protestant School*, [1928] A.C. 200, [1928] 1 D.L.R. 1041.

[11] *Esquimalt & Nanaimo Railway v. McGregor* (1985), 2 W.L.R. 530, Martin J. (B.C.S.C.); restored after intermediate reversal, [1907] A.C. 462. See also *Clearwater Election, Re* (1913), 12 D.L.R. 598, 6 Alta. L.R. 343 (C.A.); *Alloway v. St. Andrews (Rural Municipality)* (1905), 15 Man. R. 188, Perdue J. (K.B.); *Three Bills Passed by the Legislative Assembly of the Province of Alberta, Re*, [1938] S.C.R. 100, Duff C.J.C. and Davis J. at 110.

[12] *Interpretation Act*, R.S.C. 1985, c. I-23, s. 13.

11

THE PURPOSES SECTION OF AN ACT

WHAT THE PURPOSES SECTION OF AN ACT IS

By no means do all Acts have purposes sections. When an Act does have such a section it is to be treated as "a tool of interpretation".[1]

In those instances in which an Act of Parliament has a purposes section it is included in the Act to give the reader a statement of what Parliament considers were the purposes it sought to achieve by passing that Act.

A typical example of a purposes section is provided by the Ontario *Advocacy Act*, S.O. 1992, s. 1:

"1. The purposes of this Act are,
   (a) to contribute to the empowerment of vulnerable persons and to promote respect for their rights, freedoms, autonomy and dignity;
   (b) to provide advocacy services,
      (i) to help individual vulnerable persons express and act on their wishes, ascertain and exercise their rights, speak on their own behalf, engage in mutual aid and form organizations to advance their interests,
      (ii) to help individual vulnerable persons who are incapable of instructing an advocate, if there are reasonable grounds to believe that there is a risk of serious harm to the health or safety of those persons, and
      (iii) to help vulnerable persons to bring about systematic changes at the governmental, legal, social, economic and institutional levels;
   (c) to ensure that community development strategies are applied in the provision of advocacy services;
   (d) to take into account the religion, culture and traditions of vulnerable persons;
   (e) to ensure that aboriginal communities are enabled to provide their own advocacy services whenever possible;
   (f) to acknowledge, encourage and enhance individual, family and community support for the security and well-being of vulnerable persons."

THE PURPOSES SECTION IS PART OF THE ACT

Since the purposes section is a section of the Act it must be treated not as a preamble or a long title but as a substantive part of the Act.

---

[1] *St. Peters Estates Ltd. v. Prince Edward Island (Land Use Commission)* (1990), 2 M.P.L.R. (2d) 58 at 71 (P.E.I.S.C.).

WHERE TO FIND THE PURPOSES SECTION

If an Act does have a purposes section — the reader will find many that do not — it is reasonable to expect to find it at or near the beginning of the Act. However, there is no requirement that it be placed in any particular part of the Act or that an Act have such a section at all. If the Act does have a purposes section it could be applicable to part only of the Act and therefore set out in that part, or it could indeed be anywhere in the Act.

HOW TO USE THE PURPOSES SECTION

One of the major principles used in statutory interpretation is the purposive approach:[2] "We must give to the words . . . a reasonable interpretation with reference to the subjectmatter and the public objective that the legislative authority had in view".[3] If a section in an Act is ambiguous, and one possible interpretation of that section is in accordance with Parliament's purpose in passing the Act while an alternative interpretation would not achieve that purpose, the first interpretation is to be preferred. In applying this principle of interpretation it may be of assistance that Parliament has stated its purpose in a purposes section rather than leaving that purpose to be deduced by the court.[4]

TRAPS TO USING THE PURPOSES SECTION

The most obvious trap to a purposes section is that only some Acts have one. However, even if there is no purposes section in the Act being interpreted it is still possible to interpret it according to what the court finds to be the purpose of the Act.[5]

Another trap which may not be as obvious is that there may be matters dealt with in the substantive sections of the Act which do not fall within the purposes section. The longer the Act is, the greater is the likelihood of provisions falling outside the scope of the purposes section, and that likelihood could be increased if the Act proves to be one that is amended frequently by Parliament. Probably in order to try to meet the problem, some purposes sections are expressed in such wide terms as to be difficult to apply.

---

[2] See chapter 26.

[3] *Ottawa (City) v. Canada Atlantic Railway Co.* (1903), 33 S.C.R. 376, Taschereau C.J. at 381.

[4] Note, however, that a purposes section can have the opposite effect: see **A section specifying the purposes of the Act** in chapter 26.

[5] This is known as the purposive approach and is considered in chapter 26.

For example, a statute enacted by the legislative assembly of British Columbia, in a provision notable for its wide and contradictory terms states:

"Purpose of Act
3.   The purpose of this Act is to establish a program that will ensure fair compensation for public sector employees based on the taxpayers', and therefore the public sector employers', ability to pay and will contribute towards an economy competitive in the global marketplace."[6]

---

[6] *Compensation Fairness Act*, S.B.C. 1991, c. 1, s. 3.

12

THE ANALYSIS

OTHER NAMES FOR THE ANALYSIS

What we refer to in this chapter as the analysis may also be referred to as the table of contents, and in some statutes it is referred to simply as the contents. In Québec it is known as sommaire.

THE NATURE OF THE ANALYSIS

An Act of Parliament has something of the same nature as a book of reference. Like books of reference, most Acts of Parliament are not meant to be read right through. An Act of Parliament may deal with a large number of matters, and the person reading the Act of Parliament will turn to the particular sections in the Act that deal with the matters that concern him or her. Particularly in the case of a lengthy Act, therefore, it is very useful if the Act contains an analysis.

The following is an example of an analysis from the *Hazardous Waste Management Corporation Act*, S.B.C. 1990:

"Contents

Section

1. Interpretation
2. Corporation established
3. Objectives of the corporation
4. Powers and capacity
5. Duties of the corporation
6. Meetings and quorum
7. Powers of board
8. Board remuneration
9. Officers and employees
10. Fees for service
11. Borrowing powers

Section

12. Financial administration
13. Superannuation
14. Benefits
15. Application of other Acts
16. Confidentiality
17. Regulations
18. Transitional
19. Expiry
20. Consequential amendment
21. Commencement"

A more expansive approach is that embodied in the bilingual *Waste Management Act*, S.O. 1992:[1]

---

[1] As to bilingual Acts see chapter 46.

"CONTENTS

PART I
INTERIM WASTE
AUTHORITY LTD

1. Definition
2. Crown agency
3. Expropriation
4. Closing of Roads
5. Hardship
6. Non-application
7. Inspectors
8. Power of entry
9. Inspection without warrant
10. Inspection warrant
11. Inspection with warrant
12. Obstruction

PART II
WASTE DISPOSAL
SITES

13. Application
14. Waste diversion estimate

15. Environmental assessment
16. Policies
17. Participant funding

PART III
IMPLEMENTATION OF
MINISTER'S REPORT

18. Waste management
   systems
19. Certificates of approval
20. Hearing for Keele
   Valley
21. Regulations

PART IV
AMENDMENTS TO THE
ENVIRONMENTAL
PROTECTION ACT

22-35 Amendments to the
   Environmental
   Protection Act
36. Commencement
37. Short title

SOMMAIRE

PARTIE I
OFFICE PROVISOIRE DE
SÉLECTION DE LIEUX
D'ÉLIMINATION DES
DÉCHETS LTÉE

1. Définition
2. Organisme de la Couronne
3. Expropriation
4. Fermeture de routes
5. Préjudice
6. Non-application
7. Inspecteurs
8. Pouvoir d'entrée
9. Inspection sans mandat
10. Mandat d'inspection
11. Inspection avec mandat
12. Entrave

PARTIE II
LIEUX D'ÉLIMINATION
DES DÉCHETS

13. Application
14. Estimation du réacheminement des
   déchets
15. Évaluation environmentale
16. Lignes directrices
17. Aide financière aux
   participants

PARTIE III
MISE À EXÉCUTION DU
RAPPORT DU MINISTRE

18. Systémes de gestion des
   déchets
19. Certificats d'autorisation
20. Audience au sujet de
   Keele Valley
21. Réglements

PARTIE IV
MODIFICATIONS
APPORTEES Á LA LOI
SUR LA PROTECTION DE
L'ENVIRONNEMENT

22-35. Modifications
   apportées à la *Loi sur la*
   protection de l'environnement
36. Entrée en vigueur
37. Titre abrégé"

THE USE OF THE ANALYSIS

The analysis gives a quick means of finding a provision in an Act of Parliament. It must be borne in mind, however, that the analysis is not a general index. There is as much difference between the analysis in an Act of Parliament and an index as there is between the table of contents and the general index in a textbook.

The fact that some particular provision cannot be found in the analysis does not mean that the Act fails to contain that provision.

THE EFFECT OF THE ANALYSIS

The analysis cannot affect the meaning of the Act itself. If some provision which is in the Act is not set out in the analysis, that provision is not robbed of its effect: it still has its full effect notwithstanding the silence of the analysis. If, on the other hand, the analysis refers to some section which does not in fact appear in the Act itself, the reference in the analysis could not have any effect, and the Act would be read as if there were no reference to that provision in the analysis.

13

SECTIONS, SUBSECTIONS AND PARAGRAPHS

SECTIONS

As a matter of convenience Acts of Parliament are divided into numbered sections. The sections are numbered consecutively. Generally in this system the numbering starts at the beginning of the Act and continues in unbroken sequence to the end of the Act.

> "There can be no question but that in Canadian legislation the numbers of sections and sub-sections are constituent parts of an Act. It often happens that one section of an Act refers to another section by its number, and it would in that case be absurd to say that the numbering formed no part of the Act. It must necessarily be deemed a part of the Act."[1]

The following are two sections taken from the Federal *Bank Act*:

> "4. A body corporate is the holding body corporate of any body corporate that is its subsidiary.
>
> 5. A body corporate is a subsidiary of another body corporate if it is controlled, determined without reference to paragraph 3(1)(d), by the other body corporate."

SUBSECTIONS

To make the provisions of an Act easier to refer to, the sections themselves may be divided into smaller segments which are known as "subsections". The following is an example taken from the Federal *Bank Act* of a section divided into two subsections:

> "83 (1) A security is a negotiable instrument but, in the case of any inconsistency between the provisions of the *Bills of Exchange Act* and this Act, this Act prevails to the extent of the inconsistency.
>
> (2) A security is in bearer form if it is payable to bearer according to its terms and not by reason of any endorsement."

---

[1] *Washington v. Grand Trunk Railway* (1897), 28 S.C.R. 184, unanimous decision at 188.

PARAGRAPHS

The subsections may themselves be divided into smaller segments which are known as "paragraphs". The following is an example taken from the Federal *Cooperative Credit Associations Act* of a section divided into subsections one of which is divided into two paragraphs:

> "(2) Without limiting the generality of subsection (1), any agreement, commitment or understanding by or between two or more persons who beneficially own shares of an association or shares or ownership interests of any entity referred to in paragraph (1)(*b*) or (*c*),
> (*a*) whereby any of them or their nominees may veto any proposal put before the board of directors of the association, or
> (*b*) pursuant to which no proposal put before the board of directors of the association may be approved except with the consent of any of them or their nominees, shall be deemed to be an agreement, commitment or understanding referred to in subsection (1)."

Paragraphs of an Act may themselves be divided into sub-paragraphs, and those subparagraphs may even be divided further.

The effect of the setting out of the Act in numbered sections, subsections, and paragraphs

The numbers of the sections and subsections "are constituent parts of an Act." [2] The setting out of the Act in numbered sections, subsections (and, sometimes, paragraphs) can be of importance to its proper interpretation. For example, a proviso in one subsection has been held not to apply to another subsection of the same section,[3] and that principle has been applied to subparagraphs within the same subsection.[4]

An Act should be so construed as to avoid conflict between its sections,[5] and this principle applies to the avoidance of conflict between subsections of the one section:[6]

> "Where a Court finds that general words . . . of an Act may be so construed as to be in apparent conflict, it will not select or insist upon an interpretation of either set of words so as to establish that conflict, but will rather select or insist upon such an interpretation as will prevent the conflict."[7]

---

[2] *Washington v. Grand Trunk Railway* (1898), 28 S.C.R. 184, Sedgwick J. at 184.
[3] *Washington v. Grand Trunk Railway* (1898), 28 S.C.R. 184, Sedgwick J. at 184.
[4] *Yorkshire & Pacific Securities Ltd. v. Fiorenza*, [1938] 1 W.W.R. 390 (B.C.S.C.).
[5] *Gladysz v. Gross*, [1945] 3 D.L.R. 208 (B.C.C.A.).
[6] *Victoria (City) v. Bishop of Vancouver Island* (1921), 59 D.L.R. 399 (P.C.).
[7] *R. v. Howe* (1890), 2 B.C.R. 36 (S.C.)

CONFLICTING SECTIONS IN THE ONE ACT

If two sections in the one Act of Parliament are in conflict with each other the person seeking to find their meaning should first look to the nature of each of those sections. If one makes a general provision on the matter and the other deals with the matter specifically, the specific section will prevail over the general one: "if [there is] a special section, . . . the general sections of the Act must be read as best they can, subject to this [special section]".[8]

If the case of conflict is one in which both the sections are general sections or both are specific ones, the ordinary meaning of the words may be departed from,[9] and later Act may be given effect over the earlier Act.[10]

Another principle enunciated by the courts to overcome what would otherwise be a conflict between sections of an Act is that, if two sections confer the same power, one being subject to conditions and the other being free of any conditions, the power fettered by conditions must prevail over the other:

> "We have then in the Act two sections dealing generally with the purchase of lands for the purposes of the corporation, one under which it is necessary to obtain the assent of the electors, and the other in which it is not.

> In such a case . . . the section which imposes a restriction must prevail over that which is silent as to restriction to the extent of requiring the assent of the electors."[11]

These principles are the same as those a court will apply to a conflict between two statutes. That conflict is dealt with in chapter 37.

THE WAY IN WHICH SECTIONS, SUBSECTIONS, PARAGRAPHS AND SUBPARAGRAPHS ARE REFERRED TO

If a section is divided into subsections, paragraphs, and subparagraphs, one of the subparagraphs could be referred to in writing in the usual abbreviated form as follows:

s. 20(1)(b)(iv).

However, in spoken form that becomes:

section twenty, subsection one, paragraph b, subparagraph four.

---

[8] *Freedman v. Howard*, [1935] 2 D.L.R. 285, Macdonald J.A. (later Macdonald C.J.) at 287, 49 B.C.R. 417 (C.A.).

[9] *R. v. Oberlander* (1910), 13 W.L.R. 643, 15 B.C.R. 134 (S.C.).

[10] *Marr, Re*, [1990] 2 All E.R. 880.

[11] *Meldrum v. Black* (1916), 27 D.L.R. 193, Galliher J. at 195, 22 B.C.R. 574 (C.A.). See also Martin J.A. at 194.

14

PARTS AND DIVISIONS

THE NATURE OF PARTS AND DIVISIONS

In the longer Acts of Parliament it is quite common to find a number of sections treated as a group. That group is known as a "part".

If the number of sections in a part is sufficient to justify doing so, that part may itself be divided into smaller groups of sections and those smaller groups are known as "divisions".

An idea of the way in which an Act is divided into parts and divisions may be gained from the following extracts from the analysis of the *Substitute Decisions Act*, S.O. 1992:

"CONTENTS

GENERAL

1. Definitions
2. Presumption of capacity
3. Counsel for persons whose capacity is in issue

PART I
PROPERTY

GENERAL

4. Application of Part
5. Age
6. Incapacity to manage property

CONTINUING POWERS OF ATTORNEY
FOR PROPERTY

7. Continuing power of attorney for property
8. Capacity to give and revoke continuing power of attorney
9. Validity despite incapacity
10. Execution
11. Resignation of attorney
12. Termination
13. Exercise despite termination, invalidity or ineffectiveness
14. Certain existing powers of attorney preserved

STATUTORY GUARDIANS OF PROPERTY

15. P.G.T. as statutory guardian
16. Assessment of capacity
17. Application to replace P.G.T.

18. Review by court
19. Where statutory guardian ceases to act
20. Termination of statutory guardianship
21. Notices

COURT-APPOINTED GUARDIANS OF PROPERTY

22. Application for appointment
23. Procedure
24. Guardian of property
25. Order
26. Variation
27. Temporary guardian in urgent case
28. Application for termination
29. Suspension of guardian's powers
30. Procedure''.

THE EFFECT OF DIVIDING AN ACT INTO PARTS AND DIVISIONS

If an Act is divided into parts and divisions the courts will ordinarily assume that the dividing of the Act in that way is intended to indicate that the group of sections in the part or in the division relates to a particular subject, and they will construe those sections in such a way as to fit into the framework created by those parts and divisions if that be possible in the particular case.[1] The courts will not read a section in one part or division as relating to a subjectmatter that is dealt with in another part or division of the Act unless it is clear from the wording of that section that it must be read in that way and that the section has therefore been placed in the wrong part or division. If, however, it is clear from the section that it has been included in an inappropriate part or division, the section will be given its full clear meaning irrespective of the part or division in which it is placed.

---

[1] *British Columbia (Attorney General) v. Canada (Attorney General)*, [1936] S.C.R. 398 at 414.

15

HEADINGS

THE NATURE OF HEADINGS

When an Act is divided into parts the custom today is to put a heading to each part. Similarly, when the sections within a part are divided into divisions the custom is to put a heading to each division.[1] The heading is in effect the title applicable to those sections within the division to which the heading is given.

THE FORM OF HEADINGS

The Federal *Corrections and Conditional Release Act* carries the heading (amongst others)

> "PART 1
> INSTITUTIONAL AND COMMUNITY
> CORRECTIONS
> *Interpretation*"

As another example, the British Columbia *Compensation Fairness Act, 1991* contains (amongst others) the following heading:

> "PART 2
> COMPENSATION GUIDELINES"

THE USE OF HEADINGS

Curiously, the use of headings in Acts of Parliament did not start until 1845. For almost a century and a half thereafter the headings could be said to "constitute an important part of the Act itself",[2] but the courts in Canada varied in their consideration of headings. Although it has been held that headings do not form part of an Act,[3] and although the use of headings as an aid to interpretation has been accepted with caution,

---

[1] See chapter 14.

[2] *Eastern Counties & London & Blackwell Railway v. Marriage* (1860), 9 H.L.C. 32, Channell B. at 41; 11 E.R. 639 at 643.

[3] *Hadden v. R.*, [1983] 3 W.W.R. 661, 21 M.P.L.R. 343, reported under the name of *R. v. Hadden* in 23 Sask. R. 303 (Q.B.).

"It may be that the headings of different portions of a statute may be referred to in order to determine the sense of any doubtful expression in a section ranged under any particular heading".[4]

It has been held that headings may legitimately be taken into account in interpretation[5] and that this is an established principle:

"That the titles, which a statute prefixes to parts of the Act, may be looked at as aids to the interpretation of the language of such parts is well settled, but the assistance to be derived from such consideration varies very much"[6]

and one judge of the Supreme Court of Canada has held cautiously that headings "may be resorted to, to restrain or extend its meaning as best suits the intention of the statute" if the words of the statute are ambiguous,[7] nevertheless, the most recent position is that in the absence of any statutory exclusion

"The courts have considered the role of statutory headings but without producing anything like a clear guideline for their use in the interpretation of statutes . . .

There are other instances in this Court where references to headings and [sic] statutes are made, but no conclusion was drawn in any of these authorities as to the principle of construction applicable to statutory headings"[8]

but when headings are "systematically and deliberately included as an integral part"

"At the very minimum, the court must take them into consideration when engaged in the process of discerning the meaning and application of the provisions".[9]

Various Parliaments have now intervened to make their own statement on the use of headings. The Federal *Interpretation Act* makes no reference to headings but only to marginal notes and to preambles. Conversely, the *Interpretation Act*, R.S.O. 1980, c. 219, s. 9 excludes headings as an aid to interpretation and states that they "form no part of the Act but shall be deemed to be inserted for convenience of reference only".

---

[4] *Connell v. Minister of National Revenue*, [1947] 1 D.L.R. 89, at 92 (Ex. Ct.).

[5] *Ryley Hotel Co., Re* (1910), 15 W.L.R. 229, 3 Alta. L.R. 281 (C.A.).

[6] *United Buildings Corp. v. Vancouver (City)* (1914), 19 D.L.R. 97, unanimous advice at 101 (P.C.).

[7] *Canada (Attorney General) v. Jackson*, [1946] S.C.R. 489, Kellock J. at 495-496.

[8] *Law Society of Upper Canada v. Skapinker*, [1984] 1 S.C.R. 357, unanimous decision at 372.

[9] *Skapinker* unanimous decision at S.C.R. 376. See also *Stephenson v. Parkdale Motors*, [1924] 3 D.L.R. 663 (Ont. H.C.); *Donly v. Holmwood* (1880), 40 O.A.R. 555.

THE EFFECT OF HEADINGS WHEN THE MEANING OF THE ACT IS CLEAR

As a general rule the heading to a part or division will not be used to alter the clear meaning of a section: "it is . . . clear that there must be some ambiguous expression in a section before the aid of the heading under which it appears can be invoked".[10] If the meaning of the section is plain, it will generally be given that plain meaning even if that meaning differs from the meaning that one would expect from reading the heading:

> "The law is quite clear that you cannot use such headings to give a different effect to clear words in the section, where there cannot be any doubt as to their ordinary meaning."[11]

THE EFFECT OF HEADINGS WHEN THE MEANING OF A SECTION IS NOT PLAIN

When it is not clear from the wording of the section how broadly it is to apply, a heading to the part or division of the Act in which that section appears can be used to help to determine the scope of the section unless Parliament has provided otherwise.[12]

Similarly, when a section has two or more possible meanings, the heading to the division or part in which that section appears can be used as a means to find out which of those possible meanings should be given to the section.[13] When the meaning of a section is not plain the heading is treated by the courts as if it were a preamble to the part or division above which it appears; and it has, indeed, been said that these headings are capable of "affording . . . a better key to the construction of the sections which follow them than might be afforded by a mere preamble".[14]

When in the course of the interpretation of a section resort is had to a heading

> "The extent of the influence of a heading in this process will depend upon many factors including (but the list is not intended to be all-embracing) the degree of difficulty

---

[10] *Cassell v. Minister of National Revenue*, [1947] 1 D.L.R. 89, at 92 (Ex. Ct.). See also *R. v. Govedarov* (1974), 3 O.R. (2d) 23 (C.A.); *Victoria and Grey Trust Co. v. Crawford* (1986), 57 O.R. (2d) 484 (H.C.); *Saskatchewan (Human Rights Commission) v. Engineering Students' Society, University of Saskatchewan* (1989), 56 D.L.R. (4th) 604, Cameron J.A. at 615 (Sask. C.A.).

[11] *R. v. Surrey Assessment Committee*, [1948] 1 K.B. 29, Lord Goddard C.J. at 32.

[12] *Sam Richman Investments (London) Ltd. v. Riedel* (1974), 6 O.R. (2d) 335 (Div. Ct.); *Auger v. St. Paul L'Érmite (Paroisse)*, [1942] Qué. K.B. 725 (C.A.).

[13] *Hammersmith & City Railway v. Brand* (1869), L.R. 4 H.L. 171.

[14] *Eastern Counties & London & Blackwell Railway v. Marriage* (1860), 9 H.L.C. 32, Channell B. at 41; 11 E.R. 639 at 643.

by reason of ambiguity or obscurity in construing the section; the length and complexity of the provision; the apparent homogeneity of the provisions appearing under the heading; the use of generic terminology in the heading; the presence or absence of a system of headings which appear to segregate the component elements of the [document]; and the relationship of the terminology employed in the heading to the substance of the headlined provision. Heterogeneous rights will be less likely shepherded by a heading than a homogeneous group of rights".[15]

THE EFFECT OF A HEADING WHEN THERE IS ONLY ONE SECTION UNDER IT

Even if there is only one section appearing under the heading, the heading may be used to find the true meaning of that section if there is doubt about the meaning.

---

[15] *Law Society of Upper Canada v. Skapinker*, [1984] 1 S.C.R. 357, unanimous decision at 377.

16

MARGINAL NOTES

THE NATURE OF MARGINAL NOTES

Marginal notes (or, as they are sometimes called, "sidenotes") appear, as their name indicates, in the margin of the Act of Parliament. At one time it was clear that marginal notes "form no part of the Act"[1] and that view has persisted until recent times. However, the situation has been altered by legislation in some jurisdictions, and in others there is judicial support for changing what used to be the law.

> "In modern times a statute passed by Parliament is as recorded in the copy printed by the Queen's Printer. That being so the rule which treats the title to an Act, the marginal notes, and the punctuation, not as forming part of the Act, but merely as *contemporanea expositio* ought not to be applied with its former rigidity. These were formerly appendages useful to a hasty enquirer but in my view they are no longer merely appendages and as such may be useful in construing a statute or a section."[2]

Not only is there a changing attitude on the part of the courts but Parliaments themselves have intervened in some instances. For example, the Federal Parliament has enacted a provision that marginal notes "shall be read as part of the enactment intended to assist in explaining its purport and object."[3] Contrast the *Interpretation Act*, S.O. 1980, s. 9 which states explicitly that "The marginal notes . . . form no part of the Act but shall be deemed to be inserted for convenience of reference only."

THE FORM OF A MARGINAL NOTE

The marginal note is intended to give a brief indication of the matters dealt with in the section or subsection against which it appears. A typical example of this terse type of marginal note is:

---

[1] *R. v. Govedarov* (1974), 3 O.R. (2d) 23, Martin J. at 48 (C.A.). See also *Fullum v. Waldie Brothers* (1909), 13 O.W.R. 236 (Ex. Ct.); *Hadden v. R.*, [1983] 21 M.P.L.R. 243, reported under the name of *R. v. Hadden* in 23 Sask. R. 303 (Q.B.).

[2] *Insurance Corporation of British Columbia v. Canada (Registrar of Trade Marks)*, [1980] 1 F.C. 669 at 673-674 (T.D.).

[3] *Interpretation Act*, R.S.C. 1985, c. I-23, s. 13.

"Agency   **3** (1) There is hereby established a corporation without share capital to
established   be known as the Waterfront Regeneration Trust Agency in English and
Agence fiduciaire de régénération de secteur riverain in French.

Appointment   (2) The Agency shall consist of as many members, not fewer than five,
of members   as the Lieutenant Governor in Council may appoint.

Term of   (3) The members shall be appointed for a term designated by the Lieute-
appointment   nant Governor in Council.

Head office   (4) The Agency shall have a head office in such location in Ontario
as the Lieutenant Governor in Council designates.

Non-applica-   (5) The *Corporations Act* and the *Corporations Information Act* do
tion   not apply to the Agency."[4]

PARLIAMENT AND THE MARGINAL NOTES

The marginal notes may perhaps give Members of Parliament a quick
indication of the scope of the Bill. When, however, the marginal notes
do not form part of the Act, they are not amended by Parliament even
if the sections against which they appear are amended. As Lord Justice
Bagallay has said: "I never knew an amendment set down or discussed
upon the marginal notes to a clause. The House of Commons never has
anything to do with a marginal note."[5]

THE DANGERS OF MARGINAL NOTES

Marginal notes can be very misleading to the reader of an Act of
Parliament.[6] This danger of being misled can arise from several different
causes. While it occasionally happens that a section of an Act has no
marginal note, the lack of a marginal note occurs quite often in the case
of the subsections. Sometimes the marginal note can be misleading because
it only indicates some of the matters dealt with in the section or subsection against which it appears.

THE PROBLEM AS TO WHETHER MARGINAL NOTES CAN BE USED TO FIND THE MEANING OF AN ACT

Over many years it had been repeatedly held by the courts that the
marginal notes cannot be used as a means of finding the true meaning
of a section when the meaning of that section is in doubt.[7] More

---

[4] *Waterfront Regeneration Trust Agency Act*, S.O. 1992.
[5] *Attorney-General v. Great Eastern Railway* (1879), 11 Ch. D. 449 at 461.
[6] *Argyle Motors (Birkenhead) Ltd. v. Birkenhead Corp.*, [1975] A.C. 99, Lord Wilberforce at 131.
[7] *R. v. Batista* (1912), 9 D.L.R. 138 (Qué. C.A.).

recently, there has been some division of opinion amongst the judges as to the possibility of using a marginal note as an aid to interpretation. The Alberta Court of Appeal in unanimous reasons for decision has expressed itself as being not at all sure that the reason for the rule against the use of marginal notes is applicable to Canadian Federal and Provincial statutes.[8] The Exchequer Court has distinguished marginal notes from headings.[9] Another decision has treated the marginal notes as useful as a guide to a hasty enquirer[10] and the Ontario Court of Appeal has held that marginal notes do give some indication of the legislative purpose.[11] It is probable that a marginal note can only be used, if at all,[12] "as an indication of the mischief with which the Act is dealing".[13] Whether or not a marginal note can be used for that limited purpose "A marginal note . . . cannot make white black".[14]

THE VALUE OF MARGINAL NOTES

While the marginal notes have the very real dangers that have been pointed out at some length in this chapter, they do have a limited value provided those dangers are borne in mind.

AN ALTERNATIVE SYSTEM

The legislative assembly of British Columbia has adopted a system of "headnotes": instead of placing the note in the margin that note is placed in black type above the section to which it relates. An example of this system is found in the *Compensation Fairness Act*, S.B.C. 1991, c. 1, ss. 42 and 43:

"Evidence

42. The commissioner may receive and accept evidence and information on oath, affidavit or otherwise as the commissioner considers proper, whether or not the evidence is admissible in law.

Regulations

43. (1) The Lieutenant Governor in Council may make regulations."

---

[8] *R. v. MacKay* (1918), 40 D.L.R. 37 (Alta. C.A.).
[9] *Fullum v. Waldie Brothers* (1909), 13 O.W.R. 236 (Ex. Ct.).
[10] *Lawrie v. Rathbun* (1876), 38 U.C.Q.B. 255 (Ont.).
[11] *R. v. Govedarov* (1974), 3 O.R. (2d) 23 (C.A.).
[12] *Hirshman v. Beal* (1916), 38 O.L.R. 40, Meredith C.J.C.P. at 45, 32 D.L.R. 680 (C.A.).
[13] *R. v. Kelt*, [1977] 1 W.L.R. 1365, Scarman L.J. (later Lord Scarman) at 1368.
[14] *Hirshman v. Beal* (1916), 38 O.L.R. 40, Meredith C.J.C.P at 45, 32 D.L.R. 680 (C.A.).

REFERENCES TO FORMER ENACTMENTS

It is often useful for the reader of an Act of Parliament to know under what circumstances a particular provision was first inserted into the legislation. Knowledge of those circumstances can assist in the interpretation of the provision concerned by giving its history in short form. By looking at the preceding Acts referred to, the reader can discover any changes which have been made during the history of that provision. Unfortunately, many Acts do not contain this assistance.

17

DEFINITIONS

THE NEED FOR DEFINITIONS

Words are too often used loosely in ordinary speech; and, as a result, the layman comes to regard them as meaning something different from their real meaning. The word "orphan" is an example. The ordinary person in the street would be likely to regard the word "orphan" as meaning a person both of whose parents have died. Reference to the *Oxford English Dictionary*, however, shows that, whilst a person who has lost both parents by death is an orphan, so also is a person who has lost either parent. A person whose mother is dead but whose father is alive is, therefore, an "orphan".

Some words have a meaning that is hard to state with certainty. One of the most striking examples is the word "building". It is easy enough to say that a nine-storey office block is a "building", but there are many borderline cases. A court has held that a movable builder's pay office made of wood and on wheels is not a building;[1] but a similar construction connected to the electricity and used as a kiosk has been held to be a building.[2] In one case a greenhouse was held not to be a building,[3] but in another case it was held that it was a building.[4] The difficulty, as pointed out in various decisions of the courts, is that the question as to what is a "building" must always be a question of degree and circumstance.[5]

When the meaning of a word is open to argument, the meaning of the section in which that word is used must itself be uncertain.

To overcome difficulties of this type the drafter of an Act of Parliament uses definitions which are set out in the Act of Parliament itself. Of course the definitions set out in the Act of Parliament will only avoid argument about the meanings of the words they define if those definitions are themselves clear definitions. Drafting a clear definition is difficult, and there are definitions that create at least as much confusion as they avoid.

---

[1] *London (County) v. Pearce*, [1892] 2 Q.B. 109.
[2] *Forster v. Mornington (Shire)*, [1949] V.L.R. 150.
[3] *Hibbert v. Acton* (1889), 5 T.L.R. 274.
[4] *Smith v. Richmond*, [1899] A.C. 448.
[5] *Moir v. Williams*, [1892] 1 Q.B. 264.

Another use of definitions in an Act of Parliament is to save repetition. One common use of definitions in this way occurs when it is necessary to refer to some particular board or officeholder in a number of sections in the particular Act of Parliament. If a board or officeholder has a lengthy title, it is much easier simply to refer to "the board" or to the title of the office and to define "the board" or that office in the Act as meaning the full title of the board or office. Similarly, many Acts of Parliament give wide powers to a Minister, and the draftsman can avoid repeated references to that Minister's full title by providing a definition of "Minister". The *Compensation Fairness Act,* S.B.C. 1991, s. 1 provides a similar example: it states that " 'commissioner' means the Compensation Fairness Commissioner".

Sometimes the definition used in an Act of Parliament is a very wide one indeed, and it includes many things that would not ordinarily be thought of as falling within the meaning of the word that has been so defined. For example, in the *Compensation Fairness Act* (referred to above) s. 1, the word "compensation" is very broadly defined as meaning "all forms of pay, benefits and perquisites paid or provided, directly or indirectly, by or on behalf of an employer to or for an employee."

Anyone who wants to read an Act of Parliament must read the definitions in that Act very carefully. All through the reading of the Act the reader must remember which words and phrases are defined in the Act.

THE DEFINITIONS SECTION

Most of the longer Acts of Parliament, and many of the shorter ones, contain a section which sets out various definitions. The general practice is to set these definitions out towards the beginning of the Act, but the English Parliament sets them out towards the end of the Act.

The fact that definitions are set out in a definitions section in the Act may lead the reader of the Act of Parliament to assume that all the definitions in that Act are set out in that definitions section. There are in fact some Acts of Parliament which do put all their definitions in the definitions section, but there are many other Acts of Parliament that do not do so. How misleading this can be is well illustrated by the Federal *Interpretation Act*, R.S.C. 1985, c. I-23: it has 6 definitions in s. 2(1) and a further 35 definitions in ss. 35-39. Adopting the same misleading approach the British Columbia *Interpretation Act*, R.S.B.C., c. 206 in s. 1 sets out 6 definitions but then without any warning sets out a further 81 definitions in s. 29 and a further definition in s. 30. It is even possible for the same Act to contain two different definitions of the same word or phrase. Of course the fact that there are two different definitions of the one word in the one Act does not mean that those two definitions apply to that word at the same time — one is the meaning given to the word in one section and another is the meaning given to the same word in another section of the same Act. It does, however, illustrate the need to read the Act bearing in mind not only that words may be given unexpected meanings in the Act but that they may be given different meanings in different sections of the same Act.

When reading a definition it is important to be aware that some of the words used in that very definition may themselves be defined in another definition in the same Act. Parliament is not required to warn the reader which words are given a special definition — it is the reader's responsibility to check in order to avoid being misled. Note the following example from the *Interpretation Act*, S.O. 1980, c. 219, s. 30:

> "21. 'mental incompetent' and 'mentally incompetent person' means [sic] a person,
>> (i) in whom there is such a condition of arrested or incomplete development of mind, whether arising from inherent causes or induced by disease or injury, or
>> (ii) who is suffering from such a disorder of the mind,
>> that he requires care, supervision and control for his protection and the protection of his property.
>
> 22. 'mental incompetency' means the condition of mind of a mentally incompetent person."

Any reader who failed to check for a definition of "mentally incompetent person" would gain very little from the definition of "mental incompetency" — and in order to fully understand the meaning of "mental incompetency" the reader must also be aware of the definitions of "mental deficiency", "mental illness" and related words. At least in this example the words concerned do appear together but so fortunate an alphabetical accident cannot be relied upon.

THE EFFECT OF DEFINITIONS IN AN ACT OF PARLIAMENT

Parliament may provide that definitions in the Act do not apply if it is apparent from the way in which the word is used in any particular section that it is used with a different meaning in that section. For example, the legislative assembly of British Columbia in its *Interpretation Act*, R.S.B.C. 1979, s. 12 provides that

> "Definitions or interpretation provisions in an enactment, unless the contrary intention appears in the enactment, are applicable to the whole enactment including the section containing a definition or interpretation provision."

Notice that sections 1 (Interpretation) and 39 (Expressions Defined) in the same Act, containing numerous definitions, do not refer the reader to section 12 as quoted above. Thus, what appear to be universal definitions may be overridden by the context. Even if Parliament in its *Inter-*

pretation Act does not include a section like that, the Act still has to be read in that way:

> "an interpretation clause is not to be taken as substituting one set of words for another, or as strictly defining what the meaning of a term must be under *all* circumstances, but rather as declaring what may be comprehended within the term where the circumstances require that it should be so comprehended."[6]

Any definition set out in an Act of Parliament will be read as not applying to a particular section if that section plainly shows that the word as used in it is used in a different sense.[7] The definition contained in the Act must always yield to any contrary context in which it is used.[8] Moreover, the need to interpret a word in a sense that is different from its statutory definition may arise not only from the express words of the Act of Parliament but also by implication from the Act.

DEFINITIONS WHICH USE "MEAN" OR "INCLUDE" OR BOTH

When reading the definitions in an Act of Parliament it is most important to note the way in which each definition is expressed. The following example shows two different ways of expressing definitions, and both ways are used in the one section from which the example is taken.

> "3. 'Assembly' means the Legislative Assembly of Ontario;
>
> 4. 'county' includes two or more counties united for purposes to which the Act relates."[9]

The first of these two definitions uses the word "means" and the second uses the word "includes". Each of these definitions has, therefore, to be read in quite a different way from the way in which the other definition is to be read. A definition which uses the word "includes" has a wider scope than one which uses "means".[10]

When a definition in an Act of Parliament says that the word it defines "includes" the particular things set out in that definition, the definition itself is left open. Everything that falls within the ordinary meaning of that word still falls within the meaning of that word as it is used in that

---

[6] *Van Allen, Re; Hamilton (City) v. Children's Aid Society of Hamilton*, [1953] O.R. 569, unanimous decision at 574, [1953] 3 D.L.R. 751 (C.A.).

[7] *Meux v. Jacobs* (1875), L.R. 7 H.L. 481, at 493.

[8] *R. v. Scory* (1965), 51 W.W.R. 447 (Sask. Q.B.); *Van Allen, Re*, [1953] O.R. 569, [1953] 3 D.L.R. 751 (C.A.).

[9] *Interpretation Act*, S.O. 1980, c. 219, s. 30.

[10] Côté, P-E, *The Interpretation of Legislation in Canada* (Les Éditions Yvon Blais Inc., Cowansville, 1984) p. 43.

Act of Parliament.[11] In addition, the things which are specifically set out in the definition also fall within the meaning of that word as it is used in that Act.[12] Other matters which are not set out in the definition, and which would not fall within the ordinary meaning of the word, can also fall within the meaning of the word in that Act.[13] As a general rule, when the word "includes" is used in a definition that definition has been inserted in the Act to give that word a wider meaning than it would otherwise have.[14] Thus, it has been said that the use of the word "includes" in a definition

"includes, unless the context otherwise requires, not only those things which the interpretation clause declares that it shall include, but such things as the word signifies according to its natural import."[15]

A good example of the width of an "includes" definition can be found in the *Interpretation Act*, S.O. 1980, c. 219, s. 30:

"27. 'peace officer' includes a mayor, warden, reeve, sheriff, deputy sheriff, sheriff's officer, and justice of the peace, and also the superintendent, governor, jailer, keeper, guard or any other officer or permanent employee of a correctional institution, and also a police officer, police constable, bailiff, constable or other person employed for the preservation and maintenance of the public peace or for the service or execution of civil process."

See also the Ontario *Securities Act* s. 1 where the definition of "securities" includes a number of instruments not normally considered to be securities.

Despite the wide general meaning given to a term defined in a definition using "includes" there is a trap: in particular circumstances the context may require "includes" to be read as if it were "means and includes" and therefore to be limited to what is set out expressly in it.[16]

When the definition of a word in an Act of Parliament says that the word "means" what is set out in the definition, the definition must be read in exactly the opposite way to the way in which a definition that uses the word "includes" is to be read. The definition which uses the word "means" closes the meaning of the word. It limits the meaning of the word to what is set out in the definition. If the ordinary meaning of the word is different from that in the definition, the ordinary meaning is discarded for the purposes of the Act. No other things are to be added

---

[11] *Ricard v. Lord* (1939), [1941] S.C.R. 1, unanimous decision at 10.

[12] *Hayduk v. Pidoborozny*, [1972] S.C.R. 879.

[13] *R. v. Girone* (1953), 17 C.R. 60 (B.C.C.A.); *R. v. Beru*, [1936] 4 D.L.R. 805 (B.C.S.C.).

[14] *Ricard v. Lord* (1939), [1941] S.C.R. 1, unanimous decision at 10.

[15] *R. v. B.C. Fir & Cedar Lumber Co.*, [1932] 2 D.L.R. 241, unanimous advice at 247 (P.C.). See also *Ricard v. Lord* (1939), [1941] S.C.R. 1, unanimous decision at 10; *I.A.A.F., Local 209 v. Edmonton (City)* (1979), 9 Alta. L.R. (2d) 119 (C.A.); *Huber v. Regina (City)* (1956), 19 W.W.R. 657 (Sask. Q.B.).

[16] *R. v. Beru*, [1936] 4 D.L.R. 805 at 806 (B.C.S.C.).

to the definition in the Act: when a statute says that a word or phrase shall "mean" — not merely that it shall "include" — certain acts or things, the definition "is a hard and fast definition and the result is that you cannot give any other meaning to the word" so defined.[17]

Since "means" and "includes" as used in the definitions sections have such different meanings, the phrase "means and includes" is one which inevitably raises a doubt about the proper interpretation.[18] However, it would seem that when a phrase is defined as one which "means and includes" the matters specified in the definition, it is restricted in its meaning to what is set out in the definition.[19]

Definitions in other Acts

The fact that a word is given one meaning in one Act of Parliament does not mean that it has the same meaning in another Act of Parliament: "The same expression, of course, may well be used in different Acts with significantly different meanings,"[20] and therefore "very clearly little assistance is to be gained from them as the definition or context varies".[21] Indeed, "it is always dangerous . . . to construe the words of one statute by reference to the interpretation which has been placed upon words bearing a general similarity to them in another statute dealing with a different subjectmatter."[22] Except in a case in which two or more Acts are to be read together as one Act,[23] a definition appearing in one Act cannot be used to interpret the same word appearing in another Act. However, a distinction must be drawn between a definition appearing in another Act on the one hand and a judicial interpretation of a word in another Act on the other hand. When a judge has interpreted a word or phrase as bearing a particular meaning that same word or phrase may well be interpreted in the same way when it appears in another Act. Judicial interpretation of words and phrases in one jurisdiction carries a lot of weight when the same word or phrase has to be interpreted in another jurisdiction, especially if the Acts in which the word or phrase occurs are similar.[24] Judicial

---

[17] *Gough v. Gough*, [1891] 2 Q.B. 665, Lord Esher M.R. at 674, *I.A.F.F., Local 209 v. Edmonton (City)* (1979), 9 Alta. L.R. (2d) 119 (C.A.); *Huber v. Regina (City)* (1956), 19 W.W.R. 657 (Sask. Q.B.).

[18] *Craies on Statute Law* (Sweet & Maxwell, London, 1971, 7th ed., Edgar S.G.G.) p. 213.

[19] *R. v. Beru*, [1936] 4 D.L.R. 805 at 806. (B.C.S.C.). See also p. 142 below.

[20] *"Fairview" Church Street Bromyard, Re*, [1974] 1 W.L.R. 579, Megarry J. (later Megarry V.-C.) at 582.

[21] *R. v. Seilke*, [1930] 3 D.L.R. 630, unanimous decision at 631 (Man. C.A.).

[22] *Lanston Monotype Machine Co. v. Northern Publishing Co.* (1922), 63 S.C.R. 482, Duff J. (later Duff C.J.C.) at 497.

[23] See chapter 36.

[24] For an example compare the *Personal Property Securities Act*, R.S.O. 1990, c. PR10 and the *Personal Property Securities Act*, S.A. 1988, c. P-4.75.

dictionaries provide assistance in finding the relevant cases in which words or phrases have been interpreted.

It should be noted that most Parliaments do pass one Act that is meant to provide definitions that are to be read into most other Acts. An Act of that nature is usually known as the *Interpretation Act*. It has been said that

"An interpretation Act is a dictionary created by Parliament for the interpretation of its enactments; it gives meaning and effect to words used by it in legislation; and, if the will of the Legislature is sought, it must be sought by this key".[25]

In practice, however, an Act of that type provides very few of the definitions that are needed to interpret an Act of Parliament.

DICTIONARY DEFINITIONS AND TECHNICAL TERMS

The use of dictionary definitions, and the meaning to be given to technical terms are considered in chapter 21.

---

[25] *D. Moore Co., Re* (1927), [1928] 1 D.L.R. 383, Middleton J.A. at 394 (Ont. C.A.).

18

SCHEDULES

THE NATURE OF A SCHEDULE

There are certain things which it is more convenient to set out in something added at the end of the Act than it is to set them out in the body of the Act itself. The system used for this purpose is that of schedules.

A common use of schedules is to specify detailed provisions for the working out of the Act.

A further use of schedules is to set out lengthy provisions which persons affected by the statute can adopt if they wish to, but which they are not compelled to adopt.

Another use of schedules is to set out a scale of fees that may be charged, or to set out a lengthy technical description of some area that is defined for the purposes of the Act. Also, schedules can be used to set out the method of prosecution and the penalties for the various offences created by an Act.

Schedules may also prescribe a form to be used by persons seeking to comply with the Act,[1] the extension of a national park,[2] or a list of crimes in respect of which temporary leave from prison may be authorised by a Parole Board.[3] Schedules have also been used to set out the terms of an agreement made between a municipality (or other government authority) and a company[4] and to provide the text of an international convention.[5] One might expect to find the text of such conventions in a schedule to a Federal Act, but it is also possible to find an international convention set out as a schedule to a Provincial Act, for example to the *International Sale of Goods Act*, S.B.C. 1990, c. 20:

---

[1] *Referendum Act*, S.C. 1992, c. 30, schedule I.
[2] *National Parks Amendment Act*, S.C. 1993, c. 23, schedules V and VI.
[3] *Corrections and Conditional Release Act*, S.C. 1992, c. 20, schedule 1.
[4] *Carter v. Sudbury (City)*, [1949] 3 D.L.R. 756 (Ont. H.C.).
[5] *Canada-Finland Income Tax Convention Act*, S.C. 1991, c. 3, schedule I.

"SCHEDULE
UNITED NATIONS CONVENTION OF CONTRACTS
FOR THE INTERNATIONAL SALE OF GOODS

THE STATES PARTIES TO THIS CONVENTION,

BEARING IN MIND the broad objectives in the resolutions adopted by the sixth special session of the General Assembly of the United Nations on the establishment of a New International Economic Order,

CONSIDERING that the development of international trade on the basis of equality and mutual benefit is an important element in promoting friendly relations among States,

BEING OF THE OPINION that the adoption of uniform rules which govern contracts for the international sale of goods and take into account the different social, economic and legal systems would contribute to the removal of legal barriers in international trade and promote the development of international trade,

HAVE AGREED as follows:

PART I
SPHERE OF APPLICATION AND
GENERAL PROVISIONS
Chapter I
SPHERE OF APPLICATION

Article 1
(1) This Convention applies to contracts of sale of goods between parties whose places of business are in different States:
  (a) when the States are Contracting States; or

  (b) when the rules of private international law lead to the application of the law of a Contracting State.''

A schedule may also be used to set out a series of Acts to which a particular provision applies. An example can be found in the *Advocacy Act,* 1992 Chap. 26:

"SCHEDULE

Section 2 — 'Facility'

Alcoholism and Drug Addiction Research Foundation Act
Cancer Act
Charitable Institutions Act
Child and Family Services Act
Community Psychiatric Hospitals Act
Developmental Services Act
General Welfare Assistance Act
Homes for Retarded Persons Act
Homes for Special Care Act
Homes for the Aged and Rest Homes Act
Independent Health Facilities Act
Mental Health Act
Mental Hospitals Act
Ministry of Community and Social Services Act
Ministry of Correctional Services Act

Ministry of Health Act
Nursing Homes Act
Ontario Mental Health Foundation Act
Private Hospitals Act
Public Hospitals Act ".

ASCERTAINING THE STATUS OF A SCHEDULE

Although there are conflicting decisions, the law as applied in Canada appears now to be established that a schedule is only to be treated as part of the Act in which it appears if it is referred to in the body of the Act and is printed with it. To have that status there must be words in the Act from which there can be inferred the intention of the legislature to make the schedule part of the Act.[6] Consequently the remainder of this chapter must be read as relating only to schedules which comply with that requirement that there be statutory authority in one of the sections of the Act for the schedule.

CONFLICT BETWEEN A SECTION OF AN ACT AND A SCHEDULE TO THAT ACT

Where there is a conflict between the provisions contained in a section of an Act of Parliament and the provisions contained in a schedule to that same Act the question arises as to whether the section or the schedule is to prevail. The answer to this question is that the schedule gives way to the section, and this is so whether the schedule contains positive provisions[7] or a form.[8] However, if there is no inconsistency between the section and the schedule, the two must be read together.[9]

CONFLICT BETWEEN A PREAMBLE TO AN ACT AND A SCHEDULE REFERRED TO IN THAT ACT

If an Act has a preamble and the provisions of a schedule to that Act which is referred to in a section of that Act are in conflict with the preamble, the provisions of the schedule prevail: full effect is to be given in that case to the provisions set out in the schedule. This necessarily follows from the principle that, if the schedule is itself part of the Act

---

[6] *Winnipeg (City) v. Winnipeg Electric Railway*, [1921] 2 W.W.R. 282, 59 D.L.R. 251, Fullerton J.A. at 277 (Man. C.A.).

[7] *Houghton's Case, Re* (1877), 1 B.C.R. (Pt. 1) 89 (S.C.).

[8] *Dean v. Green* (1882), 8 P.D. 79, Lord Penzance at 89; *R. v. Baines* (1840), 12 A. & E. 210, at 227, 113 E.R. 792, Lord Denman C.J. at 799.

[9] *Dow v. Parsons* (1917), 36 D.L.R. 510, unanimous decision at 512 (N.S.S.C.).

which contains it, then, like the sections of the Act, its plain meaning cannot ordinarily be altered by a preamble.

THE USE OF SCHEDULED FORMS

The High Court of Ontario has drawn attention to "the advisability — sometimes the necessity — of following statutory forms strictly".[10]

If the statutory requirement is that a scheduled form or a form "to the like effect" be used, the insertion of additional words that do not appear in the scheduled form does not invalidate the use of the form.[11]

---

[10] *Bills v. Sims* (1922), 53 O.L.R. 57 at 86 (H.C.).
[11] *R. v. Grant* (1898), 30 N.S.R. 368 (C.A.).

19

PROVISOS

THE NATURE OF A PROVISO

A proviso is something which is included in an Act of Parliament to make certain that the Act does not have the particular effect that it might have if the proviso were not included in the Act. The proviso may be inserted in the Act, for example, to preserve existing rights. It may be inserted to make sure that certain rights of the Crown are not affected by a section which does affect rights of the Crown to some extent. It may be inserted in the Act to create exemptions from the section to which it is a proviso.

THE FORM OF A PROVISO

Provisos frequently begin with the words "Provided that". However, no particular form of words is needed: it is the effect of the words used that makes them a proviso. Thus when a subsection was not worded as a proviso but was held to be "clearly tantamount to one" it was given the effect of a proviso.[1]

THE EFFECT OF A PROVISO

A genuine proviso is something which qualifies or modifies the section to which it is a proviso. It is, therefore, to be read in the light of that section itself.[2] The usual effect of the proviso is to take out of the section something that would otherwise fall within it:

> "When one finds a proviso to a section, the natural presumption is that, but for the proviso, the enacting part of the section would have included the subjectmatter of the proviso."[3]

A proviso should not be given an extended meaning: it should have

---

[1] *Rome v. Punjab National Bank (No. 2)*, [1989] 1 W.L.R. 1211, Sir John May (formerly May L.J.) at 1219.

[2] *R. v. Wesley*, [1932] 4 D.L.R. 774, McGillivray J.A. at 782 (Alta. C.A.); *City Tours Ltd. v. Toronto Transit Commission* (1985), 51 O.R. (2d) 696 (C.A.).

[3] *Mullins v. Surrey (Treasurer)* (1880), 5 Q.B.D. 170, Lush J. (later Lush L.J.) at 173.

no greater effect than a strict interpretation of its words requires,[4] and should ordinarily be treated as affecting only the section or subsection to which it is annexed.

PROVISO INSERTED UNNECESSARILY

When a Bill is being drafted or is brought before Parliament it may happen that some persons become afraid that the provisions in the Bill will affect them even although the intention is that they should not be affected by those provisions. If that happens, the Act when it is finally passed may contain a proviso stating that the particular section does not apply in the way in which those persons were afraid it would apply. The proviso in such a case may have been put in because those persons' fears were correct, or it may have been put in because it was thought that there might be some basis for the fears and it was therefore thought better to make certain that the section did not apply to those persons. The fact that there is a proviso therefore does not necessarily affect the reading of the section itself. If the fears that led to the inclusion of the proviso were groundless, the proviso would obviously have no effect at all. In such a case the section is not to be read in such a way as to give effect to the proviso, but it is to be given its ordinary clear meaning without reference to the proviso:

> "I am perfectly clear that if the language of the enacting part of the statute does not contain the provisions which are said to occur in it, you cannot derive these provisions by implication from a proviso."[5]

Of course, if a section of the Act is ambiguous, reference can be made to a proviso to ascertain the proper interpretation of the section.

---

[4] *Washington v. Grand Trunk Railway* (1897), 28 S.C.R. 184, unanimous decision at 189.
[5] *West Derby Union Guardians v. Metropolitan Life Assurance Co.*, [1897] A.C. 647, Lord Watson at 652; *Bulman v. Anderson*, [1946] 4 D.L.R. 679 (B.C.S.C.).

20

PUNCTUATION

ACTS OF PARLIAMENT PASSED BEFORE 1850

In the case of Acts of Parliament which were passed by Parliament before 1850 the actual copies of the Acts which received the royal assent did not contain any punctuation. The reader of any of those Acts must therefore ignore any punctuation in the printed copy.[1]

PUNCTUATION IN ACTS OF PARLIAMENT PASSED IN 1850 OR LATER

If the real meaning of a section is clear but does not agree with the punctuation of the section, the section must be read as if it had no punctuation in it: punctuation cannot control the sense of the section if the meaning of that section is otherwise reasonably clear.[2] A misplaced comma cannot be allowed to destroy the reasonable inference to be deduced from the language of the whole clause.[3]

An eminent English judge has said that it is "very doubtful" whether punctuation can be used at all in finding the meaning of a section,[4] and the Alberta Supreme Court in its Appellate Division has held unanimously that "The rule adopted in the courts is . . . to pay little, if any, attention to punctuation" and that it "should, in any case, hesitate to rest much upon a difference in punctuation without an examination of the original roll [comprised of the Acts which have received assent]".[5] However, there are various cases in which punctuation has in fact been used by the courts to find the meaning of the section.[6] Typically, it has been held that "there appears . . . no valid reason why regard should be denied to punctuation

---

[1] *Inland Revenue Commissioners v. Hinchy*, [1960] A.C. 748, Lord Reid at 765; *McPherson v. Giles* (1919), 45 O.L.R. 441 (H.C.).

[2] *Houston v. Burns*, [1918] A.C. 337, Lord Finlay L.C. at 342, Lord Haldane at 344, Lord Shaw at 348; *Smart Hardware Co. v. Melfort (Town)* (1917), 32 D.L.R. 552 (Sask. C.A.).

[3] *Winding Up Act, Re* [1923] 3 D.L.R. 1052, Macdonald C.J.A. at 1055 (B.C.C.A.). See also *Smart Hardware Co. v. Melfort (Town)* (1917), 32 D.L.R. 552, unanimous decision at 554 (Sask. C.A.).

[4] *Inland Revenue Commissioners v. Hinchy*, [1960] A.C. 748, Lord Reid at 765.

[5] *Medicine Hat (City) v. Howson* (1920), 53 D.L.R. 264 at 265.

[6] See, for example, *Slaney v. Kean*, [1970] 1 Ch. 243, Megarry J. (later Megarry V-C) at 252; *Robinson v. Lumsden* (1986), 32 D.L.R. (4th) 154, unanimous decision at 157.

in construing a statute"[7] although "Punctuation cannot render a single interpretation so certainly correct as to obviate the need to refer to the entire enactment in the interpretation of one of its provisions but it is certainly to be considered."[8] Punctuation marks, it has been held, "are no longer merely appendages and as such may be useful in construing a statute or a section."[9]

The proper use of punctuation in the interpretation of a statute has been well put by Megarry V-C who said:

> "As for [counsel for the plaintiff's] point on the comma, I accept, of course, that the day is long past when the courts would pay no heed to punctuation in an Act of Parliament: see *Hanlon v. Law Society* [1981] A.C. 124 at 197-198 per Lord Lowry. Nor do I say that a mere comma can have little force; indeed, I would be the last to deny that its presence or absence may be highly significant . . . . Over two centuries ago James Burrow, the law reporter, in his *Essay on Punctuation* (1772, p. 11), gave an illustration of the potency of punctuation in a little jingle:
>
> > 'Every lady in this land
> > Hath twenty nails upon each hand
> > Five and twenty on hands and feet
> > And this is true, without deceit.'
>
> Leave this unpunctuated, or with punctuation only at the end of the lines, and it seems plainly untrue. Insert a comma or semicolon at the beginning and end of the phrase 'upon each hand five', and nonsense becomes sense, albeit at the cost of some impairment of the rhythm. Yet throughout, one must remember that punctuation is normally an aid, and no more than an aid, towards revealing the meaning of the phrases used, and the sense that they are to convey when put in their setting. Punctuation is the servant and not the master of substance and meaning. Furthermore, although a pair of commas may of course be used to enclose a parenthetic phrase, there is no rule of grammar, usage or common sense that requires words so enclosed to be treated as a parenthesis."[10]

---

[7] *Alexander v. McKenzie,* [1947] J.C. 155, Lord Jamieson at 166, quoted in *Cardinal v. R.* (1979), 97 D.L.R. (3d) 402 at 407 (F.C.C.).

[8] *Cardinal v. R.* (1979), 97 D.L.R. (3d) 402 Mahoney J. at 407 (F.C.C.).

[9] *Insurance Corporation of British Columbia v. Canada (Registrar of Trade Marks),* [1980] 1 F.C. 669, Cattanach J. at 673-674 (T.D.).

[10] *Marshall v. Cottingham,* [1982] 1 Ch. 82 at 88.

21

THE MEANING OF WORDS
NOT DEFINED IN THE ACT

THE DIFFICULTY OF FINDING THE MEANING OF WORDS

Even when reading an ordinary statement free from the complexities of an Act of Parliament it may be difficult to find the meaning of particular words. This difficulty may arise because the proper meaning of a word is different to the meaning the ordinary person in the street expects it to have or, more frequently, because the word has many possible meanings.[1] When the word the meaning of which has to be found is in an Act of Parliament the difficulty of finding that meaning may be increased by the complexities of the Act itself and by the possibility that Parliament has used the same word in different senses in the same Act. The rules of statutory interpretation evolved by the courts attempt to assist the reader to find a way through these difficulties and so to find the meaning of the words.

WHERE POSSIBLE, A WORD IS TO BE GIVEN A CONSTANT MEANING THROUGHOUT THE ACT

One of the rules used in reading an Act of Parliament is that a word should, if possible, be given the same meaning throughout the whole of the Act:[2]

"While it is quite true that a word may have different meanings in the same statute or even in the same section, it is not to be forgotten that the first inference is that a word carries the same connotation in all places where it is found in a statute."[3]

In support of this principle of giving a constant meaning to a word in a statute it has been held that

"It would, I think, be a departure from the ordinary rules of construction to give the word 'district' in that sub-section a meaning different from its meaning when used in

---

[1] See **The need for definitions** in chapter 17.

[2] *Strachan v. Lamont* (1906), 3 W.L.R. 571 (N.W.T.S.C.); *Giffels and Vallet of Canada Ltd. v. R.; Miller, ex parte*, [1952] 1 D.L.R. 620 (Ont. H.C.). The same word is even to be given the same meaning in different Acts covering the same subjectmatter if they are to be read together: *Lee-Verhulst (Investments) Ltd. v. Harwood Trust*, [1973] 1 Q.B. 204, Stamp L.J. at 218.

[3] *Giffels and Vallet of Canada Ltd. v. R; Miller, ex parte*, [1952] 1 D.L.R. 620 (Ont. H.C.).

other parts of the same section, the more especially so, as one is not driven to that end in order to give the word a reasonable meaning. I think the word must have the same meaning throughout."[4]

If it is clear that the word is not used consistently throughout the Act, the rule that it is to be treated as having a common meaning throughout the Act is of no effect. The one word has been held to have two different meanings in one and the same section of an Act:

"Counsel for the defendant contended that since . . . the word 'public' is descriptive of colleges and academies, . . . the word 'public' should be given the same meaning in both places in which it occurs in the section, public here includes a school house open to the public, though privately maintained. Something may be said for that argument, and in a doubtful case it might be given weight; but the presumption that the same word shall be given the same meaning wherever it occurs in a section is not a strong presumption. It may be used in different senses in the same section".[5]

WORDS IN AN ACT OF PARLIAMENT HAVE THE MEANING WHICH THEY BORE AT THE DATE WHEN THE ACT WAS PASSED

Words used in an Act of Parliament (if they are not defined in the Act) are to be read as having the meaning which they had in ordinary speech (or, if they are technical words, then as having their technical meaning) at the time when the Act was passed: "it is undoubtedly true that the words of a statute will generally be understood in the sense which they bore when it was passed."[6]

What the reader of the Act has to do is to employ "the best and surest method of expounding an instrument [which] is by construing its language with a reference to the time when and circumstances under which it was made."[7]

However, if social conditions have changed since the legislation was passed, and if the language of the enactment is wide enough to extend to those new circumstances, there is no reason why it should not apply.[8]

Since the meaning of a word does not change quickly, the rule about reading words in the light of the meaning which they had at the time when the Act was passed is generally of little assistance in the case of a com-

---

[4] *Archibald v. Royer*, [1924] 1 D.L.R. 897, Chisholm J. at 900 (N.S.C.A.); *Canadian National Railway v. Ottawa (City)*, [1924] 4 D.L.R. 1217, Middleton J.A. at 1221-1222.

[5] *Dartmouth v. Roman Catholic Episcopal Corp. of Halifax*, [1940] 2 D.L.R. 309, Graham J. at 315 (N.S.C.A.).

[6] *King (Township) v. Marylake Agricultural School & Farm Settlement Association*, [1939] O.R. 13, Masten J.A. at 20 (C.A.).

[7] *Canadian Pacific Railway v. James Bay Railway* (1905), 36 S.C.R. 42, Nesbitt J. at 90. See also *R. v. L.* (1922), 69 D.L.R. 618 (Ont. H.C.); *Stamford (Township) v. Welland (County)* (1916), 31 D.L.R. 206.

[8] *Colonial Commodities Ltd. v. Siporex Trade SA*, [1990] 2 All E.R. 552, Lord Bridge of Harwich at 557.

paratively recent Act.[9] However, it is possible that the rapid advance of scientific knowledge may lead to a change in the meaning given to a particular word shortly after an Act is passed: in such a case the word used in the Act is to be given the meaning that it had at the time when the Act was passed, not the current meaning and this is so even although a scientist could be confused by an understandable tendency to read the Act in its current scientific meaning.

DICTIONARY DEFINITIONS

If the meaning of a particular word is in doubt and that word is not defined in the Act of Parliament in which it occurs, it is to be interpreted on the basis that Parliament "intended [it] to bear its ordinary meaning".[10] The person reading that Act of Parliament should turn to the various law dictionaries in which the legal meanings of words are set out.[11] These dictionaries include *Black's Law Dictionary*, the *Canadian Legal Dictionary* and a number of words and phrases services.

If the word is not defined in the Act and there is no appropriate definition appearing in one of the judicial dictionaries, the reader must then turn to the ordinary standard dictionaries such as the *Oxford English Dictionary*[12] and *Webster's*.

In using either the law dictionaries or the ordinary standard dictionaries it is necessary to be careful not to place too much emphasis upon a particular word if it has to be interpreted as part of a phrase of two or more words:

> "It is often fallacious in considering the meaning of a phrase consisting of two words to find a meaning which each has separately and then infer that the two together cover the combination so arrived at. The two together may . . . have acquired a special meaning of their own."[13]

TECHNICAL TERMS AND LEGAL TERMS

The use of technical terms without definition in an Act of Parliament can also cause difficulty. If an Act of Parliament is one which relates to a particular trade or business, or to a particular type of transaction, the words used in that Act may be words which have a particular meaning in

---

[9] *Assheton Smith v. Owen*, [1906] 1 Ch. 179, Cozens-Hardy L.J. (later Baron Cozens-Hardy M.R.) at 213.

[10] *Peart v. Stewart*, [1983] 2 A.C. 109, Lord Diplock at 114.

[11] *Haigh v. Charles W. Ireland Ltd.*, [1974] 1 W.L.R. 43, Lord Diplock at 55; *McIntyre Porcupine Mines Ltd. v. Morgan* (1921), 62 D.L.R. 619, Hodgins J.A. at 624 (Ont. C.A.).

[12] Third ed., Oxford University Press, 1989. See also *Rippon Housing Order, Re*, [1939] 2 K.B. 838.

[13] *Lee v. Showmen's Guild of Great Britain*, [1952] 2 Q.B. 329, Somervell L.J. at 338.

that trade, business or transaction, but care must be taken in using it.

> "The rule that statutes are to be construed according to the meaning of the words in common language is quite firmly established and it is applicable to statutes dealing with technical or scientific matters. . . . Of course, because 'tetracycline' designates a specific substance the composition of which has been determined in terms of a chemical formula, resort may be had to the appropriate sources for ascertaining its meaning. In my view this does not imply that 'derivative' is to be construed as it might be in a scientific publication".[14]

Legal terms are given their "well-established legal meaning." [15]

---

[14] *Pfizer Co. v. Canada (Deputy Minister of National Revenue (Customs and Excise)* (1975), [1977] 1 S.C.R. 456, unanimous decision at 460.
[15] *McArthur v. R.*, [1943] Ex. C.R. 77 (Ex. Ct.).

22

THE DIFFERENCE BETWEEN THE GENERAL RULES AND THE SPECIFIC RULES

THE GENERAL RULES

There are four general rules of statutory interpretation, considered in turn in the four succeeding chapters. They are the plain meaning rule, the golden rule (that manifest absurdity and injustice are to be avoided), the mischief rule and the purposive approach. These are rules of general applicability and therefore are to be contrasted with rules which apply only if the particular circumstances to which they relate occur in the Act.

CONFLICTS BETWEEN THE GENERAL AND THE SPECIFIC RULES

It is important to remember that the general rules of statutory interpretation are the basic ones. The factual circumstances for the application of one of the specific rules may apply (as, for example, the presence of a class of two or more specific words followed by a general word which would make it possible to invoke the class rule[1]) but invoking the specific rule might have the effect of defeating the purpose of the Act, and it would therefore have to give way to the purposive basis of interpretation.[2]

---

[1] See chapter 33.
[2] See chapter 26.

23

THE PLAIN MEANING RULE

THE NAMES BY WHICH THE PLAIN MEANING RULE IS KNOWN

The plain meaning rule is generally referred to as "the plain meaning rule" but it can also be referred to as the literal rule, the ordinary meaning rule, or the grammatical rule: "In statutory interpretation, as a starting point the courts frequently apply some version of the 'plain meaning' principle of construction."[1]

THE EFFECT OF THE PLAIN MEANING RULE

The plain meaning rule is a very simple rule. It means what it says. If the meaning of the Act is plain, it is to be given that plain meaning. The words are to be given the plain and ordinary meaning applying to them the appropriate grammatical rules:[2]

> "It is an elementary principle that the grammatical or ordinary sense of words used in a statute are to be adhered to unless that would lead to some absurdity or some repugnance or inconsistency with the rest of the statute."[3]

If the meaning of the Act of Parliament is clear, the reader's opinion as to what Parliament's intention really was is not to be used to give the words of the Act a different meaning to agree with that supposed intention: "The issue . . . is not the reasonableness of the provision. The issue is what did the legislature intend, given the language it used?"[4]

The words of the Act are to be given their plain meaning even if doing so creates practical difficulties. This is so even although the application of the plain meaning rule would entail "extreme inconvenience".[5] It is

---

[1] *Newcorp Properties Ltd. v. West Vancouver (District)* (1989), 45 M.P.L.R. 297 at 300 (B.C.S.C.).

[2] *Reference re Medical Act (Ontario)* (1906), 13 O.L.R. 501, Moss C.J.O. at 504 (C.A.).

[3] *Washington v. Grand Trunk Railway* (1897), 28 S.C.R. 184, unanimous decision at 189. See also *Stamford (Township) v. Welland (County)* (1916), 31 D.L.R. 206, Riddell J. at 214 (Ont. C.A.).

[4] *University Hospital Board v. Boros* (1985), 24 D.L.R. (4th) 628, unanimous decision at 630, reported under the name of *Boros v. University Hospital*, [1986] 2 W.W.R. 587 (Sask. C.A.).

[5] *Canadian Performing Right Society Ltd. v. Famous Players Canada Corp.*, [1929] 2 D.L.R. 1 (P.C.).

for Parliament and not for the courts to cure any injustice in what Parliament has enacted.

Hardship does not preclude the application of the plain meaning rule: "Statutes have to be applied according to their terms where the terms are clear" even if hardship results to the private individual:[6]

> "Great stress is laid by the appellants on the extreme inconvenience of a literal construction . . .
>
> One answer to this argument is that it ought to be addressed to the legislature and not to the tribunal of construction, whose duty it is to say what the words mean, not what they should be made to mean in order to avoid inconvenience or hardship."[7]

The reader of an Act of Parliament may think that it is unjust, but that is no justification for giving it a meaning different to the plain meaning of its words:

> "However ridiculous and unjust the results of the . . . Act may be, and this one produces peculiarly ridiculous and unjust results, it has been enacted by Parliament and it is our duty to enforce it."[8]

Even if giving the words their plain meaning has the result that the probable intention of Parliament is defeated, the plain meaning rule may still apply:

> "It is reasonably clear what the legislature said and also what it intended; further that it did not say what it intended and that without disregarding the words of the statutes it is difficult to give effect to the intention.
>
> Although a statute is to be construed according to the intent of them that made it, if the language admits of no doubt or secondary meaning it is simply to be obeyed."[9]

In such a case "the relief must be supplied by the law makers and not by the courts, because the meaning of the statute does not appear to be obscure nor are the words employed ambiguous."[10]

It is possible, however, in such circumstances that a court will be prepared to interpret the otherwise plain words in such a way as to give effect to what the court presumes to have been the Parliament's purpose in enacting the statute as a whole or the provision in which the words occur in particular. This purposive approach is considered in chapter 26.

---

[6] *Hare v. Gocher*, [1962] 2 Q.B. 641.

[7] *Canadian Performing Right Society Ltd. v. Famous Players Canada Corp.*, [1929] 2 D.L.R. 1, unanimous advice at 3 (P.C.). See also *R. v. Dowsey* (1866), 6 N.S.R. 93 (C.A.).

[8] *Commissioner of Police of the Metropolis v. Curran*, [1976] 1 W.L.R. 87, at 103-104; see also *Cox v. Hakes* (1890), 15 App. Cas. 506, Lord Herschell at 528.

[9] *Canadian Northern Railway v. Winnipeg (City)* (1917), 54 S.C.R. 589, Fitzpatrick C.J. at 593-594.

[10] *R. v. McEachern*, [1935] 3 D.L.R. 298, Ross J. at 302 (N.S.C.A.).

THE IMPORTANCE OF THE PLAIN MEANING RULE

The plain meaning rule is one of the basic rules for the reading of any Act of Parliament. Traditionally, if the meaning of the words is plain, the plain meaning rule is applied; and on that basis there is no room to use any other rule at all. Where the words of an Act of Parliament are clear, there is no room for applying any of the other principles of interpretation, for they are merely presumptions applied in cases of ambiguity in the statute: "If the words of the statute are in themselves precise and unambiguous, then no more can be necessary than to expound those words in their natural and ordinary sense."[11]

The plain meaning rule is one of the most important rules for the reader of a statute to remember and apply. If he or she does not do so, subjective factors of hardship and unjust results may lead the reader into adopting a forced meaning that the Act does not bear and the plain meaning rule will not allow.

THE PLAIN MEANING RULE CANNOT APPLY IF THE MEANING IS NOT PLAIN

Although the plain meaning rule is a basic rule for the reading of any Act of Parliament, it can of course apply if, and only if, the meaning of the words is plain. If the statutory provision is ambiguous, the plain meaning rule cannot apply.

---

[11] *Sussex Peerage Case* (1844), 11 Cl. & Fin. 85 at 143, 8 E.R. 1034 at 1057, followed in *Dufferin Paving and Crushed Stone Ltd. v. Anger*, [1940] S.C.R. 174, Davis J. at 181; *Edmonton (City) v. Northwestern Utilities Ltd.*, [1961] S.C.R. 392, Locke J. at 403.

24

MANIFEST ABSURDITY AND INJUSTICE ARE TO BE AVOIDED

THE NATURE OF THE RULE

There is a rule that, if there is ambiguity in an Act of Parliament, the plain meaning rule cannot apply and the Act should be read in such a way as to avoid a result of manifest absurdity or injustice:

"It is [a] well settled rule of construction that when the language of the legislature admits of two constructions, and if construed one way would lead to obvious injustice, the courts act upon the view that such a result could not have been intended unless the intention has been manifested in express words."[1]

As has been expressed by Middleton JA,

"I would have no hesitation in attributing to the *Temperance Act* [S.O. 1916, s. 51] such an interpretation as would avoid the absurd result contended for the defendant . . . I think the Act must be so read as to avoid the extraordinary result suggested."[2]

This approach has the authority of the Supreme Court of Canada in a case in which it has been held that "If the construction argued for is to be placed on these sections, it would lead to such obviously absurd results that some other construction must be sought for."[3] It is a rule which could easily be carried too far, and it is a rule which must be applied very sparingly: "That sort of intervention requires two rare elements . . . : gross injustice, and a rule to select what beyond doubt would be accepted by the legislature."[4]

"The presumption is that the legislature intended what is fair, reasonable, convenient, and just."[5] The courts have

"the duty of trying to give the statute under consideration reasonable interpretation. In performance of this duty the Courts out of respect for the law givers, if for no other reason, will not assume that an absurd consequence was within the contempla-

---

[1] *Way v. St. Thomas (City)* (1906), 12 O.L.R. 240, Teetzel J. at 244 (Div. Ct.).

[2] *Sawczuk v. Padgett*, [1927] 1 D.L.R. 849, Middleton J.A. at 851; 59 O.L.R. 638 at 640 (C.A.).

[3] *Canadian Pacific Railway v. James Bay Railway* (1905), 36 S.C.R. 42, Nesbitt J. at 95.

[4] *Boykiw v. Calgary (City) Development Appeal Board* (1992), 9 M.P.L.R. (2d) 113, unanimous decision at 119 (Alta. C.A.).

[5] *Gundy v. Johnston* (1912), 28 O.L.R. 121, Lennox J. at 123 (H.C.).

tion of Parliament. On the contrary, the Courts will lean always in such cases towards an interpretation that serves to avoid absurdity, repugnance or inconsistency."[6]

It certainly does not, for example, authorise the modifying of the meaning of the words of the Act because they relate back to a period when social conditions and social problems were different from those of today.[7]

It must always be borne in mind that it is not for the person reading the Act of Parliament to substitute his or her own ideas of justice for Parliament's ideas of justice. The reader may not agree with the way in which Parliament has dealt with a matter in the Act of Parliament, but it is not open to agree or disagree on policy when seeking to find the meaning of the Act of Parliament:

"The duty of the court, and its only duty, is to expound the language of the Act in accordance with the settled rules of construction. It is . . . as unwise as it is unprofitable to cavil at the policy of an Act of Parliament, or to pass a covert censure on the legislature."[8]

For more than a century now it has been held that

"it is sufficient that the words have in their primary signification a plain obvious meaning which leads to no illegal or absurd result, and is controlled by no context requiring us to apply to them an extended or secondary meaning."[9]

It is important for the reader to appreciate that "in the absence of any reasonable alternative interpretation a sense of the possible injustice of an interpretation ought not to induce judges to do violence to well-settled rules of construction".[10]

While the reader's own ideas of justice must not be substituted for those of Parliament, this does not mean that the reader's ideas of justice are always to be set aside. It is a primary rule of construction that the meaning is to be gathered from what is said.[11] It is easy enough to say that an Act of Parliament must be read strictly as Parliament has written it if the meaning of the Act of Parliament itself is plain. If, however, a section has two or more possible meanings, the reader must choose between those meanings; and, if one of those meanings gives an absurd or an unjust result, and the other does not, the reader should choose that meaning which avoids the absurdity or injustice. The "Courts will always lean . . . towards an interpretation that serves to avoid absurdity, repugnancy, or incon-

---

[6] *McCaffry v. Law Society (Alberta)*, [1941] 1 D.L.R. 213, McGillivray J.A. at 222 (S.C.C.).

[7] *R. v. Chief Metropolitan Stipendiary Magistrate; Choudhury, ex parte*, [1990] 3 W.L.R. 986, at 999; *Boykiw v. Calgary (City) Development Appeal Board* (1992), 9 M.P.L.R. (2d) 113, unanimous decision at 119 (Alta. C.A.).

[8] *Vacher & Sons Ltd. v. London Society of Compositors*, [1913] A.C. 107, Lord Macnaghten at 118.

[9] *Walsh v. Trebilcock* (1894), 23 S.C.R. 695, Strong C.J.C. at 705. See also *R. v. Swan* (1952), 7 W.W.R. (N.S.) 1 (Sask. C.A.).

[10] *R. v. Lee Sha Fong*, [1940] 3 D.L.R. 317, Sloan J.A. at 321 (B.C.C.A.).

[11] *McCaffry v. Alberta (Law Society)*, [1941] 1 D.L.R. 213, Harvey C.J.A. at 217 (Alta. C.A.).

sistency.''[12] This approach has been adopted by the courts because if the grammatical or ordinary sense of the words used ''would lead to some absurdity or some repugnance or inconsistency with the rest of the statute, . . . the grammatical and ordinary sense of the words may be modified so as to avoid that inconsistency and absurdity, but no further''.[13] ''It is more probable that the Legislature should have intended to use the word in that interpretation which least offends our sense of justice.''[14]

Sometimes the giving of a literal meaning to the words in the Act can lead to so great an absurdity or so great an injustice that a court must give a more restricted meaning to it. Thus, as the Privy Council has pointed out,

> ''the object of the construction of a statute being to ascertain the will of the legislature it may be presumed that neither injustice nor absurdity was intended. If therefore a literal interpretation would produce such a result and the language admits of an interpretation which would avoid it, then such an interpretation may be adopted.''[15]

Applying that principle, it has been held by the British Columbia Court of Appeal in unanimous reasons for decision that

> ''The legislature cannot be presumed to act unreasonably or unjustly, for that would be acting against the public interest . . . . Words used in enactments of the legislature must be construed upon that premise. That is the real 'intent' of the legislature. That is why words in an Act of the legislature are not restricted to what are sometimes called their 'ordinary' or 'literal' meaning, but are extended flexibly to include the most reasonable meaning which can be extracted from the purpose and object of what is sought to be accomplished by the statute.''[16]

The basis upon which the court acts is that

> ''The mere fact that the results of a statute may be unjust or absurd does not entitle this court to refuse to give it effect, but if there are two different interpretations of the words in an Act, the court will adopt that which is just, reasonable and sensible rather than that which is none of those things.''[17]

A WARNING ABOUT THE RULE

Although lawyers know this rule as the golden rule, in practice it has its dangers. The reader's own ideas of justice must not be substituted for

---

[12] *McCaffry*, McGillivray J.A. at 222 (Alta. C.A.). See also *R. v. Ruddick*, [1928] 3 D.L.R. 208, 62 O.L.R. 248 (H.C.); *Quong-Wing v. R.* (1914), 49 S.C.R. 440.

[13] *Washington v. Grand Trunk Railway* (1897), 28 S.C.R. 184, unanimous decision at 189.

[14] *Simms v. Registrar of Probates*, [1990] A.C. 323, Lord Hobhouse at 335.

[15] *Mangin v. Inland Revenue Commissioners*, [1971] A.C. 739 at 746. See also *R. v. Quon*, [1948] S.C.R. 508, Kellock J. at 520.

[16] *Waugh v. Pedneault (Nos. 2 & 3)*, [1949] 1 W.W.R. 14. See also *Fort Garry (Rural Municipality) v. Fort Garry School District* (1958), 26 W.W.R. 443 (Man. Q.B.).

[17] *Holmes v. Bradfield (Rural District Council)*, [1949] 2 K.B. 1, Finnemore J. at 7. See also *Morris v. Structural Steel Co.* (1917), 35 D.L.R. 739, Macdonald C.J. at 740-741.

the ideas upon which Parliament has acted. In fact, circumstances in which it can be said that an Act is manifestly absurd or manifestly unjust (as distinct from operating harshly) rarely occur.

It must also be borne in mind that absurdity means something more than mere disagreement with what Parliament has done. Even if it can be shown that Parliament's policy is mistaken nonetheless that policy must be enforced by the courts. For example, Parliament might adopt a policy of higher tariffs in defiance of the advice of economists, or a policy of rent control which harmed both landlords and tenants: this would not entitle a court to rewrite the Act. For a court to treat a provision as so absurd that the plain meaning rule has to be departed from it is not enough to point to absurdity in the colloquial sense.

25

THE MISCHIEF RULE

THE NATURE OF THE RULE

For law students one of the best known rules to be used in reading an Act of Parliament is the mischief rule (or, as the law students know it, "the rule in *Heydon's Case"*). This is a rule which is used to find the meaning of an Act when that meaning is obscure:

"The real meaning to be attached to the words must be arrived at by consideration of the mischief that the statute was intended to remedy and the provisions of the statute as a whole, in addition to the particular language of the section in question."[1]

"It is very much part of the duty of the courts, in their task of statutory interpretation, to ascertain as best they can what was the mischief as conceived by Parliament for which a statutory remedy was being provided."[2]

What the reader of an Act of Parliament does in using the mischief rule is to

"consider how the law stood when the statute to be construed was passed, what the mischief was for which the old law did not provide, and the remedy provided by the statute to cure that mischief".[3]

To do this the reader must ask four questions:

1. What was the state of the law before the Act was passed?
2. What was the mischief or defect for which the law did not provide before the Act was passed?
3. What remedy has Parliament provided in the Act to cure the mischief or defect?
4. What is the true reason of the remedy?[4]

In applying the mischief rule to an ambiguous provision (and it can only be applied to an ambiguous provision) of an Act the court will do so to try to give such an interpretation to that ambiguous provision as

---

[1] *Glenn v. Schofield*, [1928] S.C.R. 208. See also *Wall v. Dyke*, [1949] 2 W.W.R. 1185 (Man. K.B.).

[2] *Associated Newspapers Group Ltd. v. Fleming*, [1973] A.C. 628, Lord Simon of Glaisdale at 646.

[3] *Mayfair Property Co., Re*, [1898] 2 Ch. 28, Lord Lindley M.R. at 35. See also *Smith v. Canada (Attorney General)*, [1924] Ex. C.R. 193 (Ex. Ct.).

[4] *Heydon's Case* (1584), 3 Co. Rep 7, 76 E.R. 637. See also *Hassard v. Toronto (City)* (1908), 16 O.L.R. 500 (C.A.).

will cure the mischief at which the Act is aimed. The court will therefore try to find an interpretation that will prevent the mischief continuing but without exposing to liability persons who do not fall within the mischief. Whether or not a court can achieve such a result will, of course, depend upon how intractable the ambiguous provision of the Act proves to be. As Riddell J. said in the Supreme Court of Ontario, "but it is only where the meaning of the words employed in the statute is not plain that any such rule can be invoked."[5]

THE STATE OF THE LAW BEFORE THE ACT WAS PASSED

In finding out what the state of the law was before the Act was passed the reader is not limited to the state of the Acts of Parliament as they then existed. Acts of Parliament are an important part of the law, but they are only part of it. A great deal of the law is not to be found in Acts of Parliament at all. Much of it is to be found in what is known as subordinate legislation — the mass of regulations, bylaws, proclamations and orders made not by Parliament itself but by somebody acting under the authority of an Act of Parliament. However, the greatest bulk of the law is to be found not in Acts of Parliament and not in subordinate legislation but in those fundamental principles of law which are known to the lawyers as the "common law" and which are to be found in the judgments given by judges of superior courts[6] in deciding the cases before them. The person who seeks to use the mischief rule in reading an Act of Parliament must take the common law into account just as much as the statute law and the subordinate legislation.

THE MISCHIEF OR DEFECT

It sometimes happens that the Act of Parliament itself sets out the mischief or defect that it seeks to overcome. For example, there was an English statute against soliciting by prostitutes and the question arose whether persons on balconies or behind windows were soliciting "in a street" contrary to the Act. Lord Parker C.J. said:

> "I approach the matter by considering what is the mischief aimed at by this Act. Everybody knows that this was an Act intended to clean up the streets, to enable people to walk along the streets without being molested or solicited by common prostitutes."

---

[5] *Worthington v. Robbins*, [1925] 2 D.L.R. 80, Riddell J. at 82 (Ont. S.C.).

[6] In Canada the Superior Courts are the Supreme Court, the Exchequer Court and the Federal Court and Federal Court of Appeal of Canada, the Supreme Courts of Provinces other than Québec, the Superior Court of Québec, and the Supreme Court of the North West Territories.

The persons in question were therefore held to be in breach of the Act.[7]

ASCERTAINING THE MISCHIEF OR DEFECT

If the statute does not set out the mischief or defect that it seeks to overcome, it is permissible *in order to find that mischief or defect* to look at contemporaneous circumstances and such material as the report of a royal commission which led to the enactment of that statute.[8] Of course, at common law the report of the royal commission cannot be looked at to find *the meaning of the words* in the statute. It can be looked at

> "not to ascertain the intention of the words used in the subsequent Act but because . . . no more accurate source of information as to what was the evil or defect which the Act of Parliament . . . was intended to remedy could be imagined".[9]

However, various Parliaments have enacted legislation changing the common law to allow the wider use of such reports as an aid to interpretation.

Hansard, which is the official record of the proceedings in Parliament, can be used at common law to ascertain the mischief or defect but the use of *Hansard* deserves a chapter of its own and is considered in chapter 27. Similarly, the preamble to an Act is a useful place in which to look for the mischief which that Act intends to cure.[10]

THE REMEDY PARLIAMENT HAS APPOINTED

The question as to what remedy Parliament has appointed is of course to be answered from the Act itself.

THE REASON FOR THE REMEDY

In the first part of this chapter, four questions are set out as the questions that must be asked in order to apply the mischief rule. The answer to the fourth of those questions (what is the true reason of the remedy?) should become plain once answers to the first three questions have been found, but it must be remembered that in answering that question what has to be found is not the reader's view, and not the view of the court, as to what is the appropriate remedy:

---

[7] *Smith v. Hughes*, [1960] 1 W.L.R. 830 at 832.

[8] *Black-Clawson International Ltd. v. Papierwerke Waldhof-Aschaffenburg AG*, [1975] A.C. 591, Lord Reid at 614-615.

[9] *Dullewe v. Dullewe*, [1969] A.C. 313 at 320.

[10] *Three Bills Passed by the Legislative Assembly of the Province of Alberta, Re*, [1938] S.C.R. 100, Duff C.J.C. and Davis J. at 110.

"In fact, Parliament may not have taken the same view of what is a mischief, may have decided as a matter of policy not to legislate for a legal remedy or may simply have failed to realise that the situation could ever arise."[11]

As Rogers J. held in the Supreme Court of Nova Scotia:

"If the control of traffic was an important factor for environmental regulation 'one would have expected a fairly clear indication of that in the' *Environmental Protection Act*."[12]

APPLYING THE RULE

In order to apply the mischief rule it is not enough merely to ask and to answer the four questions. Having found the reason of the remedy the reader of an Act should then be able to find that meaning which best cures the mischief and advances the remedy while at the same time not exposing to unnecessary liability persons not intended to be covered by the Act.

THE MISCHIEF CANNOT LIMIT THE MEANING OF PLAIN WORDS

Like all the other rules considered in this book the mischief rule cannot be used to limit the meaning of words when that meaning is plain. If Parliament chooses to legislate more widely than the mischief requires, effect must be given to the statute unlimited by the mischief:

"If the natural and ordinary meaning of the words is clear, I must give effect to them, even if I find their effect goes beyond what was needed to deal with the mischief."[13]

---

[11] *Carrington v. Term-a-Stor*, [1983] 1 W.L.R. 138, Sir John Donaldson M.R. (later Lord Donaldson of Lymington M.R.) at 142.

[12] *Nova Scotia (Minister of the Environment) v. Cacchione* (1987), 1 C.E.L.R. (N.S.) 177 at 194, quoting from *Alaska Trainship Corp. v. Pacific Pilotage Authority*, [1981] 1 S.C.R. 261, Laskin C.J. at 277.

[13] *Rance v. Mid-Downs Health Authority*, [1991] 2 W.L.R. 159 at 185.

26

THE PURPOSE OF THE
ACT OF PARLIAMENT

A SECTION SPECIFYING THE PURPOSES OF THE ACT

Some recent Acts contain a section near the beginning of the Act setting out the purpose or purposes of that legislation. Such a purposes section is considered in chapter 11. The present chapter considers the method of interpretation by reference to the purpose of the Act whether or not there is a purposes section in the Act.

THE ACT IS TO BE INTERPRETED ACCORDING TO ITS OBJECT AND INTENT

"The object of a statutory enactment is to be considered when endeavouring to ascertain the real meaning of the words used".[1]

> "We should try to make statutes work by determining the object or scheme of the Act and then by giving the words the meaning which best advances that object or scheme, provided only that the actual words under review can reasonably bear that interpretation . . ."[2]

As Idington J. held in the Supreme Court of Canada,

> "If we would interpret correctly the meaning of any statute or other writing we must understand what those framing it were about, and the purpose it was intended to execute."[3]

The proper interpretation of an Act of Parliament is not a mere mechanical exercise. What the court is endeavouring to do in interpreting the statute is to give effect to the object and intent of Parliament in enacting that statute: "In my view, the term . . . must be interpreted in a fashion consistent with the objects of the legislation..."[4] The cardinal rule, or

---

[1] *Minor v. R.* (1920), 52 D.L.R. 158 (N.S.C.A.).

[2] *Boykiw v. Calgary (City) Development Appeal Board* (1992), 9 M.P.L.R. (2d) 113, unanimous decision at 116-117 (Alta. C.A.).

[3] *Williams v. Box* (1910), 44 S.C.R. 1 at 10.

[4] *861168 Ontario Inc. v. Lindsay (Town) Chief Building Official* (1991), 6 M.P.L.R. (2d) 84 at 87 (Ont. H.C.).

rather the end and object of all construction of statutes, is the ascertainment of the intention of the legislature.[5] The intention of Parliament is not to be found in a vacuum: in an environmental case it was held that

> "This intention must be assessed against the background of modern industrial society which has developed a high level of concern for protection of the environment. In dealing with these environmental concerns there should be a workable balance between preservation of the environment, the needs and demands of business and industry, and preservation of private rights."[6]

Furthermore, "It is an elementary rule of statutory interpretation that 'no one should profess to understand any part of a statute . . . before he has read the whole of it' ".[7] The Supreme Court of Canada has held that an Act should not be construed so as to defeat Parliament's clear intention.[8]

The task

> "is not to speculate on the actual states of mind of draftsmen or legislators: it is to interpret [the] section, so far as its language will permit, in a way which makes the best sense of what [the judge considers] to have been the purpose of . . . the provisions."[9]

As Greenshields C.J. said in the Superior Court of Québec,

> "In an effort to interpret this Act of the Legislators, I have been guided by the well known rule, that a Court should not seek to ascertain and determine what the Author of the Act intended to say, but rather, what he intended by what he did say."[10]

The intention of the Legislature is to be ascertained as expressed by the words used. In order to understand those words the Court is to enquire regarding the subject-matter about which they are used and the object of the Act.[11]

THE PARLIAMENTARY INTENT SHOULD BE EFFECTUATED, NOT DEFEATED

Language, although the best available means of communicating an intention, has its difficulties because the one word can have different meanings and different shades of meaning. In statutes there is often the added problem of complexity. Nevertheless, if the intention of the legislature can be discovered by the court from the words that have been used, it is the duty of the court to give effect to that intention and not to defeat

---

[5] *Bradbury, Re* (1916), 30 D.L.R. 756, Harris J. at 769, 50 N.S.R. 298 (C.A.).

[6] *R. v. Consolidated Maybrun Mines Ltd.* (1993), 12 C.E.L.R. (N.S.) 171 at 176 (Ont. H.C.).

[7] *R. v. Consolidated Maybrun Mines Ltd.* (1993), 12 C.E.L.R. (N.S.) 171 at 189 (Ont. H.C.).

[8] *Ottawa (City) v. Canada Atlantic Railway* (1903), 33 S.C.R. 376.

[9] *Smith v. Schofield*, [1990] 1 W.L.R. 1447 at 1452.

[10] *Henry Morgan & Co. v. Guérin*, [1942] Qué. S.C. 444.

[11] *Excelsior Lumber Co. v. Ross* (1914), 6 W.W.R. 367 (B.C.C.A.).

it, and that intention is to be ascertained by reading and interpreting the language which Parliament itself has chosen for the purpose of expressing it.[12] The "words of an Act are to be read in their entire context and in their grammatical and ordinary sense harmoniously with the scheme of the Act, the object of the Act, and the intention of Parliament."[13] However,

"The rule of grammar . . . must give way to the rule of interpretation which requires a Court to ascertain the intention of the Legislature from the language used upon a consideration of the statute as a whole."[14]

"In the interpretation of statutes, it is the duty of the Court to ascertain the real intention of the legislature by carefully regarding the whole scope of the statute to be construed. And in each case the Court must look at the subjectmatter, consider the importance of the provision and the relation of that provision to the general object intended to be secured by the Act."[15]

In order to find the true meaning of the words used the Court should look to the context.[16] Thus in a maintenance action the relevant section was limited to the object and purpose of the legislation, which was to promote the welfare of infants and to ensure that their physical wants were met. It was held that any wider construction would be contrary to the plain intention of the legislation.[17]

THE MEANING OF "INTENTION" IN THIS CONTEXT

What Parliament intended to achieve by enacting the particular statute may not necessarily be ascertainable from the words that Parliament has used. It is not unknown for people to say one thing and to mean another. The courts cannot ask Parliament what its intention was: they have to find that intention from the words that Parliament has used or from reports of commissions or other materials which Parliament has expressly authorised to be used. As Lord Simon of Glaisdale has pointed out,

"in the construction of all written instruments including statutes, what the court is concerned to ascertain is, not what the promulgators of the instruments meant to say,

---

[12] *R. v. Dubois*, [1935] S.C.R. 378.

[13] *R. v. Enso Forest Products Ltd.* (1992), 8 C.E.L.R. (N.S.) 253 at 261 (B.C.S.C.).

[14] *Greenwood (City) v. Board of School Trustees, School District No. 18* (1965), 55 D.L.R. (2d) 663, unanimous decision at 665 (B.C.C.A.).

[15] *Morrison v. Canada (Minister of Customs and Excise)*, [1928] 2 D.L.R. 759, Audette J. at 762-763, reported under the name of *Morrison v. Canada (Minister of National Revenue)* in [1928] Ex. C.R. 759 (Ex. Ct.).

[16] *Morrison v. Canada (Minister of National Revenue)*, [1928] Ex. C.R. 759 (Ex. Ct.). See also *Hirsch v. Montreal Protestant School Board*, [1926] S.C.R. 246.

[17] *Harley v. Harley*, [1960] O.W.N. 357, reported under the name of *Harley, Re; Harley v. Harley* (1960), 24 D.L.R. (2d) 438 (C.A.).

but the meaning of what they have said. It is in this sense that 'intention' is used as a term of art in the construction of documents."[18]

In a later case that same distinguished judge said:

"The final task of construction is still, as always, to ascertain the meaning of what the draftsman has said, rather than to ascertain what the draftsman meant to say. But if the draftsmanship is correct these should coincide."[19]

The problem is that

"An enactment of the Legislature, subject as it is to the limitations which beset all things human, cannot possibly have in view every situation which may arise. A combination of circumstances may arise which on its face appears to come within the strict language of the enactment yet cannot be so included, because obviously the Legislature would not have included it, if it had such a situation in mind when the enactment was made."[20]

It is to ascertain Parliament's intention that the various rules of statutory interpretation which are considered in this book have been evolved by the courts.

If it were not for those rules, there could be the confusion of finding a number of different or varying intentions held by a number of Members of Parliament all of whom voted in favour of the enactment of the statute — a matter well expressed by Lord Diplock when he said:

"Leaving aside the rare phenomenon in modern times of a genuine Private Member's Bill, what statutes are meant to give effect to is the intention of the government in power at the time that they are passed and as respects such matters of detail as are usually the subject of interstitial law making by the judges, the intention of the government department that was responsible for the promotion of the Bill. If the language to be construed is not clear and unambiguous one may be pretty sure that those members of the legislature who voted in favour of the Bill had no common intention one way or the other as to how the unperceived obscurity or ambiguity ought to be resolved."[21]

WHEN THE PURPOSIVE APPROACH IS UNAVAILABLE

There is a real risk that the reader of legislation may be led astray by the purposive approach. Although, as we have seen, "Where there is an ambiguity . . . the court will strive to give a purposive construction"[22], applying that approach to an unambiguous provision would be wrong. Lord Donaldson of Lymington MR has observed that "If an Act of Parlia-

---

[18] *Farrell v. Alexander*, [1977] A.C. 59 at 81.

[19] *Stock v. Frank Jones (Tipton) Ltd.*, [1978] 1 W.L.R. 231 at 236.

[20] *Waugh v. Pedneault (Nos. 2 and 3)*, [1949] 1 W.W.R. 14 (B.C.C.A.).

[21] In an address in 1977 to the Fifth Commonwealth Law Conference, (1977), 26 *Town Planning and Local Government Guide*, par. 2873.

[22] *Lonhro, Re (No. 2)*, [1990] Ch. 695

ment is unambiguous . . . the policy underlying it may not be directly relevant."[23] Lord Lowry has gone further and held that

> "there is no room for a purposive construction if the words to be construed will not bear the interpretation sought to be put upon them and it must always be borne in mind that the art of statutory interpretation can be applied only when the provision to be interpreted is ambiguous"[24]

and Sir Nicholas Browne-Wilkinson V-C (now Lord Browne-Wilkinson) held that

> "however desirable it may be to construe the Act in a way calculated to carry out the parliamentary purpose, it is not legitimate to distort the meaning of the words Parliament has chosen to use in order to achieve that result. Only if the words used by Parliament are fairly capable of bearing more than one meaning is it legitimate to adopt the meaning which gives effect to, rather than frustrates, the statutory purpose."[25]

However, there are limits to the weight to be given to the grammatical meaning of a section. As was said in the Court of Appeal of Ontario,

> "To read the two subsections . . . as an impediment in an area where the legislative policy favours public hearings would be to frustrate its purpose. In reading the two-letter word 'or' between the subsections . . . social purpose is more important than a rule of grammar."[26]

and

> "In construing an enactment of this kind [the *Infants Act*, R.S.O. 1937 c 215] it must be borne in mind that very often things which are within the words of a statute are out of its purview, which extends no further than the intent of the makers of the Act, and in such a case the best way to construe an Act of Parliament is according to the intent rather than the words . . . [W]here it manifestly appears that a thing which may come within the words of a statute could not have been intended to be brought within its range of operation, a . . . principle of construction is invoked, the Court being guided by the spirit and meaning of the Act apart from the words.
> I approach my consideration of the scope of s. 1(4) of the *Infants Act* with these principles in mind. The words of a statute should not be read in their widest literal sense if when so read it seems highly improbable that they express the real intention of the legislature, but their application should be limited to the object and purpose of the legislation".[27]

A conflict of approach has emerged in Canada over how much weight is to be given to the purpose of legislation and how much to the plain meaning rule:

---

[23] *Post Office v. Union of Communication Workers*, [1990] 1 W.L.R. 981 at 989.
[24] *R. v. Inland Revenue Commissioners; Woolwich Equitable Building Society, ex parte*, [1990] 1 W.L.R. 1400 at 1428.
[25] *Bristol Airport plc v. Powdrill*, [1990] 2 W.L.R. 1362 at 1371.
[26] *Davisville Investment Co. v. Toronto (City)* (1977), 2 M.P.L.R. 81 at 87.
[27] *Harley, Re; Harley v. Harley* (1960), 24 D.L.R. (2d) 438, unanimous decision at 442, reported under the name of *Harley v. Harley* in [1960] O.W.N. 357 (C.A.).

"in contemporary jurisprudence, there exist two divergent schools of thought. Pigeon J. in *R. v. Sommerville*, [1974] S.C.R. 387, at 395, [1973] 2 W.W.R. 65; 32 D.L.R. (3d) 207:

> 'I have been unable to find any authority supporting the proposition that one can depart from the clear meaning of the enactment if this appears to be at odds with its scheme and purpose.'

And Lord Herschell in *Brophy v. Manitoba Attorney-General*, [1895] A.C. 202, at 216, . . . 'The question is, not what may be supposed to have been intended, but what has been said'. On the other hand, Spence J. in *Toronto Transit Commission v. Toronto*, [1971] S.C.R. 746, at 752, 18 D.L.R. (3d) 68:

> 'in every case the meaning of the statutory provision must be obtained by consideration not only of the actual words in a subsection but of the whole statute and by considering the purpose of the legislation.'

The dichotomy would be this: what did the legislature say, as opposed to what does it appear that the legislature intended to say? As between these two conflicting views, my preference is the former. (See *National Farmers Union v. Prince Edward Island (Potato Marketing Council)* (1989), 56 D.L.R. (4th) 753).

Accordingly, I would consider that the proper interpretative approach to be taken to the legislation . . . is, first, to have regard to what the legislature actually said: second, to apply the words used by the legislature in their clear and grammatical meaning, insofar as those words permit it to be done, towards the accomplishment of the indicated objects and purposes of the legislation itself. Finally, should there be any inconsistency between the words used and the purported purpose of the legislation, the words must prevail, and that they be not tortured in their meaning and context to suit and conform to a purpose which cannot be otherwise effected by a clear and grammatical meaning of the words used."[28]

FINDING THE INTENTION BY NECESSARY IMPLICATION

The very fact that the courts have had to evolve special rules for the interpretation of statutes shows that Parliament does not always use plain words to express its intention. When the words themselves fail to convey the intention it may be necessary for the court to ascertain that intention by necessary implication from the words that Parliament has used or from other material that Parliament has authorised to be used for that purpose. Understandably, the courts are normally reluctant to find an intention by mere implication. However,

> "where you have rival constructions of which the language of the statute is capable you must resort to the object or principle of the statute if the object or principle of it can be collected from its language; and if one finds there some governing intention . . . expressed or plainly implied then the construction which best gives effect to the governing intention or principle ought to prevail against a construction which, though agreeing better with the literal effect of the words of the enactment runs counter to the principle and spirit of it."[29]

---

[28] *St. Peters Estates Ltd. v. Prince Edward Island (Land Use Commission)* (1990), 2 M.P.L.R. (2d) 58, McQuaid J. at 72-73 (P.E.I.S.C.).

[29] *McBratney v. McBratney*, [1919] 3 W.W.R. 1000 (S.C.C.). See also *War Amputations of Canada v. Canada (Pension Review Board)*, [1980] 2 F.C. 421 (C.A.).

The courts are to look "not only at the words of the statute but at the cause of making it to ascertain the intent."[30] In seeking the intention of Parliament the court is to have regard to "the possible consequences of alternative constructions of ambiguous expressions".[31] In interpreting the language of a section one should look not only at the object of the Act as a whole but also at the specific purpose of the relevant part of the Act.[32]

CAUTION MUST BE EXERCISED IN INTERPRETING BY INTENTION

People see the same thing in different ways, approaching it from a different basis. This is particularly so in seeking an intention. The answer to the question "What was Parliament's intention?" can readily be influenced by political or other factors in the seeker's mind. If those factors were allowed to determine the meaning of the Act, two totally different results could be achieved depending upon whether the person interpreting the Act was a conservationist on the one hand or someone concerned with development on the other. It must therefore be remembered that "The final task of construction is still, as always, to ascertain the meaning of what the draftsman meant to say"[33] and that

> "dislike of the effect of a statute has never been an accepted reason for departing from its plain language. Holt C.J. said nearly three centuries ago '. . . an Act of Parliament can do no wrong, though it may do several things that look pretty odd'.[34] . . . Accordingly, even if one regarded the policy implicit in [the Act] as open to criticism, [if] the statutory language is clear beyond doubt [it] must prevail."[35]

"Intention of the Legislature" has been held to be a common but very slippery phrase, signifying anything from intention embodied in positive enactment to speculative opinion about what Parliament would probably have meant, although it had omitted to enact it.[36] As it has been held in the Supreme Court of Canada, the duty of a judge is to construe legislation, not to enact it:

> "If the language . . . is only capable of one meaning it would, of course, be our duty so to declare, irrespective of whether the effect would be to defeat the object and purpose of the Act. . . ."[37]

---

[30] *Barrett v. Winnipeg (City)* (1891), 19 S.C.R. 374.

[31] *Hickey v. Stalker* (1923), 53 O.L.R. 414 (C.A.).

[32] *Minneapolis-Honeywell Regulator Co. v. Irvine & Reeves Ltd.* (1954), 13 W.W.R. 449 (B.C.C.A.).

[33] *Stock v. Frank Jones (Tipton) Ltd.* [1978] 1 W.L.R. 231, Lord Simon of Glaisdale at 236.

[34] *London (City) v. Wood* (1701), 12 Mod. Rep. 669 at 687-688, 88 E.R. 1592 at 1602.

[35] *Stock v. Frank Jones (Tipton) Ltd.*, [1978] 1 W.L.R. 231, Lord Edmund-Davies at 238.

[36] *Hayes, Re* (1931), 12 C.B.R. 225 (Sask. K.B.).

[37] *Grand Trunk Railway v. Hepworth Silica Pressed Brick Co.* (1915), 51 S.C.R. 81.

Naturally, the court would hope to apply the words used by Parliament "towards the accomplishment of the indicated objects and purposes of the legislation itself," but

> "should there be any inconsistency between the words used and the purported purpose of the legislation, the words must prevail, and [they must not be] tortured in their meaning and context to suit and conform to a purpose which cannot be otherwise effected by a clear and grammatical meaning of the words used."[38]

> "A mere conjecture that Parliament entertained a purpose which, however natural, has not been embodied in the words it has used if they be literally interpreted is no sufficient reason for departing from the literal interpretation."[39]

It is possible that two policies may come into conflict: in such a case the court is not to speculate as to which of those two conflicting policies should prevail — it should confine itself to the construction of the language of the Act read as a whole.[40]

The dangers attending an excessive use of the purposive approach have been well set out by Ferguson J.A. in the Ontario Court of Appeal:

> "It appears that the sages of the law heretofore have construed statutes quite contrary to the letter in some appearance, and those statutes which comprehended all things in the letter, they have expounded to extend but to some things, and those which generally prohibit all people from doing such an act, they have interpreted to permit some people to do it, and those which include every person in the letter they have adjudged to reach to some persons only, which expositions have always been founded on the intent of the Legislature which they have collected sometimes by considering the cause and necessity for making the Act, sometimes by comparing one part of the Act with another and sometimes by foreign circumstances. So that they have ever been guided by the intent of the legislature, which they have always taken according to the necessity of the matter and according to that which is consonant to reason and good discretion."[41]

---

[38] *St. Peters Estates Ltd. v. Prince Edward Island Land Use Commission* (1990), 2 M.P.L.R. (2d) 58 at 73 (P.E.I.S.C.).

[39] *Royal Bank v. Acadia School Division No. 8*, [1943] 1 W.W.R. 256 (Alta. T.D.).

[40] *Toronto & Niagara Power Co. v. North Toronto (Town)*, [1912] A.C. 834.

[41] *Gordon Mackay Ltd. v. Laroque* (1926), 7 C.B.R. 384 (Ont. C.A.).

27

HANSARD

THE NATURE OF HANSARD

Everything that Members of Parliament say in the course of the proceedings in Parliament is recorded at the time and is printed as a permanent record. This record is known as *Hansard*. It takes its name from T.C. Hansard, who, with his two sons and their sons, were the compilers of this record in England from 1774.

CAN HANSARD BE USED AT COMMON LAW IN THE INTERPRETATION OF AN ACT?

There have been conflicting statements in the superior courts over whether, or to what extent, *Hansard* can be used in the process of statutory interpretation. *Hansard* has been used to find the mischief against which the Act being interpreted was directed:

> "I am strengthened in this conclusion by the clear indication of the evil sought to be remedied found in the parliamentary debates, of which as public documents this Court can take judicial notice. While the rule still remains that legislative history is not admissible to show the intention of the Legislature directly, the Supreme Court of Canada has nevertheless looked at legislative history for related purposes . . . in relation to the interpretation of statutes generally . . . The present rule would thus appear to be that *Hansard* may be used, like the report of a commission of enquiry, in order to expose and examine the mischief, evil or condition to which the Legislature was directing its attention . . . .
>
> Here, the budget statement of the then Minister of Finance . . . describes the perceived need to which the amendment to the Act was the response . . .
>
> The evil aimed at is clearly stated to be 'any slowdown in investment' ".[1]

However, in the Supreme Court of Canada, *Hansard* was "rejected as inadmissible" along with evidence tendered from two Ministers, a deputy Minister, the Clerk of the House of Commons, and a press gallery correspondent.[2] In the same court, Dickens C.J.C. held that

---

[1] *Lor-West Contracting Ltd. v. R.*, [1986] 1 F.C. 346, MacGuigan J. at 355-356 (T.D.).
[2] *Canada (Attorney General) v. Reader's Digest Association*, [1961] S.C.R. 775, Kerwin C.J.C. at 782.

"generally speaking, speeches made in the legislature at the time of enactment of the measure are inadmissible as having little evidential weight".[3]

WHY THE COMMON LAW LIMITS THE USE OF HANSARD TO FIND THE MEANING OF AN ACT OF PARLIAMENT

It is a traditional rule of the common law, regarding the reading of an Act of Parliament, that the reader must not turn to *Hansard* to find out directly what the Act means as distinct from finding out the mischief the Act was designed to cure.[4] For example, *Hansard* has been held to be admissible to examine the condition to which Parliament directed its attention when enacting a section providing for tax credits.[5] The rule applies to the Minister's speech in introducing the Bill for the Act, and perhaps to what a Member has said in Parliament.[6] The reason for this rule is clear. Before it becomes an Act of Parliament every Bill must receive three readings in each House of Parliament.[7] That does not mean, however, that every Member of Parliament can state his or her views about the Bill. In fact, by far the majority of Members of Parliament would be unlikely to speak upon any particular Bill before Parliament. The views stated by those Members of Parliament who do speak upon the particular Bill might be quite different to the views of the other Members who vote in favour of the Bill. One could not say with any certainty that the views expressed by any particular Member of Parliament were the views of Parliament as a whole. The courts have therefore repeatedly held that the reader of an Act of Parliament must not turn to *Hansard* to find out what the Act means.[8] As the Ontario Court of Appeal held in a unanimous decision,

"Undoubtedly the great weight of authority is against the use of Parliamentary debates as an aid to the interpretation of statutes. However, we would note that Lord Reid,

---

[3] *Reference to the Court of Appeal pursuant to the Constitutional Questions Act*, R.S.O. 1970, c. 79, [1981] 1 S.C.R. 714, Dickson J. (later Dickson C.J.C.) at 721. This statement appears to mean that the weight to be given to *Hansard* is so slight as to make such statements inadmissible.

[4] As Phillips J. has said, "It is an error to suppose that ministerial intentions are the equivalent of enacted legislation": *Hereford and Worcester County Council v. Craske* (1976), 75 L.G.R. 174 at 177. The minister's speech reflects what the department intended the legislation to achieve, but what the legislation actually achieves depends upon the proper interpretation of the words of the Act as passed by Parliament. As to the mischief rule, see above, chapter 25.

[5] *Lor-West Contracting Ltd. v. R.*, [1986] 1 F.C. 346 (T.D.).

[6] *Gosselin v. R.* (1903), 33 S.C.R. 255; *Smiles v. Belford* (1877), 1 O.A.R. 436 (C.A.).

[7] See chapter 1.

[8] See footnotes 2 and 3, and for English cases see *Millar v. Taylor* (1769), 4 Burr. 2303 at 2332, 98 E.R. 201 at 217; *South Eastern Railway Co. v. Railway Commissioners* (1881), 50 L.J.K.B. 201 at 203; *Lumsden v. Inland Revenue Commissioners*, [1914] A.C. 877 at 908; *Assam Railways & Trading Co. v. Inland Revenue Commissioners*, [1935] A.C. 455 at 458. It can, however, be used to find the mischief or defect the Act is supposed to cure.

although he more than once affirmed this general rule, suggested in *Warner v. Metropolitan Police Com'r*, [1969] 2 A.C. 256, at 279, that there might be some scope for an exception 'where examining the proceedings in Parliament would almost certainly settle the matter one way or the other' ".[9]

In England, however, the common law rule has been overturned by the House of Lords in a decision in which it allowed recourse to be made to *Hansard*, not only for ascertaining the mischief at which the Act is aimed but for purposes of interpretation generally.[10] It is therefore uncertain whether the Canadian courts will decide to follow the new English rule or to continue with the traditional rule concerning *Hansard*. In any event,

"The general rule which is applicable to the construction of all other documents is equally applicable to statutes and the interpreter should so far put himself in the position of those whose words he is interpreting as to be able to see what those words related to. He may well call to his aid all those external or historical facts which are necessary for this purpose and which led to the enactment and for those he may consult contemporary or other authentic writings".[11]

COMMON LAW DOES NOT USE THE HISTORY OF A BILL BEFORE PARLIAMENT TO INTERPRET THE ACT

A Bill may be amended extensively by Parliament before it finally becomes an Act of Parliament. The Bill as it is first placed before Parliament is not in words that have been approved by Parliament; indeed, at that stage, Parliament itself has not seen the Bill. Accordingly, in finding the meaning of the Act of Parliament, the common law rule is that no help can be gained from comparing the Act with the Bill from which it came;[12] and, for the same reason, the common law rule is that the courts will not consider the fate of amendments dealt with in either House of Parliament:[13] the court is there to find the meaning of the Act itself, not the meaning of the Bill as drafted by the drafter and not the separate meaning of amendments proposed in Parliament but which were not included in the Act as it was finally enacted by Parliament.

The common law rule about not considering amendments proposed in Parliament must not be confused with the case in which a later Act of Parliament amends an earlier Act. That is a different case altogether. In

---

[9] *R. v. Stevenson* (1980), 57 C.C.C. (2d) 526 at 530-531 (Ont. C.A.).

[10] *Pepper v. Hart*, [1993] A.C. 593, [1992] 3 W.L.R. 1032.

[11] *Canadian Pacific Railway v. James Bay Railway* (1905), 36 S.C.R. 42, Nesbitt J. at 89-90.

[12] *Herron v. Rathmines and Rathgar Improvement Commissioners*, [1892] A.C. 498 at 501; *Lumsden v. Inland Revenue Commissioners*, [1914] A.C. 877 at 922.

[13] *Viscountess Rhondda's Claim*, [1922] 2 A.C. 339 at 383 and 399; *Mountain Park Coals Ltd. v. Minister of National Revenue*, [1952] Ex. C.R. 560 (Ex. Ct.).

that case there are two Acts of Parliament, and both, therefore, express the will of Parliament at the time that they were passed. The amendments in fact made by Parliament *as set out in the later Act* can be used in finding the meaning of the earlier Act.

28

USING OTHER MATERIAL FROM OUTSIDE AN ACT TO UNDERSTAND THE MEANING OF THAT ACT

THE USE OF EXTRINSIC MATERIALS TO INTERPRET AN ACT

If there is an ambiguity in a statute, resort may be had to materials other than the Act itself in order to arrive at its true meaning:

"The general rule which is applicable to the construction of all other documents is equally applicable to statutes and the interpreter should so far put himself in the position of those whose words he is interpreting as to be able to see what those words related to. He may call to his aid all those external or historical facts which are necessary for this purpose and which led to the enactment and for those he may consult contemporary or other authentic works and writings."[1]

However,

"It is only when the language used in a statute presents a choice of two or more meanings equally tenable [that] it is admissible within certain limits to have resort to the aid of extraneous considerations in order to discover which meaning was most probably intended."[2]

SURROUNDING CIRCUMSTANCES

The Supreme Court of Canada has taken into account, as leading by necessary implication and logical inference to the purpose of the legislation, "the circumstances surrounding the passage of the legislation, informing as they must the context of the statute".[3]

REPORTS BY LAW REFORM COMMISSIONS

Law reform commission reports can lead to new legislation. They identify matters which the law needs to cover or which the existing law does not cover adequately, and they may make recommendations as to the form

---

[1] *Canadian Pacific Railway v. James Bay Railway* (1905), 36 S.C.R. 42, Nesbitt J. at 89-90.
[2] *Moose Jaw (City) v. British American Oil Co.*, [1937] 2 W.W.R. 309 (Sask. C.A.).
[3] *Friends of the Oldman River Society v. Canada (Minister of Transport)*, [1992] 1 S.C.R. 3.

which new legislation should take. At common law, the courts are entitled to look at any relevant report of a law reform commission, in order to discover the previous state of the law and the mischief requiring remedy as at the time when legislation consequent upon that report was enacted.

> "It now seems reasonably clear that Royal Commission Reports . . . made prior to the passing of a statute are admissible to show the factual content and purpose of the legislation."[4]

It is not sufficient merely to determine the view taken by a Law Reform Commission. Parliament need not "adopt all the interpretations of a non-legislative body, as distinguished from that body's recommendations."[5] Parliament may very well decide to modify what the Law Reform Commission has recommended. Those recommendations, therefore, are a useful starting point, rather than being in themselves a decisive factor.

REPORTS BY ROYAL COMMISSIONS AND BOARDS OR COMMITTEES OF INQUIRY

Royal commission and board or committee of inquiry reports can result in Parliament taking legislative action. Should this be so, the relevant report may be looked at by the judges in order to discover the mischief at which the subsequent legislation was aimed. As Martin C.J.B.C. said in the British Columbia Court of Appeal,

> "We think the report should be admitted in evidence insofar only as it finds facts which are relevant to the ascertainment of the . . . alleged purpose and the effect of the enactment."[6]

Such a report has been admitted as evidence of the situation and context in which an Order in Council was passed,[7] to show the "materials" the Legislature had before it when enacting certain legislation,[8] and to ascertain the true purpose and effect of the enactment.[9]

---

[4] *Reference to the Court of Appeal pursuant to the Constitutional Questions Act*, R.S.O. 1970, c. 79, [1981] S.C.R. 714, Dickson J. (later Dickson C.J.C.) at 721.

[5] *Landex Investments Ltd. v. Red Deer (City)* (1991), 6 M.P.L.R. (2d) 36, unanimous decision at 45 (Alta. C.A.).

[6] *Home Oil Distributors Ltd. v. British Columbia (Attorney General)*, [1939] 1 W.W.R. 49, at 51.

[7] *New Brunswick Broadcasting Co. v. Canada (Canadian Radio-Television & Telecommunications Commission)*, [1985] 2 F.C. 410 (T.D.).

[8] *Canadian Indemnity Co. v. British Columbia (Attorney General) (No. 3)*, [1975] 3 W.W.R. 224 (B.C.S.C.).

[9] *Home Oil Distributors Ltd. v. British Columbia (Attorney General)*, [1939] 1 W.W.R. 49 (B.C.C.A.), but see *Goulbourn (Township) v. Ottawa -Carleton Regional Municipality*, [1980] 1 S.C.R. 496.

PARLIAMENTARY COMMITTEE REPORTS

Parliamentary committee reports "made prior to the passing of a statute are admissible to show the factual content and purpose of the legislation."[10] Similarly, reports of Parliamentary committees producing draft Bills are admissible.[11]

DRAFTER'S REPORTS

The courts are now more disposed than previously to refer to the report of commissioners appointed to draft and submit a Bill for adoption.[12] The Cour supérieure du Québec is willing to consider and to weigh the reports of the codifiers from which the *Civil Code* and the *Code of Civil Procedure* of that Province were adopted when interpreting various articles of those codes.[13]

MISCELLANEOUS REPORTS

Canadian Courts have been willing to consider not only the report of Statute Revision Commissioners,[14] but also minutes of the Executive Council of a Province containing the recommendation of a committee which was communicated to the Federal Government,[15] and a letter by the Deputy Governor of the Bank of Canada read by the Minister of Justice to the House of Commons.[16] Cosgrove J., in the Ontario Court of Justice was even willing to follow a sentencing process recommended by the Canadian Sentencing Commission and by a Bill currently before Parliament, though of course recognising that the court is not bound "by legislation which is resting in Parliament that has not been passed."[17]

EXPLANATIONS BY GOVERNMENT DEPARTMENTS

When an Act has been passed by Parliament, the government department which is responsible for enforcing the Act sometimes sends out a circular explaining what the department believes the Act to mean. The fact

---

[10] *Reference to the Court of Appeal pursuant to the Constitutional Questions Act*, R.S.O. 1970, c. 79, [1981] 1 S.C.R. 714, Dickson J. (later Dickson C.J.C.) at 721.
[11] *R. v. Jeanotte*, [1932] 2 W.W.R. 283, Mackenzie J.A. at 285-286 (Sask. C.A.); *Robitaille v. Beauprés* (1937), 75 Qué. S.C. 502.
[12] *R. v. Jeanotte*, [1932] 2 W.W.R. 283 (Sask. C.A.)
[13] *Robitaille v. Beauprés* (1937), 75 Qué. S.C. 502.
[14] *Campbell v. Dowdall* (1992), 12 M.P.L.R. (2d) 27 at 38 (Ont. H.C.).
[15] *British Columbia (Attorney General) v. Canada* (1889), 14 App. Cas. 295.
[16] *R. v. Giftcraft Ltd.* (1984), 13 C.C.C. (3d) 192, Saunders J. at 196 (Ont. H.C.).
[17] *R. v. Bata Industries Ltd.* (1993), 11 C.E.L.R. (N.S.) 208 at 222 (Ont. Gen. Div.).

that the circular is issued by the department does not make it part of the Act itself. The basic rule is, that what has to be found is the meaning of the Act itself, not what the department thinks the Act does mean or should mean. In finding the meaning of the Act, therefore, the courts will not look at the departmental circular[18] except possibly for the purpose of ascertaining the mischief the Act was intended to remedy. The Supreme Court of Canada has held that the general exclusionary rule formerly applicable has been greatly modified and relaxed — the court may consider extrinsic evidence on the operation and effect of an Act, but only evidence not inherently unreliable or offending public policy should be admitted. Declarations by public figures were excluded, but a government pamphlet was accepted as evidence of Parliament's intent.[19] Acceptance of the government pamphlet raises the question as to whether Tax Interpretation Bulletins and Securities Commissions' Policy Statements will be received by the courts as evidence of the purpose of the legislative provisions with which the bulletin or policy statement is concerned.

Subordinate legislation

The use of subordinate legislation (that is, bylaws, regulations, planning schemes and all other forms of legislation made by government, semi-government and local government bodies under a power conferred upon them by Parliament) to assist in the interpretation of an Act of Parliament is considered in chapter 44.

---

[18] *London County Council v. Central Land Board,* [1959] Ch. 386.
[19] *Churchill Falls (Labrador) Corp. v. Newfoundland (Attorney General),* [1984] 1 S.C.R. 297.

29

THE ACT MUST BE READ AS A WHOLE

WORDS MUST BE READ IN THE LIGHT OF THE SECTION AS A WHOLE

Words must be read in their context. For example, in a Taxation Act "Light on the true meaning of the words used in the statute has to be sought from the context and the scheme . . . with reference to which they are used."[1] In finding the right meaning to give to an Act of Parliament the reader must give close attention to the meaning of each word that is used. This will often involve turning to the judicial dictionaries or to the standard dictionaries such as the *Oxford English Dictionary* to find the meanings to be given to individual words in the section. This attention to individual words, necessary as it is, can cause the reader to lose sight of the fact that those words are only part of the whole. What is really sought is not the meaning of individual words, but the meaning of the Act as a whole. It would be easy to assign a correct meaning to each word individually, and yet have a meaning for the section as a whole that is not the true meaning of that section. The pianist who has to play a chord does not get the proper result by playing each of the notes in that chord separately — they must be played together. So, too, the reader of an Act of Parliament must consider all the words of the section together.[2]

The true meaning of a word in a section can in fact only be found by considering that word in the context of the section in which it stands. The word "forthwith" is a good example. There are some sections in which "forthwith" must be read as meaning "immediately".[3] There are other sections in which "forthwith" does not mean immediately but instead means only "within such time as is reasonably practicable"[4] having regard to the circumstances of the case and the subject-matter.[5] An example of the importance of reading the Act as a whole is provided by the New Brunswick *Municipalities Act* (1973), in which s. 74 (3) stated that "The

---

[1] *Morrison v. Canada (Minister of National Revenue)*, [1928] 2 D.L.R. 759, Audette J. at 763 (Ex. Ct.).

[2] *Yorkshire & Pacific Securities Ltd. v. Fiorenza*, 52 B.C.R. 509 (S.C.).

[3] See, for example, *R. v. Berkshire Justices* (1879), 4 Q.B.D. 469.

[4] *Partridge v. Aylwin*, [1924] 3 D.L.R. 324, unanimous decision at 326.

[5] *R. v. Cuthbertson* [1960] Ex. C.R. 83, O'Connor J. at 87; *Southam, Re; Lamb, ex parte* (1891), 19 Ch. D. 169.

Council . . . *may appoint''* while the previous subsection stated that ''The Council . . . *shall appoint''* various other officers. The court held that the contrast between those two subsections made it clear that Parliament gave councils a discretion ''to determine whether they [required] the services of officers such as those mentioned in subs 74(3)''[6] The context of words in an Act can be vitally important:

> ''Thus the words 'while committing' could have one meaning when disembodied from the *Criminal Code* and another entirely when read in the context of the scheme and purpose of the legislation. It is the latter meaning that [the Court] must ascertain''[7]

and

> ''even the ordinary meaning of words used is to yield to the context — still the rule is not to suppose that the Legislature has been either ungrammatical or loose in its use of tenses or words, but the contrary''[8]

In some cases the reading of the word in the light of its context may give a wider meaning than it would have had if read on its own, and in other cases the meaning of the word when read in its context may be narrower than it would otherwise have been. For example, it has been held that

> ''The words 'guidelines' cannot be construed in isolation; [the section] must be read as a whole. When so read it becomes clear that Parliament has elected to adopt a regulatory scheme that is 'law' and thus amenable to enforcement . . .''[9]

A SECTION MUST BE READ IN THE LIGHT OF THE ACT AS A WHOLE

If it is necessary to read words in the light of the section as a whole, it is equally necessary to read the section in the light of the Act as a whole. When it is said that words must be read in their context, that context is not limited to the particular section or subsection but extends to the whole of the Act:

> ''In the interpretation of statutes, it is the duty of the Court to ascertain the real intention of the legislature by carefully regarding the whole scope of the statute to be construed''[10]

> ''The relation of various provisions of a statute to each other is relevant in elaborating

---

[6] *Hughes v. Moncton (City)* (1991), 6 M.P.L.R. (2d) 203 at 208.

[7] *R. v. Enso Forest Products Ltd.* (1992), 8 C.E.L.R. (N.S.) 253 at 262, quoting *R. v. Paré*, [1987] 2 S.C.R. 618, Wilson J. at 626.

[8] *McGowan v. Hudson's Bay Co.* (1901), 5 Terr. L.R. 147 (N.W.T.C.A.).

[9] *Friends of the Oldman River Society v. Canada (Minister of Transport)*, [1992] 1 S.C.R. 3, 7 C.E.L.R. (N.S.) 1 at 25.

[10] *Morrison v. Canada (Minister of National Revenue)*, [1928] 2 D.L.R. 759, Audette J. at 762-763. See also *Saskatchewan (Human Rights Commission) v. Engineering Students' Society, University of Saskatchewan* (1989), 56 D.L.R. 604 at 614.

the meaning or scope of a statute and a provision should, if possible, be construed to fit into that statute or framework."[11]

"For the purposes of construction, the context of words which are to be construed includes not only the particular phrase or section in which they occur, but also the other parts of the statute."[12]

Where there are two or more alternative meanings, "that meaning should be selected which is in harmony with the balance of the statute . . ."[13] The language of the Act must be read as a whole:

"If the clearly expressed scheme of the Act requires it, particular expressions may have to be read in a sense which would not be the natural one if they could be taken by themselves."[14]

It must be remembered that the task of the courts is to find Parliament's intention:

"In making this determination the Court must not take part of a statute and construe it without regard to its context. An Act of a legislature is to be treated as a unit and must be read as such in attempting to ascertain the meaning of a portion of such."[15]

Indeed, the decision of a lower court has been reversed on appeal because the lower court "put a narrow and technical construction upon the precise words used . . . without taking into consideration the meaning and intent of the statute as a whole."[16]

If a section is capable of two meanings, a consideration of that section in the context of the Act in which it appears may show which of the two meanings is to be given to that section:

"In deciding which of . . . two meanings the legislature intended the section to bear, I think that the construction should be adopted which, upon a reading of the Act and its amendments as an entire enactment, appears to better accord with the body of the enactment than does the alternative construction."[17]

and

"in construing statutes one has to look at the whole Act when construing a particular section to find whether or not the section must be modified by reference to the whole where either of two constructions is open for adoption."[18]

---

[11] *Ontario (Joint Board under Consolidated Hearings Act) v. Ontario Hydro* (1993), 11 C.E.L.R. (N.S.) 135, unanimous decision at 145 (Ont. Div. Ct.).

[12] *Canada (Attorney General) v. Saskatchewan Water Corp.* (1990), 5 C.E.L.R. (N.S.) 252 at 281–282 (Sask. Q.B.).

[13] *Vancouver (City) v. Grant* (1993), 17 M.P.L.R. (2d) 204 at 209 (B.C.S.C.).

[14] *R. v. Marchioness of Donegal* (1923), 51 N.B.R. 309 (C.A.).

[15] *Maguire v. Hinton (Municipality) Commissioners of Police* (1980), 14 Alta. L.R. (2d) 199 (Q.B.).

[16] *R. v. Fraser Companies Ltd.*, [1931] S.C.R. 490, Smith J. at 492.

[17] *R. v. New Brunswick (Public Utilities Commission)* (1926), 54 N.B.R. 138 (C.A.).

[18] *Chandler v. Vancouver (City)*, [1919] 1 W.L.R. 605 (B.C.C.A.).

Naturally, two sections of the same statute should be construed "so as to avoid any repugnancy or inconsistency."[19]

If the Act is one which is divided into parts, the context to be looked at is not just the part in which the particular section appears: it is the Act as a whole.

LIMITS TO THE USE OF THIS RULE

The rule that an Act of Parliament is to be read as a whole must not be used to destroy the clear meaning of a part of the Act that is being read:

> "No rule of construction can require that when the words of one part of a statute convey a clear meaning it shall be necessary to introduce another part of a statute for the purpose of controlling or diminishing the efficacy of the first part."[20]

The principle which forms the basis of this rule is clear. This principle is that

> "Every clause of a statute should be construed with reference to the context and other clauses in the Act, so as, as far as possible, to make a consistent enactment of the whole statute or series of statutes relating to the subjectmatter."[21]

Care must be taken in using this rule. Caution is particularly necessary when reading a consolidating Act, which consolidates an earlier Act with a large number of Acts amending that earlier version. In the case of an Act of Parliament of that nature, the drafting is far less likely to be consistent, and a search for consistency could lead the reader away from the real meaning of the section. This follows from the fact that a consolidating Act takes provisions drafted at different times, and appearing in different Acts, and places them together in the one statute. Those who drafted those provisions of course attempted to achieve consistency, but it is all too easy in drafting amendments and new sections to overlook other sections of the Act which bear upon the same or a similar subject-matter. Similarly, when an Act has been amended so that provisions in a schedule have been inserted at different times, were perhaps prepared by a different drafter, and dealt with different legislative provisions, they should not be read together.

---

[19] *Hamilton Harbour Commissioners v. Hamilton (City)* (1976), 1 M.P.L.R. 133 at 156.

[20] *Warburton v. Loveland* (1831), 2 D. & Cl. 489 at 500, 6 E.R. 809 at 813.

[21] *Canada Sugar Refining Co. v. R.*, [1898] A.C. 735, Lord Davey at 741. As to the interpretation when drafting precludes the giving of a consistent meaning see chapter 37.

30

EFFECT MUST BE GIVEN
TO THE WHOLE ACT

WORDS SHOULD NOT BE DISCARDED

Parliament's intention is not to be found by substituting the reader's presumption as to that intention in place of the clear meaning of the words used. Similarly, it is not for the reader to assume that Parliament has used words idly. Except when it is impossible to do so effect must be given to every word in the Act. The reader must bear in mind that "a statute is never supposed to use words without a meaning."[1] The rule is that if it can be prevented, no clause, sentence, or word shall be superfluous, void, or insignificant.[2] For example, the word "and" has been read as "or" because otherwise words in the section "would be superfluous."[3] In another example when a section used the word "replace" and also the word "fill" those two words were held to refer to two different actions.[4] "The authorities are clear that in the interpretation of statutes, to the extent reasonably possible, a meaning must be given to all portions of the statute"[5] — "no words or phrases are to be treated as insensible."[6]

SENSE SHOULD BE MADE OF A PROVISION IF POSSIBLE

Since Parliament must be assumed not to have used words idly, it must also be assumed that Parliament intended the words to make sense. It meant the Act of Parliament to be effective. Therefore, if two meanings could be given to the words used in the Act of Parliament, what the reader should do is "to adopt that construction which will give some effect to the words

---

[1] *Auchterarder Presbytery v. Lord Kinnoull* (1839), 6 Cl. & F. 646 at 686, 7 E.R. 841, Lord Brougham at 856.

[2] *Whitney v. Inland Revenue Commissioners*, [1926] A.C. 37, Lord Dunedin at 42.

[3] *Canadian Pacific Ltd. v. Canadian Transport Commission* (1983), 2 D.L.R. (4th) 630, unanimous decision at 636 reported under the name of *Canadian Pacific Ltd. v. Canada (Canadian Transport Commission)* in (1983), 49 N.R. 354 (Fed. C.A.).

[4] *New Brunswick Liquor Corp. v. C.U.P.E., Local 963* (1978), 21 N.B.R. (2d) 441 (C.A.).

[5] *Canada (Attorney General) v. Saskatchewan Water Corp.* (1990), 5 C.E.L.R. (N.S.) 252 at 281 (Sask. Q.B.). See also *Reese v. Alberta* (1992), 7 C.E.L.R. (N.S.) 89 at 124 (Alta. Q.B.).

[6] *Ottawa-Carleton v. Goulbourn (Township)* (1978), 5 M.P.L.R. 195 at 204.

rather than that which will give none".[7] This rule is a basic one, and nothing short of impossibility should allow a judge to declare a statute unworkable; even though an enactment is unclear and ambiguous that does not provide grounds for holding the enactment to be unenforceable — only if it is truly impossible to find the meaning may a judge refuse to apply the enactment.[8] However, if despite the efforts of the court there is a word or phrase which does not lend itself to a sensible construction that word or phrase should be eliminated:[9]

> "To treat any part of a statute as ineffectual, or a mere surplusage, is never justifiable if any other construction be possible. The rejection or excision of a word or phrase is permissible only where it is impossible otherwise to reconcile or give effect to the provisions of the Act."[10]

The courts will not assume an intention by Parliament to enact a meaningless provision. However, where there is such repugnancy that certain words (if effect were given to them) would empty the section of all meaning and destroy the intended effect of the Act, those words should be totally disregarded.[11]

REPETITION AND SURPLUSAGE

Although the reader of an Act of Parliament must try to give a sensible meaning to all the words of the Act, there are cases in which one is forced to find that Parliament has repeated itself or that surplus words have been included in the Act. This is a reading of the Act which should only be used as a last resort.[12]

Thus, a court will interpret a word in an Act in such a way as to avoid it being synonymous with another word in the same provision.[13] Nevertheless, there have been cases in which the courts have been forced to treat words in an Act of Parliament as repetition or as surplus words. As one of the greatest of the judges has admitted, it may not always be possible to give a meaning to every word used in an Act of Parliament. Nevertheless, it is a bold step to treat words as if they were not in the Act, and it is a step that should only be taken in a case of necessity.[14]

---

[7] *Gaudet v. Brown; Cargo ex "Argos"* (1873), L.R. 5 P.C. 134 at 153. See also *Him, Re* (1910), 15 B.C.R. 163 (S.C.).

[8] *R. v. Dagley* (1979), 32 N.S.R. (2d) 421 (C.A.).

[9] *Newman v. Grand Trunk Railway* (1910), 20 O.L.R. 285 (C.P.).

[10] *Williams v. Box* (1910), 44 S.C.R. 1.

[11] *Reference re Alberta Legislation*, [1938] S.C.R. 100.

[12] *R. v. St. John, Westgate, Burial Board* (1862), 2 B. & S. 703 at 706, 121 E.R. 1232, Erle C.J. at 1234.

[13] *Income Tax Commissioners v. Pemsel*, [1891] A.C. 532, Lord Macnaghten at 589.

[14] *Cowper-Essex v. Acton Local Board* (1889), 14 App. Cas. 153, Lord Bramwell at 169.

A warning to be regarded

The principles enunciated in this chapter are principles that have stood the test of time. They are principles that will be accepted and applied by the courts whenever they are appropriate.

However, a note of caution should be sounded:

"It is the business of the court to interpret legislation that has been enacted if it is possible. It is not the duty of the court to entirely rewrite an unworkable statute."[15]

---

[15] *Flood v. Monargo Mines Ltd.*, [1938] 2 D.L.R. 460, reported under the name of *Flood & Monargo Mines Ltd., Re*, [1938] O.R. 282 (C.A.).

31

OMISSIONS FROM THE ACT

THE RULE AS TO THINGS LEFT OUT OF THE ACT

All the rules for reading an Act of Parliament have been laid down by the courts to enable the reader to discern what Parliament meant by the words that it actually used in the Act. It must always be borne in mind that what the reader must try to do is to find the meaning of the words actually used, not the meaning of the words he or she thinks should have been used.

No matter how carefully an Act of Parliament may be drafted, and no matter how carefully it may be considered by Parliament, there is always the chance that something will be overlooked or forgotten. There have been various Acts of Parliament which have failed to deal with matters that they could reasonably have been expected to deal with. When that happens, it is certainly not for the reader to deal with the matter personally; the Act of Parliament must be read as it stands, and must be read as failing to deal with that matter. This is a rule that has been reiterated time and time again by the courts.[1] When it is clear that Parliament "had not in mind a case of this kind and made no provision for it" the court "cannot add, and mend, and, by construction, make up deficiencies which are left there."[2] It has been held that even to avoid an obvious mischief, the court cannot extend the language of an Act to meet a case for which, clearly and undoubtedly, provision has not been made.[3] A court which departs from the plain and obvious meaning of a statute is exceeding its function by altering the Act rather than interpreting it — if the court supplies a defect which Parliament could have supplied, that court is no longer interpreting, but making, the law.[4]

---

[1] See, for example, *Mersey Docks & Harbour Board v. Henderson* (1888), 13 App. Cas. 595, Lord Halsbury at 603; *Crawford v. Spooner* (1846), 6 Moore P.C. 1 at 8-9, 13 E.R. 582 at 585; *Western Bank Ltd. v. Schindler*, [1977] Ch. 1, [1976] 3 W.L.R. 341, Scarman L.J. (later Lord Scarman) at 355; *Craies on Statute Law* (Sweet & Maxwell, London, 1971, 7th ed., Edgar S.G.G., 1971) p. 70.

[2] *Stadnic v. Bifrost (Rural Municipality)*, [1929] 2 D.L.R. 703, unanimous decision at 705 (Man. C.A.).

[3] *Pickles v. Barr*, [1957] 2 W.W.R. 272 (B.C.S.C.).

[4] *Halifax Branch of Navy League of Canada, Re* (1927), 59 N.S.R. 212 (C.A.).

"If there is a gap in the legislation it is for Parliament and not for the courts to fill it."[5] There are many cases in which the courts have drawn Parliament's attention to the need to amend an Act to deal with something that has been overlooked in the Act, but this is as far as the courts can normally go. For example, in a case before the Supreme Court of Canada, Sedgewick J. said:

> "We know of many cases where Legislatures without doubt intended to say one thing but signally failed to say it. We should not say it for them. The misfortune is curable by the legislatures only, not by the courts."[6]

> ". . . In my view it is for the legislature in unambiguous terms to impose that duty . . . .. If it has not done so, the courts cannot do it".[7]

Of course, if Parliament itself has legislated to overcome the gap, the courts can take Parliament's intention into account in interpreting the later Act by which Parliament has tried to cover the gap:

> "In interpreting [the section] it is essential to bear the statutory objective in mind. This was to make good the lacuna to which attention had been drawn in [a previous judicial decision]. If the words . . . can extend to cover [the gap in the legislation] they should therefore be so construed."[8]

IMPLIED TERMS

A distinction has been drawn between filling a gap which Parliament itself has failed to fill (which is something that is not permissible in the interpretation of a statute) on the one hand and supplying a missing word or words on the other. In the latter case, there are very limited circumstances in which it may be possible for the court to supply the missing words. For example, the courts will avoid absurdity, repugnance or inconsistency, even to the extent of supplying a clerical omission which the context clearly shows to have been unintended.[9] In a case in which the Act to be interpreted provided that a certain thing should not be done without applying to a named tribunal for approval, there was held to be a necessary implication that an application on its own was not enough — the Tribunal's approval had to be obtained.[10] Words can only be implied

[5] *R. v. Richards*, [1974] 3 All E.R. 696, Lawton L.J. at 700; *R. v. Soon*, [1919] 1 W.W.R. 486 (B.C.C.A.).

[6] *Midland Railway v. Young* (1893), 22 S.C.R. 190 at 198.

[7] *Midland Railway*, at 197.

[8] *Director of Public Prosecutions of Jamaica v. White*, [1978] A.C. 426 at 433-434.

[9] *M. v. Law Society (Alberta)*, [1940] 3 W.W.R. 600 (Alta. C.A.).

[10] *Canadian Pacific Railway v. Northern Pacific & Manitoba Railway* (1888), 5 Man. R. 301 (Q.B.).

into a statute if it is necessary to do so.[11] Before this can be done three conditions must be fulfilled:

> "it must be possible to determine from a consideration of the provisions of the Act read as a whole precisely what the mischief was that it was the purpose of the Act to remedy; [it must be] apparent that the draftsman and Parliament had by inadvertence overlooked, and so omitted to deal with, an eventuality that required to be dealt with if the purpose of the Act was to be achieved; [it must be] possible to state with certainty what were the additional words that would have been inserted by the draftsman and approved by Parliament had their attention been drawn to the omission before the Bill passed into law."[12]

As Davies C.J.C. said in the Supreme Court of Canada,

> "I cannot admit the right of the Courts where the language of a statute is plain and unambiguous to practically amend such statute either by eliminating words or inserting limiting words unless the grammatical and ordinary sense of the words as enacted leads to some absurdity or some repugnance or inconsistency with the rest of the enactment, and in those cases, only to the extent of avoiding that absurdity, repugnance and inconsistency."[13]

Strong C.J.C., also in the Supreme Court of Canada, said:

> "I know of no principle upon which we are entitled so to alter the prima facie meaning of the words in which the intent of the Legislature is expressed by adding other words."[14]

Today the courts are readier than in the past to try to meet the problem of omissions from the Act, and it has been said that they

> "should now be very reluctant to hold that Parliament has achieved nothing by the language it used, when it is tolerably plain what Parliament wished to achieve."[15]

Of course, a term cannot be implied into a statute if the court is unable to determine what words have been omitted by Parliament,[16] or where there is nothing from which Parliament's intention can be gathered — "the Courts cannot give effect to what cannot be ascertained."[17]

---

[11] *Bell-Irving v. Vancouver (City)* (1892), 4 B.C.R. 219 (S.C.). In Britain, the House of Lords has applied the more stringent test of "clear necessity" (*Thompson v. Goold & Co.* [1910] A.C. 409, Lord Mersey at 420; *Northman v. Barnet London Borough Council*, [1979] 1 W.L.R. 67, Lord Salmon at 72) and so has the Privy Council (*BP Refinery (Westernport) Pty. Ltd. v. Shire of Hastings* (1977), 52 A.L.J.R. 20 at 25).

[12] *Jones v. Wrotham Park Settled Estates*, [1980] A.C. 74, Lord Diplock at 105 (H.L.).

[13] *Grand Trunk Pacific Railway v. Dearborn*, [1919] 1 W.W.R. 1005, 58 S.C.R. 315 at 320-321.

[14] *Walsh v. Trebilcock* (1894), 23 S.C.R. 695.

[15] *BBC Enterprises Ltd. v. Hi-Tech Xtravision Ltd.*, [1990] Ch. 609, Staughton L.J. at 615 (Eng. C.A.); on appeal, [1991] 2 A.C. 327; *Century Aviation Services Ltd. v. British Columbia (Industrial Relations Board)* (1976), 69 D.L.R. (3d) 176 (B.C.S.C.).

[16] *Commercial Credit Corp. v. Niagara Finance Co.*, [1940] S.C.R. 420.

[17] *Lethbridge (City) v. Northern Trusts Co.*, [1925] 4 D.L.R. 422 (Alta. C.A.); *Commercial Credit Corp. v. Niagara Finance Co.*, [1940] S.C.R. 420.

Similarly, "you must not imply a term in a statutory enactment if it is likely to defeat the purpose of the enactment as disclosed by the words actually used."[18] Furthermore, the courts are reluctant to imply terms into a penal statute[19] or a tax Act.[20] When a term was used in parts of a statute but omitted, apparently deliberately, in other parts of that statute, it was held that the court has no right to supply the supposed omission.[21]

---

[18] *Canadian Northern Railway, Re* (1909), 42 S.C.R. 443, Duff J. (later Duff C.J.C.) at 466.
[19] *R. v. Thompson* (1913), 5 W.W.R. 157 (Alta. C.A.).
[20] *BP Refinery (Westernport) Pty. Ltd. v. Shire of Hastings* (1977), 52 A.L.J.R. 20 (P.C.).
[21] *McCallum v. Hurry* (1911), 17 W.L.R. 533 (Alta. C.A.).

32

MISTAKES IN AN ACT OF PARLIAMENT

COMMON CAUSES OF MISTAKES IN ACTS OF PARLIAMENT

The mass of legislation which has to be drafted and printed today is so great that it is not surprising that some mistakes do occur in it. Mistakes can be made by the drafter, by Parliament itself, and by the printer who is responsible for printing the Act after Parliament has passed it. Mistakes by the drafter or by Parliament itself can arise, either through ignorance of the true position, or by oversight.

THE EFFECT OF A MISTAKE AS TO THE FACTS

It has been said that the British Parliament can do anything except make a man a woman. Obviously, if an Act of Parliament stated that a person named in that Act was a woman whereas in fact he was a man, the wrong statement in the Act of Parliament could not make him a woman in fact. The facts would remain unchanged notwithstanding the Act of Parliament. Similarly, if an Act of Parliament wrongly stated that a road was in a certain township whereas in fact it was not, the statement in the Act of Parliament could not have the effect of putting that road into that township. As a result, a court which was called upon to find the meaning of that Act of Parliament would have to consider that Act in the light of the true fact that the road was not in the township.[1]

If the Act of Parliament says that something is so, when in fact it is not so, the person reading that Act of Parliament may read it in the light of the true facts. Quite a different case arises, however, when Parliament has passed the whole Act of Parliament under a mistake as to what the real facts are. The judge who is called upon to say what an Act of Parliament means cannot take into account the fact that the whole Act of Parliament being considered was passed by Parliament by mistake. If, for example, Parliament thought that somebody who had entered into a contract with the government had made an exorbitant profit out of that contract, and it therefore passed an Act of Parliament reducing the total contract price by $100,000, the courts would have no power to set aside the Act of Parliament even if it was fully proved that the contractor, instead

---

[1] *R. v. Houghton (Inhabitants)* (1853), 1 E. & B. 501, 118 E.R. 523.

of making an exorbitant profit, had in fact made a loss; and the question as to whether the contractor had made a profit or loss could not be brought up in court in considering the true meaning of the Act.

"Even if it could be proved that the Legislature was deceived, it would not be competent for a Court of law to disregard its enactments. If a mistake has been made, the Legislature alone can correct it . . . . The Courts of law cannot sit in judgment on the Legislature, but must obey and give effect to its determination."[2]

For example, when Parliament made a factual error in referring to the date, it was held that factual error could only be corrected by Parliament, not by the Court:[3]

"The problem presented to me is whether I can regard the plan filed on September 18th as being comprehended by the statutory reference to the plan 'filed . . . on September 8th' . . . [T]hough there is a power to correct some obvious misprints or slips . . . I can find nothing to justify me in accepting the phrase 'plan filed . . . on the 8th day of September, 1956' as if it read 'plan filed . . . on the 18th day of September 1956'.

. . . I feel constrained to hold that any error of fact contained in the reference to the plan as filed on September 8th is not subject to judicial correction. In such a case the sufferer must appeal to the lawgiver."[4]

THE EFFECT OF A MISTAKE AS TO THE LAW

It has been pointed out that "it is, of course, true that Parliament may misconceive the existing law."[5] If an Act of Parliament is prepared upon a mistake as to the legal position, the result is just the same as if the Act had been prepared upon a mistake as to the facts. If Parliament, in making a new Act, includes a statement that the existing law before the passing of that Act had a certain effect, whereas actually it did not have that effect, the wrong statement in the Act of Parliament does not ordinarily alter the law: "if the view be truly erroneous the section has misfired."[6]

"The enactment is, no doubt, entitled to great weight as evidence of the law, but it is by no means conclusive; and when the existing law is shown to be different from that which the Legislature supposed it to be, the implication arising from the statute cannot operate as a negation of its existence."[7]

---

[2] *Labrador Co. v. R.*, [1893] A.C. 104.
[3] *Azar v. Sydney (City)* (1958), 15 D.L.R. (2d) 124 (N.S.T.D.).
[4] *Azar v. Sydney (City)* (1958), 15 D.L.R. (2d) 124, MacDonald J. at 129 (N.S.T.D.).
[5] *First National Securities Ltd. v. Chiltern District Council*, [1975] 1 W.L.R. 1075 at 1082.
[6] *County of London Housing Order, Re*, [1956] 1 W.L.R. 499, Upjohn J. (later Lord Upjohn) at 503.
[7] *Cope & Taylor v. Scottish Union & National Insurance Co.* (1897), 5 B.C.R. 329 (C.A.).

In such a case, the law must be applied correctly, and not according to the erroneous statement of it in the new statute.[8]

When an Act has been drafted upon a wrong basis so far as the law is concerned, it may be difficult to give a meaning to the Act. The reader of the Act must, however, try to do so:

> "It is . . . a very serious matter to hold, that where the main object of a statute is clear, it shall be reduced to a nullity by the draftsman's unskilfulness or ignorance of law. It may be necessary for a court of justice to come to that conclusion, but . . . nothing can justify it except necessity, or the absolute intractability of the language used."[9]

However, in an extreme case the mistake made by Parliament may be so fundamental to the operation of the new Act as to change the previous law by implication.

THE EFFECT OF A MISTAKE AS TO POLICY

It is for Parliament, not the courts, to decide on the policy underlying an Act of Parliament. Even if the judge is sure that Parliament's policy is misguided, he or she must nevertheless accept the Act as it stands. There is no right of appeal from Parliament to the courts.

> "Some people may think the policy of the Act unwise and even dangerous to the community. Some may think it at variance with principles which have long been held sacred. But a judicial tribunal has nothing to do with the policy of any Act which it may be called upon to interpret . . . The duty of the court, and its only duty, is to expound the language of the Act in accordance with the settled rules of construction. It is, I apprehend, as unwise as it is unprofitable to cavil at the policy of an Act of Parliament, or to pass a covert censure on the legislature."[10]

THE EFFECT OF A DRAFTER'S OVERSIGHT

Working against time, the drafter of Acts of Parliament can be led into error by oversight. No matter how careful the drafter may be, mistakes can and do happen. An interesting example is provided by a section of an Act passed by the British Parliament[11] which provided that the loans dealt with in that Act must be secured by a mortgage "in the form set forth in the third schedule hereto". The Act did not in fact have a third schedule, and no forms were set out in the Act. Some four years later

---

[8] *West Midland Baptist (Trust) Association Inc. v. Birmingham Corp.*, [1970] A.C. 874, Lord Reid at 898 (H.L.). See, for example, *Norton v. Spooner* (1854), 9 Moore P.C. 103, 14 E.R. 237.

[9] *Salmon v. Duncombe* (1886), 11 App. Cas. 627 at 634.

[10] *Vacher & Sons Ltd. v. London Society of Compositors,* [1913] A.C. 107, Lord Macnaghten at 118.

[11] *Artisans and Labourers' Dwellings Act,* 1875 (U.K.), s. 22(3).

Parliament passed another Act[12] which stated that the words referring to the third schedule had been "inserted by mistake" and that the Act of 1875 had to be read as if the words in that section "had not been inserted therein".

When a drafter mistakenly used the word "hereinafter" in place of "hereinbefore" the court corrected that mistake in order to avoid an absurdity:[13]

> "Another question of law was raised depending on the construction of sec. 4 of our Act. That section provides that the Act shall apply only to employment by the undertakers as *hereinbefore defined* on, in or about a railway, . . . or engineering work, and to employment by the undertakers as *hereinafter defined* about any building which exceeds a certain height.
>
>   . . . [A] curious mistake seems to have been made . . . by the draftsman . . . Undertakers are defined in sec. 2 of the Act and in no other place, yet sec. 4, in the first part of it . . ., refers to them correctly as *'hereinbefore defined'*, while in the second part of the section it refers to them as *'hereinafter defined'*. The question, therefore, is whether I ought to read the word 'hereinafter' as 'hereinbefore'.
>
>   . . . I have no doubt that the draftsman of our Act made a slip when copying this section [from an English Act].
>
>   . . . It is not a [case of omission], but the using of the wrong word by mere accident. . .
>
>   I am, therefore, of opinion that I am not precluded from reading the word 'hereinafter' as meaning 'hereinbefore'."[14]

MISPRINTS

It is a well-known fact that, no matter how careful the printer, and no matter how carefully the proofs are checked before the document is finally printed, misprints do occur. Many of the misprints that occur in newspapers have their humorous side, one of the milder examples being the statement that "the dogs, patrolling day and night, kept an area of more than 5,000 acres free of *rates.*"[15] Misprints in statutes, however, are seldom of a humorous nature.

The real problem of course arises if an Act has to be considered by the courts at a time when it contains a misprint, and that misprint has not been corrected by Parliament. The rule is that, if the misprint is plain, the Act of Parliament is to be read as if the misprint had not been made. In England, more than a century ago, an Act of Parliament repealed several earlier Acts. Owing to a misprint, one of the Acts to be repealed was

---

[12] 43 Vict. c. 8.

[13] *Morris v. Structural Steel Co.,* [1917] 2 W.W.R. 749, 35 D.L.R. 739 (B.C.C.A.). See also *R. v. Flaman* (1978), 43 C.C.C. (2d) 241 (Sask. C.A.).

[14] *Morris v. Structural Steel Co.,* [1917] 2 W.W.R. 749, 35 D.L.R. 739, Macdonald C.J.A. at 740-1 (B.C.C.A.).

[15] *The Liverpool Echo,* quoted in 5 *Town Planning and Local Government Guide* par. 685.

referred to as "13 Geo 3 c 56" but it should have been referred to as "17 Geo 3 c 56". Lord Chief Justice Denman said:

> "A mistake has been committed by the legislature; but having regard to the subject-matter, and looking at the mere contents of the Act itself we cannot doubt that the intention was to repeal the Act of 17 Geo 3,"[16]

and the Act was accordingly held to repeal the Act to which it should in fact have referred, namely 17 Geo 3 c 56.

As Morse J. said in the Manitoba Court of Queen's Bench: "I should say that s. 625(7) refers to s. 625(3). This is obviously a typographical error"[17], and he read it accordingly. In another example, the Divisional Court of Ontario in unanimous reasons for decision delivered by Estey C.J.H.C. stated that

> "The respondent agrees that . . . the objective of the Legislature . . . was not attained because of the reference in s. 194(1) to s-s (2) instead of s-s (3) of s. 189 . . . By reason of this typographical error, or drafting oversight, the respondent submits the statutory pattern . . . has not been achieved and that By-law 88-69 is void.
>   . . . This kind of interpretative difficulty was encountered in *The Queen v. Wilcock* (1845), 7 Q.B. 317; 115 E.R. 509. Denman L.C.J. at p. 338, stated that an obvious printer's error can be corrected by the courts . . .
>   For these reasons I interpret the reference in s. 194 to be to s-s. (3) of s. 189".[18]

THE EXTENT TO WHICH THE COURTS WILL CORRECT MISTAKES IN ACTS OF PARLIAMENT

When it is called upon to find the meaning of an Act of Parliament, a court is bound to proceed upon the assumption that the legislature is an ideal person that does not make mistakes.[19]

> "I think it extremely probable that, if the attention of Parliament had been drawn to the possibility of a case like the present arising, it would have worded the section so as to cover it, but that probability does not justify a Court in extending the enactment to a case that the legislature has left unprovided for. Even if quite satisfied that the omission on the part of Parliament was a mere oversight, I cannot supply the defect."[20]

However, there are circumstances in which, despite that principle, it must be recognised that a mistake has been made. The extent to which

---

[16] *R. v. Wilcock* (1845), 7 Q.B. 317 at 338, 115 E.R. 509 at 518.

[17] *Singh v. Winnipeg (City)* (1992), 80 Man. R. (2d) 132 at 140, 11 M.P.L.R. (2d) 236 at 247. See also *R. v. Donald B. Allen Ltd.* (1975), 11 O.R. (2d) 261 (Div. Ct.); *R. v. Wolfe*, [1928] 2 W.W.R. 689 (Alta. T.D)

[18] *R. v. Donald B. Allen Ltd.* (1975), 11 O.R. (2d) 271 at 275 and 276 (Div. Ct.). See also *R. v. Wolfe*, [1928] 2 W.W.R. 689 (Alta. T.D.).

[19] *Income Tax Commissioners v. Pemsel*, [1891] A.C. 531, Lord Halsbury L.C. at 549.

[20] *Larence v. Larence* (1911), 17 W.L.R. 197 (Man. K.B.). See also *R. v. Irwin*, [1926] Ex. C.R. 127 (Ex. Ct.).

the courts will go in cases in which there has been a mistake as to the facts or as to the law has been considered earlier in this chapter. So far as mistakes in words, or misprints, are concerned, the courts are limited to the correction of obvious slips.[21] The courts have no power to treat an Act of Parliament as being altered in such a way as to agree with the judge's idea of what is right or reasonable.[22]

---

[21] *Salmon v. Duncombe* (1886), 11 App. Cas. 627 at 634.
[22] *Abel v. Lee* (1871), L.R. 6 C.P. 365 at 371.

33

THE CLASS RULE

THE NATURE OF THE CLASS RULE

Where there are two or more specific words forming a class, followed by general words, the courts may limit the scope of the general words to the scope of the class constituted by the specific words.[1] This rule of interpretation is known as the class rule.

The class rule is a rule that is used to find the meaning of a broad general word when that word follows after a group of specific words. Typically, the class rule applies where there is a group of specific words followed by the words "or other" and then general words. Note, however, that the use of the words "or other" is not a condition precedent to the applicability of the class rule.

The word "building" is a typical word to which the class rule could be applied. The difficulty of finding the meaning of the word "building" has already been referred to earlier in this book.[2] The word "building" is a word the meaning of which can vary a great deal depending on the context in which it is used. If a section of an Act states that it applies to

"any building"

and there are no words to limit the meaning of "building", that word would be given a broad general meaning. It would include houses, and it would also include, for example, shops, factories, office blocks and hotels. If, on the other hand, the words used in the section were

"any house flat maisonette villa-pair or other building"

the class rule could be used to find the meaning of the word "building", and the use of the class rule would show that the word "building" is limited in that context to things of the same class as the class which precedes it — things of the same class as any "house flat maisonette" or "villa-pair", that is, residential buildings.

An Act required any legal action against a "Hospital, Nursing Home

---

[1] For an application of this principle see *Re Saskatchewan Human Rights Commission and Engineering Students' Society* (1989), 56 D.L.R. (4th) 604, Cameron J.A. at 625, reported under the name of *Saskatchewan Human Rights Commission v. Engineering Students' Society* in 72 Sask. R. 161 (C.A.).

[2] See chapter 17.

or other Institution'' to be brought within three months after damage had been sustained. The court held that ''other Institution'' meant an institution having the same characteristics and designed to provide the same services as a hospital or nursing home, so that an action against a medical clinic of general practitioners and specialists was not barred by the statutory provision.[3] The Saskatchewan *Human Rights Code*, s. 14 prohibited newspaper publication of ''any notice, sign, symbol, emblem or other representation'' ridiculing persons because of their sex. It was held that the words ''or other representation'' do not have an independent meaning regardless of context, so that articles in a student newspaper ridiculing women were not prohibited by s. 14.[4] A conflict of interest provision defined ''local board'' by giving examples followed by the phrase ''any other board''. It was held that a member of a committee was not within the conflict of interest provision because the committee did not fall within the same class as the boards named in the definition, as it had no power to make decisions.[5] It has also been held that a slough was not included within the phrase ''rivers, streams, watercourses, lakes and other bodies of water'' because it did not share the common features of the other bodies of water named.[6]

A very good example of the way in which the class rule operates is to be found in a decision in a case in which the court had to determine the meaning of the words ''and other provisions'' in the phrase ''meat, fish, poultry, vegetables, fruit and other provisions''. Mr. Justice Buckley said:

> ''This is a case in which the . . . rule must certainly apply for I think that the composite expression 'for the sale of meat, fish, poultry, vegetables, fruit and other provisions' is just such an expression as to be appropriate for the application of the doctrine. The problem is to decide what is the true nature of the [class] to which 'other provisions' is to be confined. [Counsel] has suggested that the common characteristic of meat, fish, poultry, vegetables and fruit is that they are all solids used for human consumption. That is quite true. But I think the class is more restrictive than that, for they seem to be all solids fit for human consumption which are natural products. They have not been subjected to a manufacturing process. They are what one might describe as the raw materials of the kitchen, and not finished articles which would be put on the table . . . I think that applying the . . . rule here 'other provisions' must be confined to other natural products of a kind which go to fill the larder and not extend it to anything like bread or confectionery which is the product of a baker's activities, converting natural flour into a finished article.''[7]

---

[3] *Francouer v. Prince Albert Community Clinic* (1986), 52 Sask. R. 221 (Q.B.).

[4] *Re Saskatchewan Human Rights Commission and Engineering Students' Society* (1989), 56 D.L.R. (4th) 604, reported under the name of *Saskatchewan (Human Rights Commission) v. Engineering Students' Society* in 72 Sask. R. 161 (C.A.).

[5] *Westfall v. Eedy* (1991), 7 M.P.L.R. (2d) 226 (Ont. Gen. Div.).

[6] *Alberta v. Very*, [1983] 6 W.W.R. 143 (Alta. Q.B.).

[7] *Hy Whittle Ltd. v. Stalybridge Corp.* (1967), 65 L.G.R. 344 at 353-354.

THE CLASS RULE 133

THERE MUST BE A GENERAL WORD

The class rule only applies to the case of a word which is a general one and which therefore has a somewhat indefinite meaning. It cannot be used to find the meaning of a word which is of a specific nature.

THE GENERAL WORD MUST FOLLOW AFTER A CLASS OF SPECIFIC WORDS

The class rule can of course only be used if there is a class of words in the section. In the example already given ("any house flat maisonette villa-pair or other building") the class is to be found in the words

"any house flat maisonette villa-pair".

Those words form a common class which might be said to be the class of buildings used for residential purposes.

It can happen that a general word in an Act of Parliament follows a number of specific words but those specific words do not form a class. Again using the word "building" as the general word, the lack of a class can be shown in the following example:

"any house flat factory bridge jetty aviary kennel or other building".

In that example the words "any house flat factory bridge jetty aviary kennel" do not form a class at all. They are all specific words, but they cannot be made to form a class. In fact, in the example given, there are two words which are of the one class ("house flat") but the other words do not fall into that class. Therefore, even although some of the words can form a class the whole of the specific words cannot and accordingly there is nothing on which to base a use of the class rule. In other words, all the specific words that come before the general word must be of the one class.[8]

Another example of the principle that the class rule cannot be applied if the specific words do not form a class is to be found in a case in which the words which the court had to consider were

"loss of time from deficiency of men, or owner's stores, breakdown of machinery, or damage to hull or other accident preventing the work of the steamer".

The court had to find the meaning of the words "or other accident". It held that the words "loss of time from deficiency of men, or owner's stores, breakdown of machinery, or damage to hull" did not form a class and that therefore the class rule could not be used to find the meaning of the

---

[8] *United Towns Electric Co. v. Newfoundland (Attorney General)*, [1939] 1 All E.R. 428 at 428 (P.C.); *Minor v. R.* (1920), 52 D.L.R. 158, Harris C.J. at 161-162 (N.S.S.C.); *British Columbia (Attorney General) v. R.* (1922), 63 S.C.R. 622, Anglin J. (later Anglin C.J.C.) at 637.

words "or other accident".[9] These examples illustrate the basic proposition, that unless there is "a genus, or, as it has been otherwise expressed, one category with 'some common and dominant feature' the rule cannot be applied."[10]

THERE MUST BE TWO OR MORE SPECIFIC WORDS BEFORE THE GENERAL WORD

Since the class rule can only apply if there is a class of specific words before the general word, it cannot be used in the case in which there is only one specific word before the general word. If the phrase used in the Act of Parliament is

"any house or other building",

the word "building" is a general word and the word "house" is a specific word, but the word "house" has no other specific word with it and it therefore cannot form a class. The class rule therefore does not apply to the phrase "house or other building".

This aspect of the class rule arose in a case in which the words which the court had to consider were

"theatres and other places of public entertainment".

The court of course held that the class rule could not be used to find the meaning of the phrase "other places of public entertainment" because the one word "theatres" could not form a class.[11]

"The rule ejusdem generis [the class rule] is one that is to be applied with caution and not to be pushed too far. It is a rule that ought not to be invoked unless the intention of the legislature is ambiguous."[12]

A COURT WILL NOT NECESSARILY APPLY THE CLASS RULE

If the specific words form two distinct classes instead of one, the class rule is inapplicable: all the specific words must fall within a single class for the rule to operate. Moreover, even if there is only one class comprised by the specific words, the boundaries of the class may be difficult to determine with accuracy and the choice between different limits for the class

---

[9] *"SS Magnhild" (The) v. McIntyre Brothers & Co.*, [1920] 3 K.B. 321; *Tiedmann v. Basiuk* (1977), 4 Alta. L.R. (2d) 12 (T.D.); *Bains v. British Columbia (Superintendent of Insurance)* (1973), 38 D.L.R. (3d) 756 (B.C.C.A.).

[10] *Would v. Herington*, [1932] 4 D.L.R. 308, Trueman J.A. at 314 (Man. C.A.).

[11] *Allen v. Emmerson*, [1944] 1 K.B. 262.

[12] *King (Township) v. Marylake Agricultural School & Farm Settlement Association*, [1939] O.R. 13, Middleton J.A. at 16 (C.A.).

constituted by the specific words may be fraught with such difficulty as to render the use of the class rule unwise. The purposive approach (chapter 26 [13]), mischief rule (chapter 25) or golden rule (chapter 24) may be of assistance in deciding whether to apply the class rule and, if so, which formulation of the class to adopt.

The class rule does not apply to limit general words following specific words, if those specific words embrace all objects of their class. To apply the class rule in those circumstances would be to make the general words superfluous. The court will therefore assume that those general words must have been intended to have a different meaning from the meaning of the specific words.[14] Also, Parliament may, if it wishes, indicate an intention that the class rule shall not apply to a particular provision.[15]

THE CLASS RULE DOES NOT GIVE GUIDANCE ON THE MEANING OF SPECIFIC WORDS WITHIN THE CLASS

The class rule is a rule for the finding of the scope to be given to the general words. It is not a rule to be used to find the meaning of any of the specific words.[16] Indeed, if the meaning of the specific words is ambiguous, it may well be impossible to find a class.

THE NAME WHICH LAWYERS GIVE TO THE CLASS RULE

The class rule is known to lawyers as the ejusdem generis rule — ejusdem generis being two Latin words meaning "of the same class".

---

[13] *Bell v. North Vancouver School District 44* (1979), 16 B.C.L.R. 94 (S.C.).
[14] *Gravestock v. Parkin* (1943), [1944] O.R. 49 (C.A.).
[15] *R. v. Barber Asphalt Paving Co.* (1911), 23 O.L.R. 372 (C.P.).
[16] In such a case the rule "words of similar meaning" may be of use—see chapter 34.

34

WORDS OF SIMILAR MEANING

THE NATURE OF THE RULE

This is a rule that is somewhat like the class rule[1], but it is a "related and more general rule of construction."[2] It is known to lawyers as the *noscitur a sociis* rule, and is sometimes known as "birds of a feather flock together". It is a rule for finding the meaning of a word which could have one of several meanings, and which finds that meaning by considering the meaning of other words with which that word is associated in the section. Unlike the class rule, however, this rule does not depend upon having a broad general word following after two or more specific words; the question resolved by this rule is likely to be a question as to the width or scope to be given to a specific word within a group of specific words.[3]

THE MEANING OF SIMILAR WORDS WHEN THEY ARE ASSOCIATED WITH EACH OTHER

When words of similar meaning are set out together in one section of an Act, and they are words which could bear several meanings, the meaning of any of them could be found by considering the general nature of the others:

"It is an ancient rule of statutory construction (commonly expressed by the Latin maxim, *noscitur a sociis*) that the meaning of a doubtful word may be ascertained by reference to the meaning of words associated with it. . . When two or more words which are susceptible of analogous meanings are coupled together they are understood to be used in their corporate sense. They take their color from each other, the meaning of the more general being restricted to a sense analogous to the less general."[4]

---

[1] Most textbook writers treat the rule about words of similar meaning and the class rule as being the same, *Maxwell on Interpretation of Statutes* (N.M. Tripathi, Bombay, 12th ed., Langan P. St. J., 1976), p. 289, however, treats them as being different rules; and it seems preferable to treat them as separate rules.

[2] *Warren v. Chapman* (1985), 17 D.L.R. (4th) 261, unanimous decision at 264 (Man. C.A.).

[3] For an example of the application of this rule see *Re Saskatchewan Human Rights Commission and Engineering Students' Society* (1989), 56 D.L.R. (4th) 604, Cameron J.A. at 625, reported under the name of *Saskatchewan Human Rights Commission v. Engineering Students' Society* in 72 Sask. R. 161 (C.A.).

[4] *R. v. Goulis* (1981), 125 D.L.R. (3d) 137, unanimous decision at 142-143, 33 O.R. (2d) 55 (C.A.).

A good example of the use of this rule occurs in a case in which the court had to find the meaning of the word "footways". The section in which that word occurred used the words

"roads, highways, footways, commons, streets, lanes, alleys, passages, and public places".

The question which the court had to decide was whether the word "footways" was wide enough in its meaning to include a path available to the public but running through a private field. The court held that it was not wide enough to include that path. It made that decision because it found that the word "footways" must be taken to have a meaning similar to that of the other words with which it was associated in the section:[5]

"Construing the word 'footway' from the company in which it is found . . . the legislature appears to have meant those paved footways in large towns."

The *Criminal Code* (Ontario), s. 350(a)(ii) stated:

"350. Everyone who,
(*a*) with intent to defraud his creditors,
    (i) . . .
    (ii) removes, conceals or disposes of any of his property, . . .
is guilty of an indictable offence and is liable to imprisonment for two years."

It was held that

"In this case, the words which lend color to the word 'conceals' are, first, the word 'removes', which clearly refers to a physical removal of property, and second, the words 'disposes of', which, standing in contrast to the kind of disposition which is expressly dealt with in subpara. (i) of the same para. (*a*), namely, one which is made by 'gift, conveyance, assignment, sale, transfer or delivery', strongly suggests the kind of disposition which results from a positive act taken by a person to physically part with his property. In my view the association of 'conceals' with the words 'removes' or 'disposes of' in s. 350 (*a*)(ii) shows that the word 'conceals' is there used by Parliament in a sense which contemplates a positive act of concealment."[6]

The basis of the rule is that the coupling together of words which are similar in their nature shows that Parliament means them to be read in the same sense.

THE RULE IS TO BE APPLIED WITH CAUTION

Like the class rule, the rule governing words of similar meaning has been said to be a rule to be applied with caution:

---

[5] *Scales v. Pickering* (1828), 4 Bing. 448 at 452 and 453, 130 E.R. 840, Best C.J. at 841, Park J. at 842.

[6] *R. v. Goulis* (1981), 125 D.L.R. (3d) 137, unanimous decision at 143 (Ont. C.A.). See also *Dawson Creek (City) v. Lougheed* (1959), 19 D.L.R. (2d) 249 (B.C.C.A.).

"Without belittling the rule of construction — *noscitur a sociis* — care must always be taken that its application does not defeat the true intention of the legislature."[7]

---

[7] *British Columbia (Attorney General) v. R.* (1922), 63 S.C.R. 622, Anglin J. (later Anglin C.J.C.) at 638.

35

EXPRESS INCLUSIONS AND IMPLIED EXCLUSIONS

THE EFFECT OF THE RULE

There is a rule that, if a section of an Act of Parliament sets out certain specific things as being within its scope, it impliedly excludes all others from its operation. Thus, for example, a section which stated that it applied to

"every factory shop office and workroom"

would not apply to a hotel: the express statement of "every factory shop office and workroom" would impliedly exclude the hotel from the operation of the section.[1]

> "I apprehend it to be a rule, as universal as it is wise, that, where a written instrument contains a specific provision as to a particular subjectmatter, the provision as to that matter, which the law would imply if the instrument were silent, cannot be resorted to."[2]

For example, a local authority was given power by statute to make a gift to "one of those bodies or parties listed in s. 128(4)." However, as "the defendant[was] not one of the bodies or parties listed, it follows, the plaintiff did not have power to make a gift" of the land to the defendant.[3]

The rule of course can only operate if Parliament in the particular section is giving a complete list of what it intends to refer to. If Parliament, rather than giving a complete list, is giving examples, the rule cannot apply. Thus when an Act referred to "housing, town planning, etc"[4] those words could not be used to restrict the operation of the Act to housing and town planning.

---

[1] *Whiteman v. Sadler*, [1910] A.C. 514, Lord Dunedin at 527.

[2] *Kadishewitz v. Laurentian Insurance Co.*, [1931] O.R. 529, Riddell J.A. at 536 (C.A.).

[3] *Spruce Grove v. Yellow Head Regional Library Board* (1982), 18 M.P.L.R. 278 at 281-282 (Alta. Q.B.). See also *LeBlanc Estate v. Bank of Montreal*, [1989] 1 W.W.R. 49 (Sask. C.A.).

[4] *Housing, Town Planning, etc, Act*, 1909 (U.K.).

THE USE OF THE RULE IN RELATION TO DEFINITIONS

It is important to note how the rule operates when what is to be interpreted is a definition. In chapter 17, attention was drawn to the fact that definitions in Acts of Parliament sometimes use the word "means", sometimes use "includes", and sometimes use "means and includes". If the definition uses the word "means" (whether with or without "includes"), the rule as to express inclusions and implied exclusions applies because the definition is giving the complete list. If, however, the definition uses the word "includes", Parliament is merely giving examples and the rule cannot operate. There can be no implied exclusion when Parliament intends to include more things than are specifically stated in the definition.

THE RULE MUST BE APPLIED WITH CAUTION

The rule that the express inclusion of certain matters in a section operates to impliedly exclude all others is a useful one but like most generalisations has its dangers:

> "The maxim has not . . . in recent years received such universal support as would warrant one in accepting it as an unerring canon of construction."[5]

It has been described as "a valuable servant, but a dangerous master":

> "The maxim *expressio unius est exclusio alterius*, enunciates a principle which has its application in the construction of statutes and written instruments, and no doubt it has its uses when it aids to discover the intention; but, as has been said, while it is often a valuable servant, it is a dangerous master to follow. Much depends on the context."[6]

It is "not to be applied, when its application . . . leads to absurdity or injustice"[7] or where the alleged limiting words are intended to be illustrative only. The reason why it can be a "dangerous master" is that Acts of Parliament are not always drafted as precisely as would be desirable. Because of the rush in which Acts of Parliament have often to be written it is not possible to produce the careful wording to which this rule could be applied with confidence. Thus it has been said:

> "I may observe that the method of construction summarised in the maxim expressio unius exclusio alterius is one that certainly requires to be watched. Perhaps few so-called rules of interpretation have been more frequently misapplied and stretched beyond their due limits. The failure to make the expression complete very often arises from accident, very often from the fact that it never struck the draftsman that the thing supposed to be excluded needed specific mention of any kind; and the application of this and every other technical rule of construction varies so much under differing

---

[5] *R. v. Boudreau*, [1924] 3 D.L.R. 75, unanimous decision at 78 (N.B.C.A.).
[6] *Turgeon v. Dominion Bank*, [1930] S.C.R. 67, unanimous decision at 70-71.
[7] *Colquhoun v. Brooks* (1888), 21 Q.B.D. 52, Lopes L.J. (later Lord Ludlow) at 65.

circumstances, and is open to so many qualifications and exceptions, that it is rarely that such rules help one to arrive at what is meant."[8]

The maxim should only be applied if, having regard to the subject-matter, it would not lead to inconsistency or injustice.[9] It has been held that it is "not enough that the express and the tacit are merely incongruous; it must clearly appear that they cannot reasonably be intended to co-exist."[10] The Ontario Court of Appeal has held that the maxim "has often been overworked; useful as it sometimes is, it is often misleading".[11]

The dangers of the rule, however, do not preclude its use when it does afford guidance in interpreting an Act. The rule must be applied with caution, but it "has been applied . . . to the interpretation of statutes in many cases."[12]

The rule is one that is likely to become of increasing importance because of the growth of both environmental and town planning controls. Environmental controls are often a complex series of specific controls, often site-specific. Town planning by-laws are often drafted on the basis of setting out expressly those uses which are permitted, or setting out expressly those uses which are prohibited. When such documents drafted in that way have to be considered by the courts, it can be expected that the rule considered in this chapter will be used.

THE NAME LAWYERS GIVE THE RULE

Lawyers know this rule by the Latin words expressio unius exclusio alterius est — to express the one is to exclude all others. The rule is also known by the Latin words expressum facit cessare tacitum — the expressed renders the unexpressed silent.

---

[8] *Colquhoun v. Brooks* (1887), 19 Q.B.D. 400 at 406. Wills J.'s dissenting judgment was upheld on appeal; (1888), 21 Q.B.D. 52 at 65. See also, for example, *First National Bank of Idaho Springs v. Curry* (1910), 16 W.L.R. 102 (Man. C.A.).

[9] *Harvie v. Calgary (City) Regional Planning Commission* (1978), 8 M.P.L.R. 227 at 253.

[10] *First National Bank of Idaho Springs v. Curry* (1910), 16 W.L.R. 102 (Man. C.A.).

[11] *Toronto (City) v. Toronto & York Radial Railway* (1918), 42 O.L.R. 545 (C.A.). See also *R. v. Cummings,* [1925] 1 W.W.R. 325 (Alta. C.A.).

[12] *R. v. Graves* (1910), 21 O.L.R. 329, Riddell J. at 355-356 (C.A.).

36

INTERPRETING AN ACT IN THE LIGHT OF OTHER ACTS

ACTS WHICH ARE RELATED TO THE ACT BEING CONSIDERED

From time to time it becomes necessary for Parliament to pass a series of Acts on the one topic, or to pass a series of Acts that are so far related to each other as to form a system of legislation. Such Acts are referred to by lawyers as Acts in pari materia. The proper way to read Acts of that kind is to read them together. They "are to be taken together as forming one system, and as interpreting and enforcing each other":[1] "One must assume that various pieces of legislation, bearing on the same subject, are intended to create a consistent scheme so as to achieve the logical purposes of all the legislation".[2]

All Acts of Parliament that relate to the same person are treated as related for the purpose of this rule, as are all Acts which relate to the same class of persons.[3] Acts of Parliament relating to the same subject-matter are, of course, related to each other for the purposes of this rule, and various Acts of Parliament relating to pilotage have therefore been read together.[4]

Acts of Parliament upon the same branch of the law are, of course, to be read together.[5]

While related Acts are to be read together in this way, it must be remembered that the basic rules still apply: if an Act has a plain meaning it is to be given that plain meaning. Therefore, if any section of one of the related Acts has a plain meaning it should be given that plain

---

[1] *Palmer's Case* (1784), 1 Leach C.C. (4th ed.) 355, quoted in *Craies on Statute Law* (Sweet & Maxwell, London, 7th ed., Edgar S.G.G., 1971) p. 134. See also *R. v. Loxdale* (1758), 1 Burr. 445 at 447, 97 E.R. 394, Lord Mansfield at 395-396.

[2] *Alberta (Board of Directors of the Western Irrigation District) v. Trobst* (1990), 49 M.P.L.R. 93 at 105 (Alta. Q.B.). See also *R. v. Alberta Railway & Irrigation Co.* [1912] A.C. 827; *Smith v. National Trust Co.* (1912), 1 W.W.R. 1122 (S.C.C.); *Bourke v. Murphy* (1856), 1 P.E.I. 126.

[3] See, for example, *R. v. Loxdale* (1758), 1 Burr. 445, 97 E.R. 394; *Davis v. Edmondson* (1803), 3 B. & P. 382, 127 E.R. 209.

[4] *Redpath v. Allan* (1872), L.R. 4 C.P. 518. See also *Capital Grocers Ltd. v. Saskatchewan (Registrar of Land Titles)* (1952), 7 W.W.R. (N.S.) 315 (Sask. C.A.); *Coleman (Town) v. Head Syndicate*, [1917] 1 W.W.R. 1074 (Alta. C.A.).

[5] *Copeland, ex parte* (1852), 22 L.J. Bcy. 17, Knight-Bruce L.J. at 21.

meaning without reference to any other of the related Acts at all.[6]

The fact that related Acts are to be read together to cure any uncertainty about the meaning to be given to any of the sections does not mean that they are to be treated in the same way as they would be treated if they were just one single Act of Parliament. For example, if one of the related Acts contains a particular provision, and another does not, that particular provision cannot be read into the Act that lacks it. The Act that does not have that provision must be read without it, however unfortunate that may be from the viewpoint of enforcing the Act.[7]

The fact that related Acts are to be read together in this way means that guidance about the meaning of the earlier Acts can be obtained by reading the later Acts, and similarly, guidance about the meaning of the later Acts can be obtained by reading the earlier Acts:[8]

> "a reference to previous legislation may be forced upon a court by reason of the ambiguity employed in the use of terms which the mind could not readily grasp without a previous preliminary interpretation. But it is always a process of construction which is accompanied with much danger."[9]

> "In interpreting a statute, particularly a statute . . . which has evolved to its present form over a period of some 400 years, regard must be had to the history of the enactment."[10]

> "There is an intimate connection between the present law and the previous one. In ascertaining the meaning of an ambiguous expression in a statute an earlier Act dealing with the same subject should be referred to."[11]

However, not every difference between two related provisions necessarily implies a difference in meaning:

> "Essential difference . . . does not . . . explain every variation between the two enactments.

> . . .[I]t may be taken that . . . the great difference between the two subsections consists in this — that the subsection appears in the Ontario statute as an original enactment with no trace of its origin or history to be found either in its terms or in any other Ontario legislation, whereas the British subsection is, on its face, an amendment of an existing Act of Parliament which, as so amended, remains the substantive operative enactment."[12]

---

[6] *R. v. Titterton*, [1895] 2 Q.B. 61, Lord Russell of Killowen C.J. at 67.

[7] *Casanova v. R.* (1866), L.R. 1 P.C. 268. See also *Cheyney v. Inuvik (Town)* (1992), 11 M.P.L.R. (2d) 267 at 275 (N.W.T.S.C.).

[8] *Clark v. Docksteader* (1905), 36 S.C.R. 622; *Windsor (City) Board of Education v. Ford Motor Co.*, [1939] S.C.R. 412.

[9] *Ouellette v. Canadian Pacific Railway*, [1925] 2 D.L.R. 677 at 681 (P.C.).

[10] *Pic-N-Save Ltd., Re* (1972), 32 D.L.R. (3d) 431 at 435 (Ont. S.C.).

[11] *R. v. Dojacek* (1919), 49 D.L.R. 36, Perdue C.J.M. at 39 (Man. C.A.).

[12] *Ontario (Attorney General) v. Perry*, [1934] 4 D.L.R. 65 at 69 (P.C.).

There is a presumption that a change of wording implies a change of meaning ,[13] but that presumption is not very strong.[14]

When the language of the statute to be interpreted is not ambiguous, there is no room for presumptions drawn from a comparison with previous legislation.[15] The principle is in any event not of great weight: "A comparison of like statutes enacted by the same Legislature is at most of peripheral assistance in determining the proper interpretation of [one of them]."[16] Nonetheless the principle has been applied in the Supreme Court of Canada:

> "Now when we see in statutes in pari materia, by the very same legislature, additional words of that nature to a prior enactment, we would be setting at naught the very clear intention of the legislature if we gave to the last enactment the same construction that had been judicially given to the prior one."[17]

In the case of two separate but similar enactments, the history of those enactments was examined by the court in order to discover whether Parliament intended that each should form a separate code.[18]

Unproclaimed sections, however, are not to be used in interpreting an Act:

> "No argument about the meaning of a statute can be validly based upon sections of it which might some time in the future become law, but are not law now, and may never become law."[19]

When a subsection was introduced for the first time in a particular Province, it was held to be contrary to principle to look at the evolution even of the corresponding British enactment.[20]

---

[13] *Holton, Re*, [1952] O.W.N. 741 (H.C.); *Conger v. Kennedy* (1896), 26 S.C.R. 397.

[14] *Dublin Continuation School Board v. Seaforth (District) High School Board*, [1952] O.R. 229 (H.C.); *Burnham v. Stratton* (1908), 17 O.L.R. 612 (K.B.); *West York (District), Re* (1907), 15 O.L.R. 303 (C.A.).

[15] *Ouellette v. Canadian Pacific Railway*, [1925] 2 W.W.R. 494 (P.C.); *Canadian Pacific Railway v. R.* (1906), 38 S.C.R. 137, Davies J. at 142; *R. v. American News Co.*, [1957] O.R. 145, Schroeder J.A. at 173 (C.A.).

[16] *Goulbourn (Township) v. Ottawa-Carleton (Regional Municipality)* (1979), 101 D.L.R. (3d) Estey J. at 15 (S.C.C.).

[17] *Ottawa (City) v. Hunter* (1900), 31 S.C.R. 7, Taschereau J. (later Taschereau C.J.C.) at 10. See also *R. v. American News Co. Ltd.*, [1957] O.R. 145, Schroeder J.A. at 175 (C.A.).

[18] *Reference re Liquor License Act (Manitoba)* (1913), 4 W.W.R. 551 (Man. C.A.).

[19] *Murphy v. Canadian Pacific Railway* (1955), 17 W.W.R. 593, 1 O.L.R. (2d) 197 at 202 (Man. Q.B.), affirmed (1956), 19 W.W.R. 57, 4 D.L.R. (2d) 443 (Man. C.A.).

[20] *Ontario (Attorney General) v. Perry*, [1934] 3 W.W.R. 35 (P.C.).

INCORPORATING ONE ACT INTO ANOTHER

Parliament may provide that an earlier Act is to be read as one with a later Act on the same topic, or it may provide that the later Act is to be read as incorporated in the earlier one. In either case, the effect is the same, namely to transpose the one into the other Act, or to write every provision of the one Act into the other Act as if they had been actually printed within it.[21]

THE EFFECT OF ACTS WHICH ARE NOT RELATED TO THE ACT UNDER CONSIDERATION

Even if some section of an Act of Parliament is one which is capable of having two or more meanings, no help can be gained by comparing that section with sections in other Acts of Parliament that are not related to the Act in which that section appears: "It is trite law that it is not permissible to construe the language of one statute by reference to the language of another."[22]

---

[21] *Knowles & Sons v. Lancashire & Yorkshire Railway Co.* (1889), 14 App. Cas. 248, Lord Halsbury at 253.

[22] *Ministry of Housing and Local Government v. Sharp*, [1970] 2 Q.B. 223, Salmon L.J. (later Lord Salmon) at 272. See also *Lake v. Bennett*, [1970] 1 Q.B. 663, Salmon L.J. (later Lord Salmon) at 672.

37

ACTS INCONSISTENT WITH
EACH OTHER

CONFLICTS BETWEEN DIFFERENT ACTS OF PARLIAMENT

As is only to be expected, Parliament is continuing to make new Acts of Parliament every year. Some of the new Acts replace older ones, but most of the new Acts are in addition to the Acts of Parliament already in existence. Year by year, therefore, the total number of Acts of Parliament continues to increase. Even if a Parliament were to carry out a thorough springcleaning of its statute books, its statutes would fill a very large number of pages.

When the Acts of Parliament are so numerous and increase at such a rate, it is not surprising that some of them are in conflict with each other; with the number of amending Acts, conflicting provisions within the same Act are also common. It would be an almost impossible task to ensure that no conflict at all arose. The courts have developed rules for the reading of Acts of Parliament whose provisions are in conflict, and those rules are considered in this chapter.

A CONFLICT BETWEEN A GENERAL ACT AND A SPECIFIC ACT

In chapter 13 the rule for interpreting a conflict between a general provision and a specific provision in the same Act is set out. The same rule applies when the general provisions and the specific provisions are contained in different Acts of Parliament:

> "When there are general words in a later Act capable of reasonable and sensible application without extending them to subjects specially dealt with by earlier legislation, you are not to hold that earlier and special legislation indirectly repealed, altered, or derogated from merely by force of such general words, without any indication of a particular intention to do so."[1]

That principle has been described as "A cardinal rule for interpretation of statutes."[2]

---

[1] *Seward v. "Vera Cruz" The* (1884), 10 App. Cas. 59, Lord Selborne L.C. at 68.

[2] *Union Gas Ltd. v. Dawn (Township)* (1977), 2 M.P.L.R. 23 at 38 (Ont. Div. Ct.); *Valley View Heritage Association Inc. v. Estevan (City) (No. 2)* (1989), 47 M.P.L.R. 24 at 35 (Sask. Q.B.).

"The principle is . . . that where there are provisions in a special Act and in a general Act on the same subject which are inconsistent, if the special Act gives a complete rule on the subject, the expression of the rule acts as an exception of the subjectmatter of the rule from the general Act."[3]

For example, the Ontario *Planning Act* has been held to be "of a general nature," with the result that the powers of land use control granted under that Act had to be read subject to special legislation such as the *Energy Act* and the *Petroleum Resources Act*.[4]

OTHER CONFLICTS BETWEEN ACTS OF PARLIAMENT

A conflict may, of course, occur between Acts of Parliament when the Acts concerned do not fall into the classes of a general Act on the one hand and a specific Act on the other hand. The courts will first attempt to reconcile the apparently conflicting provisions:

"It take it to be a cardinal principle in the interpretation of a statute that if there be two inconsistent enactments it must be seen if one cannot be read as a qualification of the other."[5]

In such a case, if it is impossible to read the two Acts together without conflict, it has been held both in England and in Canada that the later Act prevails over the earlier one.[6]

IMPLIED REPEAL

The conflict between one Act and another may lead to the conclusion that the later Act impliedly repeals the earlier to the extent of the conflict: "all legislation carries in its inherent nature the power of amendment."[7] Therefore, "every presumption must be made in favour of the

---

[3] *Ottawa (City) v. Eastview (Town)*, [1941] S.C.R. 448, Rinfret J. (later Rinfret C.J.C.) at 462; *Way v. St. Thomas (City)* (1906), 12 O.L.R. 240, Teetzel J. at 242 (Div. Ct.). See also *Morley v. Story Mountain Institution* (1981), 8 Man. R. (2d) 258, reported under the name of *Morley v. R.* in 59 C.C.C. (2d) 361 (Man. Q.B.); *R. v. L. (M.J.)* (1986), 46 M.V.R. 301, 77 N.B.R. (2d) 212 (Q.B.).

[4] *Union Gas* at 38.

[5] *Gladysz v. Gross*, [1945] 3 D.L.R. 208, Bird J.A. at 210, [1945] 2 W.W.R. 266 (B.C.C.A.). See also *Neuhaus Estate, Re*, [1923] 3 W.W.R. 873, [1923] 4 D.L.R. 1190 (Man. K.B.); *British Columbia (Law Society) v. Lawrie*, [1988] 1 W.W.R. 351 (B.C.S.C.).

[6] *Argyll (Duke) v. Inland Revenue Commissioners* (1913), 109 L.T. 893, Scrutton J. (later Scrutton L.J.) at 895; *Kariapper v. Wijesinha*, [1968] A.C. 716; *Point Grey By-law No. 15, Re* (1911), 19 W.L.R. 638 (B.C.C.A.). However, without referring to any of those decisions the English Court of Appeal refused to apply what it described as the "so called" rule to a conflict between provisions in the same Act: *Marr, Re*, [1990] 2 All E.R. 880.

[7] *Foxcroft v. London (City)*, [1928] 1 D.L.R. 849, Middleton J.A. at 850 (Ont. C.A.).

constitutional right of a legislative body to repeal the laws which it has itself enacted."[8]

Generally speaking, "repeal by implication is not favoured":[9] "some strong reason should exist before a statute should be held to produce such a result."[10] Implied repeal by a later Act is an approach of last resort:

"Revocation or supersession of an earlier enactment as the result of a later statute occurs only when the words of the latter cannot otherwise be given reasonable effect."[11]

"It is not within the competence of the Legislature to pass a statute binding itself never to pass a contradictory statute. That would be to fetter itself in matters in which it is supreme . . . If therefore, there is that repugnancy between the two statutory provisions . . . the result must be that the provision of the older statute will go."[12]

In deciding whether there is an implied repeal, it is not a matter of mechanically applying the rule that one statute is later than the other or that one is more general than the other: all the circumstances are to be taken into consideration, especially when the later Act contains no express statement of Parliament's intention to repeal or amend the earlier Act.[13]

The result is that the person or body which argues in favour of an implied repeal of a statutory provision must discharge a heavy onus or burden of proof.

WHICH ACT IS THE LATER?

In order to determine which Act prevails, it is not enough to discover the dates of the original enactment of the statutes said to be in conflict. More pertinent is the consideration of the enactment of the particular provisions said to give rise to the implied repeal. If two provisions become law at the same moment, no doubt one will come after the other in the relevant Act, but the rule that the later provision prevails over the earlier does not apply.[14] A special rule has been held to apply to a Statute Law Revision Act, which "does not alter the law, but simply strikes out certain enactments which have become unnecessary" — the inclusion of an Act in such a revision is therefore not a repeal and re-enactment of the old Act, and does not make it a "later" Act than one passed between the enactment of the first Act and its revision.[15]

---

[8] *Statutes of the Province of Manitoba Relating to Education, Re* (1894), 22 S.C.R. 577, Strong C.J.C. at 654.

[9] *Meldrum v. Black* (1916), 27 D.L.R. 193, Martin J.A. at 194, 22 B.C.R. 574 (C.A.).

[10] *R. v. Ruddick* (1928), 62 O.L.R. 248, Wright J. at 253 (S.C.).

[11] *Canadian Westinghouse Co.*, [1927] S.C.R. 625, Anglin C.J.C. at 630. See also *Ells v. Ells* (1979), 99 D.L.R. (3d) 686, unanimous decision at 687 (N.S.S.C.).

[12] *R. v. Broughton*, [1951] O.R. 263 (C.A.).

[13] *Old Kildonan (Municipality) v. Winnipeg (City)*, [1943] 2 W.W.R. 268 (Man. K.B.).

[14] *Ottawa (City) v. Hunter* (1900), 31 S.C.R. 7.

[15] *Villeneuve v. Pageau*, [1956] Qué. Q.B. 847 (C.A.).

38

EIGHT CLASSES OF ACTS
OF PARLIAMENT

AMENDING ACTS

An Act of Parliament may of course be amended by any other Act of Parliament. The amending Act will not necessarily have the same sort of short title as the Act which it amends. For example, an Act of Parliament dealing with hotels may alter the Act of Parliament dealing with local government, so as to permit local government authorities to establish community hotels.

The Act which is amended by the later Act is generally referred to as the "principal Act".

Parliament of course has power to pass an amending Act even though that Act has the effect of amending a statute that has been enacted but has not yet come into force. Amendments to a statute

"are to be construed together with the original Act to which they relate as constituting one law and as part of a coherent system of legislation; the provisions of amendatory and amended Acts are to be harmonized, if possible, so as to give effect to each and to leave no clause of either inoperative."[1]

Furthermore,

"When an amending Act alters the language of the principal statute, the alteration must be taken to have been made deliberately."[2]

For example, when the word "for" in an Act was replaced by the word "of" the court held that this was done with the intention of changing the law, and it construed the section so as to give full effect to that intention.[3]

CODES

Unlike a revised Act, which is basically a putting together of an original Act and all the amendments to it, a code is an attempt by Parliament

---

[1] *G. T. Campbell & Associates Ltd. v. Hugh Carson Co.* (1979), 99 D.L.R. (3d) 529, Houlden J.A. at 539 (Ont. C.A.).

[2] *D. R. Fraser & Co. v. Canada (Minister of National Revenue)*, [1948] 4 D.L.R. 776 at 781.

[3] *Baker, Re* (1907), 7 W.L.R. 69 (Sask. C.A.).

to enact legislation to set out the whole of the law to cover a particular subject-matter or field, and in doing so, to cover not only any existing statutory provisions, but also the common law. The courts therefore take the basic approach to a code, that it is to be interpreted in the light of its own language without resort to the previously existing law whether statutory or common law.[4] However, if a provision in the code is ambiguous or uncertain of meaning, the courts may still have to take the pre-existing law, and particularly the pre-existing common law, into consideration.

DECLARATORY ACTS

If doubts arise as to the state of the law, Parliament may decide to pass a declaratory Act setting out what the law is. Parliament can do so, and is not limited to setting out what the state of the law as written in Acts of Parliament is: it can also set out the state of the common law:

> "For modern purposes a declaratory Act may be defined as an Act passed to remove doubts existing as to the common law or the meaning or effect of any statute. Such Acts are usually held to be retrospective."[5]

A declaratory Act usually sets out that the law is, and always has been, what it is said to be in the declaratory Act itself. A typical example is the Act which says: "Whereas the rightful jurisdiction of Her Majesty, her heirs and successors, extends and has always extended . . ."[6] The very nature of a declaratory Act is such that it will usually be found to operate from a date before the date on which it is passed by Parliament.[7] If a declaratory Act is to apply only from the date on which it is passed, there should be something on the face of that Act to show that that is Parliament's intention.[8]

ENABLING ACTS

An enabling Act is passed to empower the performance of an action which would not otherwise be lawful. For example, Parliament may enact legislation empowering a company to lay a pipeline through private property for the very long distance from its oil refinery to a major distribution point, or from a gas field to a capital city. Ordinarily, powers conferred by such an Act will be interpreted strictly. However, there is a different

---

[4] *Northern Crown Bank v. International Electric Co.* (1911), 24 O.L.R. 57, Teetzel J. at 59-60 (C.A.).

[5] *Mortgage Corp. of Nova Scotia v. Walsh* (1925), 57 N.S.R. 547, [1925] 1 D.L.R. 665 (C.A.).

[6] *Territorial Waters Jurisdiction Act* 1878 (U.K.), quoted in *Craies on Statute Law* (Sweet & Maxwell, London, 7th ed., Edgar S.G.G., 1971), p. 59.

[7] *Attorney-General v. Theobold* (1890), 2 Q.B.D. 557. See also chapter 40.

[8] *Earl of Mountcashel v. Grover* (1847), 4 U.C.Q.B. 23.

class of enabling Act which is one conferring jurisdiction upon a court or other body, and in respect of this type of legislation the jurisdiction conferred is construed liberally.

EXPLANATORY ACTS

Sometimes Parliament passes an Act to explain the meaning of an earlier Act of Parliament. When that happens, the earlier Act is to be read in the light of the explanatory Act, and it is to be read as if that explanation in the explanatory Act had been available to the reader at the time when the original Act was passed.[9]

If a law case has already been decided on the basis of the earlier Act, before the explanatory Act is passed, the passing of the explanatory Act does not alter the decision in that law case unless Parliament expressly says so in the explanatory Act. The explanatory Act does, however, affect any law cases which were started before the explanatory Act came into force but which had not been completed at that time, for the law cases must then proceed upon the basis of the original Act as read in the light of the explanatory Act. It would seem that, if a case had been decided on the basis of the earlier Act before the explanatory Act is passed, but was the subject of an appeal which had not been decided before the coming into force of the explanatory Act, the appeal court would have to apply the law as set out in the explanatory Act unless the explanatory Act contains a transitional provision to cover such a case.

REMEDIAL ACTS

The term remedial Act refers to an Act introduced by Parliament to remedy what Parliament perceives to be an existing problem. Such an Act should, so far as reasonably possible, be given a wide construction and application.[10] It should be construed so as to give the fullest relief which the fair meaning of its language will allow:

> "It should receive a generous interpretation so as, if possible, to carry out the intention of the Legislature . . ."[11]

However, while a court will extend the legislation so far as Parliament intended, it must be recognised that Parliament's words may be inept or otherwise fail to achieve its intention — in such a case the court must give effect to the words used according to their fair import and understanding.[12]

---

[9] *R. v. Dursley (Inhabitants)* (1832), 3 B. & Ad. 465, 110 E.R. 168.

[10] *Karch, Re* (1921), 50 O.L.R. 509, Middleton J. at 513, 64 D.L.R. 541 (C.A.).

[11] *Peterson v. Bitulithic Co.* (1913), 4 W.W.R. 223 (Man. C.A.).

[12] *R. v. Jasperson*, [1958] O.W.N. 360 (H.C.).

The remedy provided by the remedial Act is prima facie to be regarded as the exclusive remedy,[13] but only if the right and the remedy are in the same remedial Act.

REVISED ACTS

When an Act of Parliament has been amended by a number of later Acts, it becomes awkward to use. The reader either has to paste the amendments into the principal Act, or else has to chase from one Act to another while reading the principal Act. There is also the risk that the reader may miss some amendment and thereby be misled. There are two ways of meeting this difficulty. One way is for Parliament to authorise the printer to print the principal Act with all the amendments actually worked into it. The other way is for Parliament itself to pass a new Act of Parliament, consolidating into one Act the original Act and the various amendments to it.

The object of a revised Act is "to consolidate and reproduce the law as it stood before the passing of that Act".[14]

> "The purpose of the revision was to revise, classify, and consolidate the public general statutes of the Dominion, and the repeal of the old statutes incorporated in the revision was rather for convenience of citation and reference by giving a new starting point than with a view of abrogating the former law."[15]

The rule for reading a revised Act is to start on the basis that the revised Act is merely intended to consolidate, into one Act, the principal Act and its various amending Acts, and that the revised Act is not intended to make any alterations to the law:

> "all matters are to be carried out under the Revised Statutes as if no repeal had taken place, for the Revised Statutes are not new laws, but a consolidation and declaratory of the law as contained in the former Acts."[16]

When a Commission was constituted to revise and consolidate the existing statutes

> "the powers of the Commissioners were intended to be restricted: their work was merely to consolidate already existing statutory law; they were not authorised to change the law; they were not to assume the functions of the Legislature."[17]

---

[13] *Bishop Rochester v. Bridges* (1831), 1 B. & Ad. 847 at 859, 109 E.R. 1001, Lord Tenterden C.J.K.B. at 1005; *Pasmore v. Oswaldtwistle Urban District Council*, [1898] A.C. 387 at 394 and 397.

[14] *Gilbert v. Gilbert and Boucher*, [1928] P. 1 at 7.

[15] *Frontenac (District) License Commissioners v. Frontenac (County)* (1887), 14 O.R. 741 (Ch.).

[16] *R. v. Durnion* (1887), 14 O.R. 672, Wilson J. at 681 (Q.B.).

[17] *Boutilier v. Nova Scotia Trust Co.*, [1940] 2 D.L.R. 221, Chisholm C.J. at 224 (N.S.C.A.).

This rule is applied so that the revised Act is treated as not being intended to alter the law, even if there is a change of wording from the preceding legislation.[18] As an example, a change in wording occurred in the Revised Statutes of Alberta 1955, the change being the elimination of the concluding word, namely "howsoever". It was held that that change "should not . . . be considered as altering the spirit or meaning of the law as expressed in the previous [Act]" as in force at the time that the revised statutes took effect.[19]

Even although an Act is described by Parliament as a revised Act, there is nothing to prevent Parliament from including in that revised Act provisions which do make changes — and even major changes — in the law. If a revised Act contains a section the words of which are plain and which, if given their plain meaning, would make a change in the law, the plain meaning rule must be applied to give the words their plain meaning.

The fact that a revised Act can alter the law may prove to be a trap for the unwary. An amendment placed in a revised Act would be placed in a statute where the public and the profession would not in the least be on their guard to look for it.

The revised Act will, of course, repeal all the Acts which it is consolidating. They go out of force, and the revised Act comes into force, at one and the same time. There is, therefore, no break in the law: its effect continues unchanged and it is merely the place where it is to be found that is altered. There is no moment of time at which the law as formerly set out in the principal Act, and its amendments as now set out in the revised Act, ceases to have effect. As Lord Simon of Glaisdale said:

> "All consolidation Acts are designed to bring together in a more convenient, lucid and economical form a number of enactments related in subjectmatter (and often by cross-reference previously scattered over the statute book. All such previous enactments are repealed in the repeal schedule of the consolidation Act. It follows that, once a consolidation Act has been passed which is relevant to a factual situation before a court, the 'intention' of Parliament as to the legal consequences of that factual situation is to be collected from the consolidation Act, and not from the repealed enactments. It is the relevant provision of the consolidation Act, and not the corresponding provision of the repealed Act, which falls for interpretation. It is not legitimate to construe the provision of the consolidation Act as if it were still contained in the repealed Act — first, because Parliament has provided for the latter's abrogation; and secondly, because so to do would nullify much of the purpose of passing a consolidation Act."[20]

---

[18] *Rolls-Royce Co., Re*, [1976] 1 W.L.R. 1584 at 1590-1591.

[19] *Construction Equipment Co. v. Bilida's Transport Ltd.* (1966), 57 W.W.R. 513, Allen J. at 522 (Alta. T.D.). See also *Cedar Rapids Saving Bank v. Dominion Pure Bred Stock Co.*, [1923] 3 W.W.R. 1214 (Alta. C.A.).

[20] *Farrell v. Alexander*, [1977] A.C. 59 at 82.

VALIDATING ACTS

If something has been done invalidly, Parliament has the power to pass an Act of Parliament saying that it is to be treated as if it had been done validly. An example of this type of Act is to be found in legislation passed to cure an alleged defect in letters patent authorising a municipality to instal a sanitary sewer system — the authorisation for that system thereafter had to be treated as valid as from the date the letters patent had been originally issued.[21]

A validating Act may be passed because someone has discovered the invalidity, although the matter has not been taken to court, or it may be passed because some court has held that the particular thing has been done invalidly.

A validating Act must, by its very nature, be treated as coming into force on a day before the date on which it was actually passed.

---

[21] *Saltspring Island Sewer Alternatives Committee v. Capital Regional District* (1982), 134 D.L.R. (3d) 751 (B.C.S.C.).

39

ACTS WHICH ARE READ NARROWLY

THE KINDS OF ACTS THAT ARE READ NARROWLY

There are some kinds of Acts to which the courts may give a narrow meaning rather than a wide meaning if the words used by Parliament are capable of either meaning. The major examples of these Acts[1] are:

— Acts which impose a penalty;

— Acts which empower arrest or detention;

— Acts which impose a tax, or charge;

— Acts which impose pecuniary obligations;

— Acts which take away vested rights; and

— Acts affecting a fundamental principle of the common law.

The way in which to read these Acts is to give the words a narrow meaning rather than a wide one; but, of course, that can only be done if the words used in the Act are words that are capable of having the narrow meaning. If the words which Parliament has used are plain, they must be given that plain meaning even although they do impose a tax or a penalty or take away existing vested rights.

The giving of a narrow meaning to Acts of this kind is a rule which the courts once applied far more strongly than they do today. The position today is that the rule still applies, and that the Act is therefore to be read in favour of the individual rather than of the state, but that the rule only applies in that way if the words used by Parliament are clearly words of doubtful meaning. Acts of this kind must never be read narrowly so as to limit their plain meaning or so as to thwart Parliament's intention.

ACTS WHICH IMPOSE A PENALTY

What the rule really amounts to is that, if an Act imposes a penalty for a criminal offence, a person who is charged with that offence is entitled to the benefit of any doubt as to the meaning of the Act:

---

[1] Reference should also be made to retrospective Acts (considered in chapter 40) and extraterritorial Acts (considered in chapter 41).

"Where there is an enactment which may entail penal consequences, you ought not to do violence to the language in order to bring people within it, but ought rather to take care that no one is brought within it who is not brought within it by express language."[2]

"Where the words of a penal statute create an ambiguity, or where the words are capable of interpretation so as to equally reflect a penalty on the one hand and not on the other, then either that ambiguity or the balance must be resolved in favour of an interpretation avoiding the penalty in a particular case."[3]

A note of caution has been sounded by Howland C.J.O., who agreed that it was "beyond dispute" that a penal statute must be construed "strictly", but stressed the importance of understanding what that principle really means, and what it does not mean:

"What it does mean is that where a person is charged with an offence created by a statute, the conduct of that person . . . must be such as can be clearly and unmistakably demonstrated to fall within the kind of conduct which is proscribed by the statute. What the principle does *not* mean is that because a statute is 'penal' or contains provisions to which penal consequences for breaches are attached, the meaning that is to be given . . . is to be determined in accordance with a rule of construction that is somehow 'stricter' than, or is to be applied more stringently than, the ordinary rules which apply to determine the meaning to be given to language used in statutes."[4]

In one case a dispute arose as to whether a penal section covered council meetings only, or included meetings of subcommittees: the court held that, taking into account the penal nature of the Act, if Parliament wanted to cover subcommittees "then it clearly should have set out . . . that all levels of meeting, including those of subcommittees, were to be caught".[5] Another Act was held to be a penal statute because a breach of that Act could deprive a person of the right to serve on a council — the court therefore held that any ambiguity must be interpreted as favourably as possible to the person liable to the penalty.[6]

In determining whether a section is penal it is important to read the Act as a whole: it is quite possible that one section might specify that breaches of various other sections constitute a criminal offence, and in such a case those other sections would have to be read narrowly as penal sections.[7]

Of course, although ambiguity in an Act imposing a penalty is to be

---

[2] *Rumbolt v. Schmidt* (1882), 8 Q.B.D. 603, Huddleston B. at 608. See also *Westfall v. Eedy* (1991), 6 O.R. (3d) 422, Carter J. at 425 (H.C.); *Sharp v. McGregor* (1988), 50 D.L.R. (4th) 183, Craig J. at 187.

[3] *R. v. Johnston* (1979), 52 C.C.C. (2d) 57 at 61 (Alta. Q.B.). See also *Westfall v. Eedy* (1991), 7 M.P.L.R. (2d) 226 at 230 (Ont. H.C.).

[4] *R. v. Budget Car Rentals (Toronto) Ltd.* (1981), 15 M.P.L.R. 172 at 180.

[5] *Mangano v. Moscoe* (1991), 6 M.P.L.R. (2d) 29, at 34 (Ont. Gen. Div.).

[6] *Van Schyndel v. Harrell* (1991), 7 M.P.L.R. (2d) 97 at 98 (Ont. Div. Ct.).

[7] *Québec (Attorney General) v. Eastmain Band* (1992), 9 C.E.L.R. (N.S.) 257, Décary J. at 283 (Fed. C.A.).

resolved in favour of the individual by giving a strict interpretation to the Act, nevertheless this rule of interpretation must not be used to defeat the apparent intention of Parliament. For example, when a statute made any person committing a stated action "liable upon summary conviction" those words were held to be sufficient to create an offence; there was no added requirement that the statute actually used the words "is *guilty of an offence and* is liable."[8]

> "This court has on many occasions applied the well-known rule of statutory construction that if a penal provision is reasonably capable of two interpretations, that interpretation which is the more favourable to the accused must be adopted . . . I do not think, however, that this principle always requires a word which has two accepted meanings to be given the more restrictive meaning. Where a word used in a statute has two accepted meanings, then either or both meanings may apply . . . It is only in the case of an ambiguity which still exists after the full context is considered, where it is uncertain in which sense Parliament used the word, that the above rule of statutory construction requires the interpretation which is the more favourable to the defendant to be adopted."[9]

It is not for the court to find or make doubt or ambiguity in a penal Act if the words are such that, if they had been used in an Act that does not impose a penalty, no doubt or ambiguity would be found to exist. As Lord Reid said:

> "As the section creates a criminal offence it must not be loosely construed. Each word must be given its ordinary or natural meaning. It may be permissible, where necessary, to give some word a secondary meaning of which it is reasonably capable in ordinary speech. But we must not substitute for any word some other word or phrase or write in anything which is not there."[10]

ACTS WHICH EMPOWER ARREST OR DETENTION

Allied with the principle that Acts which impose a penalty should be interpreted, in case of ambiguity, in such a way as to give the individual the benefit of the doubt created by that ambiguity, is the principle that ambiguity in an Act should be resolved against implying a power to arrest or to detain.

ACTS WHICH CREATE A TAX OR CHARGE

Acts of Parliament which impose a tax or charge (whether imposed at Federal, Provincial or local government level) are also read narrowly if they are in words which could bear both a wide and a narrow meaning.

---

[8] *R. v. Doreen Rungay Ltd.* (1974), 51 D.L.R. (3d) 240, unanimous decision at 243 (Man. C.A.).
[9] *R. v. Goulis* (1981), 125 D.L.R. (3d) 137, unanimous decision at 141-142 (Ont. C.A.). See also *R. v. Govedarov* (1974), 3 O.R. (2d) 23 (Ont. C.A.).
[10] *Director of Public Prosecutions v. Turner*, [1974] A.C. 357 at 364.

Certainly "the subject is not to be taxed unless the language of the statute clearly imposes the obligation."[11] A tax or charge is not to be read into an Act — it must appear from the express words used in the Act itself.[12]

> "In a taxing Act one has to look merely at what is clearly said. There is no room for any intendment. There is no equity about a tax. There is no presumption as to a tax. Nothing is to be read in, nothing is to be implied. One can only look fairly at the language used."[13]

However, the principle that, if there is a real doubt as to the meaning of the words of the section, the meaning which is more favourable to the taxpayer should be adopted, cannot mean that taxpayers are to be allowed to avoid their clear obligations:

> "it is no longer correct to simply say that any ambiguity must be resolved in favour of a taxpayer. If there are two interpretations, the more reasonable one must prevail even if it imposes a tax. When there are two interpretations and one cannot be said to be more reasonable than the other, the choice should then be resolved in favour of the taxpayer."[14]

Although ambiguities in taxation Acts are to be "strictly construed against the taxing authority" the rules of construction applying to all statutes are nevertheless available.[15]

A court is less likely to read a taxing or charging provision narrowly if the case before it involves a tax evasion scheme.

The position in relation to tax exemptions is different, and much less favourable to the taxpayer:

> "The burden of establishing its right to the exemption claimed is upon the plaintiffs [claimants] and in determining that right the statutory provision creating such exemption is to be strictly construed against the person seeking it."[16]

---

[11] *Hull Dock Co. v. Browne* (1831), 2 B. & Ad. 43, 109 E.R. 1059. See also *D'Avigdor-Goldsmid v. Inland Revenue Commissioners*, [1953] A.C. 347; *Grinnell v. R.* (1888), 16 S.C.R. 119, Ritchie C.J. at 136; *Dartmouth (Town) v. Roman Catholic Episcopal Corp. of Halifax*, [1940] 2 D.L.R. 309, Graham J. at 313 (N.S.C.A.).

[12] *Morguard Properties Ltd. v. Winnipeg (City)* (1983), 24 M.P.L.R. 219, unanimous decision at 236 (S.C.C.); *Morgan v. Winnipeg (City) Assessor* (1990), 2 M.P.L.R. (2d) 169 at 175 (Man. Q.B.); *Lions v. Meaford (Town)* (1977), 2 M.P.L.R. 121 at 127 (Ont. Div. Ct.); *Green Meadows Estate Ltd. v. Nova Scotia (Director of Assessment)* (1982), 17 M.P.L.R. 296, unanimous decision at 302 (N.S. C.A.).

[13] *Cape Brandy Syndicate v. Inland Revenue Commissioners*, [1921] 1 K.B. 64, Rowlatt J. at 71; approved in *Canadian Eagle Oil Co. v. R.*, [1946] A.C. 119, Viscount Simon L.C. at 140.

[14] *Gossner v. Ontario Regional Assessment Commissioner* (1983), 22 M.P.L.R. 281 at 286-287 and 289 (Ont. Div. Ct.).

[15] *Trizec Equities Ltd. v. Area Assessor Burnaby–New Westminster* (1983), 22 M.P.L.R. 318 at 322 (B.C.S.C.); *R. v. Crown Zellerbach Canada Ltd.* (1954), 14 W.W.R. 433 at 439 (B.C.S.C.); *R. v. Budget Car Rentals (Toronto) Ltd.* (1981), 15 M.P.L.R. 172 at 180-181.

[16] *Saskatoon (Episcopal Corp.) v. Saskatoon (City)*, [1936] 2 W.W.R. 91, Mackenzie J.A. at 96 (Sask. C.A.); *Mennonite Collegiate Institute v. Gretna (Village)* (1990), 2 M.P.L.R. (2d) 209, at 214 (Man. Q.B.); *Hamilton (City) v. Hamilton Harbour Commissioners* (1984), 28 M.P.L.R. 1 at 13 (Ont. S.C.); *Moose Jaw (City) v. British American Oil Co.*, [1937] 2 W.W.R. 309 (Sask. C.A.).

ACTS IMPOSING PECUNIARY OBLIGATIONS

There are Acts which impose pecuniary obligations outside the scope of taxing and charging provisions. Town planning Acts are likely to do so. Requirements imposed under environmental legislation may also do so. Child welfare legislation is another field of pecuniary obligations, it being held in respect of an Act imposing liability for the maintenance of children "of a woman in receipt of an allowance" that the Act did not apply when the mother had died and the children thereafter were living with a sister: "As the statute is one which imposes pecuniary obligations it is subject to the rule of strict construction."[17]

ACTS WHICH AFFECT VESTED RIGHTS

The rule is that, if the Act is one which could take away vested rights, its words should only be given that effect if they clearly require it: "Statutes should be interpreted, if possible, so as to respect vested rights."[18] Indeed, "If a vested right is to be defeated, the section must plainly say so."[19] This rule has been stated by the courts over and over again:

> "The burden lies on those who seek to establish that the Legislature intended to take away the private rights of individuals, to show that by express words, or by necessary implication, such an intention appears."[20]

> "speaking generally it should not only be widely inconvenient but a flagrant violation of natural justice to deprive people of rights acquired by transactions perfectly valid and regular according to the law of the time."[21]

Legislation should be interpreted in that manner which interferes least with the common law rights of subjects.[22] In particular, limitations on the right to sue in the courts are narrowly interpreted[23] as a means of protecting the rights of persons whose opportunity to gain the protection of the courts for those rights would otherwise be destroyed. Nevertheless, of course, the words can be so plain and so strong that they have to be given their effect of taking away vested rights,[24] even if those rights are under an existing

---

[17] *Child Welfare Act, Re*, [1945] 1 W.W.R. 252 at 255 (Alta. S.C.).

[18] *Hough v. Windus* (1884), 12 Q.B.D. 224 at 237.

[19] *Engineering Industry Training Board v. Samuel Talbot (Engineers) Ltd.* [1969] 2 Q.B. 270, at 275. See also *Upper Canada College v. Smith* (1920), 61 S.C.R. 413, Duff J. (later Duff C.J.C.) at 419; *Montreal (City) v. Civic Parking Centre Ltd.* (1981), 18 M.P.L.R. 239, unanimous decision at 256 (S.C.C.); *McKittrick v. Byers*, [1926] 1 D.L.R. 342, unanimous decision at 344-345 (Ont. C.A.).

[20] *Berton Dress Inc. v. R.*, [1953] Ex C.R. 83 at 92 (Ex. Ct.).

[21] *Upper Canada College v. Smith* (1920), 61 S.C.R. 413, Duff J. (later Duff C.J.C.) at 419.

[22] *Greater Niagara Transit Commission v. Matson* (1977), 16 O.R. (2d) 351 (H.C.).

[23] *Williams v. Canadian National Railway* (1976), 75 D.L.R. (3d) 87, unanimous decision at 92.

[24] *Cheyney v. Inuvik (Town)* (1992), 11 M.P.L.R. (2d) 267 at 276 (N.W.T.S.C.).

court order. Such a provision taking away vested rights is to be strictly construed and applied.[25] "Moreover, legislation which clearly interferes with property rights should not . . . be interpreted in such a way as to interfere with those rights to any greater degree than is necessarily consistent with a fair interpretation of the words used."[26]

THE RIGHTS TO BE PROTECTED MUST BE VESTED RIGHTS

The rule that, when choosing between different meanings of a section, that meaning is to be chosen which will not take away existing vested rights, and is limited to those rights which have actually vested when the Act of Parliament has come into force. The rule deals only with *vested* rights. It does not deal with existing rights that have not vested at the date when the Act comes into force. A moment's thought shows that this must necessarily be so, for "most Acts of Parliament in fact do interfere with existing rights",[27] and in fact must do so.

EXPROPRIATING PROPERTY

The rule is that, in case of doubt, Acts which could have the effect of taking away vested rights must be given a narrow meaning in favour of the person who is entitled to those rights. This is a rule that applies with particular force in the case of an Act of Parliament that could have the effect of expropriating property.[28]

"A statute should not be held to take away private rights of property without compensation unless the intention to do so is expressed in unambiguous terms."[29]

---

[25] *R. v. Robb* (1925), 57 O.L.R. 23, Riddell J. at 25 (S.C.); followed in *R. v. Robinson*, [1939] O.R. 235, Urquhart J. at 239 (S.C.); *Silliker v Newcastle* (1974), 10 N.B.R. (2d) 118 (Q.B.).

[26] *Haldimand-Norfolk (Regional Municipality) v. Copland* (1992), 12 M.P.L.R. (2d) 85 at 89 (Ont. Gen. Div.).

[27] *West v. Gwynne*, [1911] 2 Ch. 1, Buckley L.J. (later Lord Wrenbury) at 12.

[28] *Colonial Sugar Refining Co. v. Melbourne Harbour Trust Commissioners*, [1927] A.C. 343 at 359; *Westminster Bank Ltd. v. Minister of Housing and Local Government*, [1971] A.C. 508 at 529; *British Columbia (Attorney General) v. Bailey*, [1919] 1 W.W.R. 191 (B.C.S.C.); *Thomson v. Halifax Power Co.* (1914), 47 N.S.R. 536 (C.A.); *Kirby v. Portugal Cove (Municipality)* (1989), 41 M.P.L.R. 142, unanimous decision at 149 (Nfld. C.A.).

[29] *Hartnell v. Minister of Housing and Local Government*, [1963] 1 W.L.R. 1141 at 1147, affirmed on appeal, [1965] A.C. 1134; *Gundy v. Johnston* (1913), 28 O.L.R. 121 (C.A.); *Central Ontario Coalition Concerning Hydro Transmission Systems v. Ontario Hydro* (1984), 10 D.L.R. (4th) 341, 27 M.P.L.R. 165, unanimous decision at 197 (Ont. Div. Ct.); *McIntyre Ranching Co. v. Cardston No. 6 (Municipality)*, [1982] 20 M.P.L.R. 49 at 59 (Alta. Q.B.).

THE PURPOSIVE APPROACH MAY DEPRIVE A LANDOWNER OF THE PROTECTION AFFORDED BY NARROW INTERPRETATION OF EXPROPRIATION PROVISIONS

Although the general rule is that provisions authorising expropriation of property, if ambiguous, should be interpreted in favour of the landowner rather than the expropriating authority, there are exceptions which are likely to cause increasing erosion of the protection principle within their fields. Thus, town planning powers have been given the "interpretation [which] is most consistent with the scheme of the legislation and intent of the Legislature" and therefore allows an implied basis for expropriation.[30] That this type of erosion is likely to increase in scope is well illustrated by heritage legislation, of which it has been held that "it must be given a wide and liberal interpretation"[31] because

"To do otherwise would frustrate the very purpose and intent of the Act. The property designation can and undoubtedly will often refer to both the interior and the exterior of the designated building . . . Not only should s 33 of the *Ontario Heritage Act* be given a wide and liberal interpretation, but so too should the reasons for designation . . . It would be illogical to give the statute a wide and purposive interpretation and yet narrowly construe the brief reasons required by the Act for the designation of a building as one of historical and architectural importance".[32]

Legal rules as to court procedure or as to law costs do not create "vested rights"

The rule for reading an Act of Parliament in such a way as to protect vested rights does not apply to an Act which lays down a new court procedure[33] or which makes a new provision about law costs.[34] What is protected is the right in respect of which the court proceedings are taken, not the way in which those court proceedings are to be conducted: "alterations in the form of procedure are always retrospective, unless there is

---

[30] *Leiriao c. Val-Bélair (Ville)*, [1991] 3 S.C.R. 349, 7 M.P.L.R. (2d) 1 at 38.

[31] *Toronto College Street Centre Ltd. v. Toronto (City)* (1986), 31 D.L.R. (4th) 402 at 414, 34 M.P.L.R. 138, unanimous decision at 153 (Ont. C.A.).

[32] *Toronto College Street Centre Ltd. v. Toronto (City)* (1986), 31 D.L.R. (4th) 402 at 414, 34 M.P.L.R. 138, unanimous decision at 153 (Ont. C.A.); *St. Peter's Evangelical Lutheran Church (Trustees) v. Ottawa (City)* (1980), 12 M.P.L.R. 241 at 244 (Ont. S.C.), reversed without affecting this aspect (1982), 20 M.P.L.R. 121 at 133.

[33] *R. v. Rivet*, [1944] 3 D.L.R. 353, Harvey C.J.A. at 354, [1944] 2 W.W.R. 132 (Alta. C.A.); *Tritt v. United States* (1989), 68 O.R. (2d) 284 (H.C.); *Baniuk v. Carpenter* (1987), 85 N.B.R. (2d) 385 (C.A.). An Act affecting the admissibility of evidence in court proceedings is an Act governing court procedure and not one relating to "vested rights": *Selangor United Rubber Estates Ltd. v. Craddock (No. 2)*, [1968] 1 W.L.R. 319.

[34] *Kanerva v. Ontario Association of Architects* (1986), 56 O.R. (2d) 518, unanimous decision at 521 (Ont. Div. Ct.). See also *Alkali Lake Indian Band v. Westcoast Transmission Co.*, [1986] 1 W.W.R. 766 (B.C.C.A.).

some good reason or other why they should not be."[35] The distinction between vested rights on the one hand and questions of court procedure on the other hand is best understood by bearing in mind that an Act which affects vested rights alters those rights themselves or the entitlement to them, whereas an Act which affects procedure does not assume to alter any rights, it merely invests the court with a measure of jurisdiction to ascertain and compel the observance of rights.

An Act which relates to procedure relates not to the rights themselves, but to the method of enforcing the existing rights. Therefore, legislation "creating or abolishing a right of appeal does not relate merely to procedure."[36]

Statutes which deal with procedure should, if possible, be construed so as to affect procedure only.[37]

ACTS AFFECTING A FUNDAMENTAL PRINCIPLE OF THE COMMON LAW

Clear words are necessary for an Act to be interpreted as setting aside a fundamental principle of the common law:

"statutes being in restriction of the common law liberty of the subject should, I think, speaking in general terms, be strictly construed."[38]

"In the construction of statutes there is a presumption that the Legislature does not intend to alter the common law beyond what it explicitly declares."[39]

One example is the common law right to privacy in a person's own home:

"The present appeal is concerned exclusively with the subject's right to the privacy of his home. . . . The appeal turns on the respect which Parliament must be understood, even in its desire to stamp out drunken driving, to pay to the fundamental right of privacy in one's own home, which has for centuries been recognised by the common law."[40]

Similarly, a statute would not deprive persons of the right to carry on a lawful occupation unless by express words or necessary implication.[41]

---

[35] *Gardner v. Lucas*, [1878] 3 App. Cas. 582, Lord Blackburn at 603; *I.A.F.F., Locals 913, 953, 1399, 1746 v. Okanagan Mainline Municipal Labour Relations Assn.* (1988), 30 B.C.L.R. (2d) 320 (S.C.).

[36] *R. v. Rivet*, [1944] 3 D.L.R. 353, [1944] 2 W.W.R. 132 (Alta. C.A.).

[37] *Leiriao c. Val-Bélair (Ville)* (1991), 7 M.P.L.R. (2d) 1 at 43 (Qué. C.A.).

[38] *R. v. Western Canada Liquor Co.*, [1920] 3 W.W.R. 352 (B.C.C.A.); *Anderson v. Lacey*, [1948] 2 W.W.R. 317 (Man. C.A.).

[39] *Toronto General Trusts Corp v. Shaw; Shaw, Re*, [1942] 2 D.L.R. 439, Martin C.J.S. at 443 reported under the name of *Shaw Estate, Re* in [1942] 1 W.W.R. 818 (Sask. C.A.).

[40] *Morris v. Beardmore*, [1981] A.C. 446, Lord Scarman at 465.

[41] *Commercial Taxi v. Alberta (Highway Traffic Board)*, [1950] 2 W.W.R. 289 (Alta. T.D.).

"Legislation . . . which interferes with or takes away rights as between parties dealing with one another in legitimate business . . . ought to be construed strictly in favour of the party whose rights are invaded."[42]

Another example is the right to silence — the right of a person not to answer questions if that person might be incriminated by the answers. This privilege against self-incrimination can only be abrogated by the manifestation of a clear legislative intention, express or implied. However, if the language of the Act is plain, Parliament clearly can abrogate even such a fundamental principle of the common law for, "if there be a clash, the statute prevails as the legislative will of Parliament".[43]

"It is true that the legislation is an encroachment on the common law doctrine, . . . but if it is clear that it was the intention of the legislature in passing a statute to abrogate the common law, it must give way, and the provisions of the statute must prevail."[44]

but the fundamental common law principle will still be supported by the courts to the extent that Parliament has not overridden it in a particular statute: "it is against principle . . . to infringe any further than is necessary for obtaining the full measure of relief the Act was intended to give."[45]

Should an Act take away a right which a person has secured by his or her own diligence, in order to bestow it on a person who has shown no diligence at all, that Act should be construed strictly and literally.[46]

Some of the rights and freedoms which have been considered in this chapter, and other rights and freedoms, are also contained in the *Canadian Charter of Rights and Freedoms* the interpretation of which is considered in chapter 45.

ACTS THAT APPLY FROM BEFORE THE DATE ON WHICH THEY WERE PASSED

The proper interpretation of Acts that apply from before the date on which they were passed is considered in chapter 40.

---

[42] *Richard Brothers Co. Estate, Re*, [1917] 2 W.W.R. 722, Hyndman J. at 725; *R. v. Chambers*, [1948] 2 W.W.R. 246, Dysart J.A. at 256.

[43] *Bromley London Borough Council v. Greater London Council*, [1983] 1 A.C. 768, Lord Scarman at 838.

[44] *Schiell v. Morrison*, [1930] 4 D.L.R. 664, Martin J.A. at 668 (Sask. C.A.).

[45] *Gray v. Ingersoll (Town)* (1888), 16 O.R. 194 (Ch.).

[46] *Muirhead v. Lawson* (1884), 1 B.C.R. (Pt. 2) 113 (S.C.).

40

ACTS THAT APPLY FROM BEFORE THE DATE ON WHICH THEY WERE PASSED

RETROACTIVE OR RETROSPECTIVE?

Contending that there is a distinction between retrospective and retroactive legislative provisions, Emeritus Professor Driedger wrote:

> "A retroactive statute is one that operates as of a time prior to its enactment. A retrospective statute is one that operates from the future only. It is prospective, but imposes a new result in respect of a past event. A retroactive statute operates backwards. A retrospective statute operates forwards, but looks backwards in that it attaches new consequences for the future to an event that took place before the statute was enacted. A retroactive statute changes the law from what it was; a retrospective statute changes the law from what it otherwise would be with respect to a prior event."[1]

His contention was accepted in two decisions[2] and was described as an "eminently sensible analysis" in another.[3] Other judges took opposing views: in a survey we made of 60 decisions by the Supreme Courts across Canada, 35 percent used "retroactive," but 65 percent used "retrospective". In another case, reasons for judgment under the heading "The issue of retroactivity" in the first five paragraphs used "retrospective" twice and "retroactive" twice.[4] Professor Driedger himself admits that "Two words are used . . ., namely, *retroactive* and *retrospective*. Although these words are used interchangeably in the reports and texts, and even in the dictionaries", he contends that "there is a subtle difference between them, as indicated by the Latin root words from which they are derived."[5] A book such as the present is not written for "subtle differences" of "Latin root words". We have therefore used "retrospective" throughout this chapter

---

[1] Driedger, Emeritus Professor EA, "*Statutes: Retroactive Retrospective Reflections*", 56 Can. Bar Rev. 264 at 268-269 (1978). Driedger's view was accepted in *Sandhu v. Mann* (1986), 34 D.L.R. (4th) 717 (B.C.S.C.) and in *Happy Investments Management Ltd. v. Dorio* (1987), 46 D.L.R. (4th) 381 at 383-384 (S.C.).

[2] *Sandhu v. Mann* (1986), 34 D.L.R. (4th) 717 (B.C.S.C.) and in *Happy Investments Management Ltd. v. Dorio* (1987), 46 D.L.R. (4th) 381 at 383-384 (B.C.S.C.).

[3] *Shuniah (Township) v. Richard* (1982), 37 O.R. (2d) 471, Maloney J. at 478.

[4] *Rempel-Trail Transportation Ltd. v. Neilsen* (1978), 93 D.L.R. (3d) 595, Taylor J. at 598-599 (B.C.S.C.).

[5] Driedger, Emeritus Professor EA, *Construction of Statutes* (Butterworths, Toronto, 1983) pp. 185-186.

— an approach which accords with the *Oxford English Dictionary* which states:

> **"Retroactive**
> *1.a* Of enactments, etc.: Extending in scope or effect to matters which have occurred in the past; retrospective."
>
> **"Retrospective**
> *2.* Of statutes, etc.: Operative with regard to past time; retroactive"[6]

and which has the support of Meredith C.J.C.P. in his treatment of "retrospective, retroactive, or ex post facto" as synonymous.[7]

THE POWER OF PARLIAMENT TO MAKE ACTS THAT APPLY FROM A DATE BEFORE THE DATE ON WHICH THEY WERE PASSED

Parliament has power to make an Act apply from a date earlier than the date on which the Act itself was passed by Parliament. An Act of this kind is known as a retrospective Act. Not only the federal but also the provincial legislatures have power to enact retrospective Acts.[8]

THE PRESUMPTION THAT STATUTES ARE NOT INTENDED TO BE RETROSPECTIVE

There is a presumption that statutes do not operate with retrospective effect.[9] This presumption has been described as "a strong *prima facie* presumption",[10] and as "an extremely strong one". [11] "The principle is too well established to require authority that a statute is *prima facie* prospective".[12] "The law is leery of retrospective legislation".[13] However, it is "a presumption which yields to the clear contrary expression of the legislature".[14]

---

[6] OED 2nd ed. (1989), (Clarendon Press London vol. 13) p. 796.

[7] *Lambert v. Anglo-Scottish General Commercial Insurance Co.*, [1930] 1 D.L.R. 284 at 286.

[8] *Boulanger v. Québec (Federation des Producteurs d'oeufs de consommation)* (1982), 141 D.L.R. (3d) 72, leave to appeal refused 141 D.L.R. (3d) 72 (note) (S.C.C.).

[9] *Sun Alliance Insurance Co. v. Angus*, [1988] 2 S.C.R. 256, unanimous decision at 262, reported under the name of *Angus v. Hart* in 52 D.L.R. (4th) 193.

[10] *Upper Canada College v. Smith* (1920), 61 S.C.R. 413, Duff J. (later Duff C.J.C.) at 421.

[11] Côté, P-E, *The Interpretation of Legislation in Canada* (Les Éditions Yvon Blais Inc., Cowansville, 1984) p. 100.

[12] *Maxwell v. Callbeck*, [1939] S.C.R. 400, Davis J. at 444.

[13] *Sun Alliance* at [S.C.R.] 266.

[14] *T. G. Bright & Co. v. Institut National des Appellations d'Origine des vins et eaux-de-vie* (1981), 130 D.L.R. (3d) 12, L'Heureux-Dubé J.A. (later a judge of the Supreme Court of Canada) at 18 (Qué. C.A.).

CLEAR WORDS ARE NEEDED TO MAKE AN ACT OPERATE FROM BEFORE THE DATE ON WHICH IT WAS PASSED

It is a very far-reaching step to make an Act of Parliament operate from a date prior to the day on which it was passed by Parliament. Clear words are therefore necessary before an Act can be read as having that effect:

"Unless there is some declared intention of the legislature — clear and unequivocal — or unless there are some circumstances rendering it inevitable that we should take the other view, we are to presume that an Act is prospective and not retrospective."[15]

The practice of the courts is to restrict "the application of statutes to the future unless the intention that they are to have a wider effect is perfectly plain."[16]

"The principle is too well established to require authority that a statute is *prima facie* prospective unless it contains express words or there is the plainest implication to the contrary effect."[17]

If, therefore, the Act is in words which could fairly be read either as operating from before the passing of the Act or as operating only from the passing of the Act, it should be read as applying only from the date of the passing of the Act.[18] Sheppard J.A. in the British Columbia Court of Appeal said that

"the section confers substantive rights and should be construed as operating prospectively unless a contrary intention is plainly manifested by express terms or clear implication."[19]

and Duff (later Duff C.J.) in the Supreme Court of Canada, held that

"where an enactment, admittedly retrospective, is expressed in language which leaves the scope of it open to doubt, and according to one construction it imposes retrospectively a new liability, while upon another at least equally admissible, it imposes no such burden, the latter construction is that which ought to be preferred."[20]

The need for clear words does not, however, mean that the word "retrospective" has to be used or that the Act has to say expressly that it operates from some date prior to the date of its passing: its necessary intendment may show that it is to be retrospective.[21]

---

[15] *Gardner v. Lucas* (1878), 3 App. Cas. 582, Lord O'Hagan at 601; *Nova Scotia (Public Utilities Board) v. Nova Scotia Power Corp.* (1976), 75 D.L.R. (3d) 72, unanimous decision at 81-82 (N.S.C.A.).

[16] *Upper Canada College v. Smith* (1920), 61 S.C.R. 413, Duff J. (later Duff C.J.C.) at 421. See also *Smith v. London (City)* (1909), 20 O.R. 133, unanimous decision at 164 (Div. Ct.).

[17] *Maxwell v. Callbeck*, [1939] S.C.R. 440, Davis J. at 444.

[18] *Main v. Stark* (1890), 15 App. Cas. 384, Lord Selborne at 387.

[19] *Stratton v. Trans-Canada Air Lines* (1962), 37 W.W.R. 577 at 590 (B.C.C.A).

[20] *Kent v. R.*, [1924] S.C.R. 388 at 397.

[21] *Zainal bin Hashim v. Malaysia (Government)*, [1980] A.C. 734 at 742.

TAKING AWAY EXISTING RIGHTS

Unfortunately, Parliament's power to pass retrospective Acts is not limited to cases in which no one will be harmed. Parliament has power not only to make an Act operate from any date that it chooses, even from a date earlier than the date on which the Act first came before Parliament as a Bill, but it has power to take away existing rights. It can even set aside the result of litigation, so that someone who has been successful in litigation can have the benefit of the court order taken away from him or her and the court order itself set aside by the statute. Plain words would, of course, be necessary in order to achieve such an effect, even in the case of litigation which is still in progress before any court order has been made:

> "As I understand the established rule of construction, statutes should not, in the absence of anything in the Act to show that it is to have a retrospective operation, be so construed as to have the effect of altering the law applicable to pending actions."[22]

> "Statutes are not to be interpreted so as to have a retrospective operation unless they contain clear and express words to that effect, or the object, subjectmatter or context shows a contrary intention. Even where a statute is, in some degree, retrospective, a larger retrospective operation should not be given than that which it can plainly be seen the Legislature meant."[23]

PROVIDING PENALTIES FOR THINGS DONE BEFORE THE COMING INTO FORCE OF THE ACT

Parliament has power not only to make an Act take effect from a date before the Act itself was passed, but it also has power to use that Act to make something a criminal offence, even although it was not a criminal offence at the time it was done. It would take clear words to have that effect, for as Lord Reid has said "there has for a very long time been a strong feeling against making legislation, and particularly criminal legislation, retrospective".[24] Therefore, it is unusual to give a penal statute any retrospective operation, except for the benefit of an accused or convicted person.

The retrospective destruction of existing substantive rights should be applied only with the greatest caution, and subject to Parliament's intention, but there are cases in which it has been done.

A horrifying example is that of the retrospective tax imposed by the British Parliament, which increased the amount to be paid on a previous year's income even though the taxpayer had already paid everything he owed. The courts do not like this kind of Act, but when the words are

---

[22] *Gauthier v. McRae* (1977), 82 D.L.R. (3d) 671, Nicholson C.J.P.E.I. at 676 (P.E.I.S.C.).

[23] *Toronto (City) v. Presswood Brothers*, [1944] 1 D.L.R. 569, unanimous decision at 583 (Ont. C.A.).

[24] *Waddington v. Miah*, [1974] 1 W.L.R. 683 at 694.

clear, the judges have no choice but to enforce them. Mr. Justice Slade[25] said:

"I am bound to say that I have a measure of sympathy with this submission, since section 8 of the Act of 1974 does appear to me to represent retrospective legislation of a fairly extreme kind. As the taxpayer said, if Parliament was content in the Act of 1974 retrospectively to increase surtax liabilities laid down by the Act of 1973 for the fiscal year 1972-1973, there seems in principle no reason why it should not hereafter increase surtax laid down by earlier Finance Acts, for even more distantly past fiscal years. It is obvious that retrospective legislation of this kind can operate harshly in individual cases, particularly, as the taxpayer pointed out, in a case where, at the time when the new legislation is introduced, the taxpayer has actually discharged the whole of his liability for the relevant fiscal year on the basis of the previously existing law; that being so, he may naturally have regarded his liability for that year as finally settled once and for all and may have arranged his affairs on that basis. No doubt with considerations such as this in mind, the court, in construing a taxing statute, will be very reluctant to construe it as having a retrospective effect and will construe it as not having such effect if the words used allow such construction. As Lord Atkinson said in *Ingle v. Farrand* [1927] A.C. 417 at 428: 'Your Lordships were referred to several authorities laying down the principle upon which the question should be determined whether a statute acts retrospectively or not. Amongst those authorities the case of *Smith v. Callander* [1901] A.C. 297, and Lindley L.J.'s[26] judgment in *Lauri v. Renad* [1892] 3 Ch. 402 at 421 were included. The rule which according to those authorities is to be applied is thus stated in *Maxwell on Statutes* p. 382: ''It is a fundamental rule of English law that no statute shall be construed so as to have a retrospective operation unless such a construction appears very clearly in the terms of the Act, or arises by necessary and distinct implication.' "

This, however, marks the limit of the court's powers to refuse to give effect to retrospective legislation. As Lord Atkinson went on to say in *Ingle v. Farrand:* 'If a clause in a statute says in so many plain words that the statute shall have retrospective operation, then it must not be construed so as to defeat those express words.'

Thus, in answer to submissions to the contrary made by the taxpayer, it is in my judgment clear that, as the constitutional law of England stands today, Parliament has the power to enact by statute any fiscal law, whether of a prospective or retrospective nature and whether or not it may be thought by some persons to cause injustice to individual citizens. If the wording of that legislation is clear, the court must give effect to it, even though it may have, or will have, a retrospective effect.'[27]

The power to make an Act operate from a date earlier than the date on which the Act itself was passed by Parliament naturally extends to anything that Parliament thinks fit to include in the Act. There are various cases, for example, in which the courts have held to be valid provisions which increase the penalties for things done before the coming into force of the provisions that increased those penalties.[28]

---

[25] Later Slade L.J.
[26] Later Lord Lindley M.R.
[27] *James v. Inland Revenue Commissioners*, [1977] 1 W.L.R. 835 at 838.
[28] *Director of Public Prosecutions v. Lamb*, [1941] 2 K.B. 89; *Buckman v. Button*, [1943] K.B. 405; *Mischeff v. Springett*, [1942] 2 K.B. 331; *R. v. Oliver*, [1944] K.B. 68.

ACTS DECLARING THE EXISTING LAW ARE RETROSPECTIVE

Parliament may be concerned to make clear what the existing law is. The need for it to do so may arise because a court decision has shown it to be unclear, or because there is a dispute amongst people who have to use the Act as to what its meaning is. In such a case, Parliament can resolve the difficulty by passing a declaratory Act which says that the law is and always has been what that Act declares it to be.

ACTS RELATING TO PROCEDURE OR EVIDENCE ARE USUALLY RETROSPECTIVE

The person who finds that his or her rights in litigation are changed because Parliament has passed an Act changing the procedure may well consider that Act to be unfair, but the courts treat a procedural Act as prima facie intended to be retrospective:[29]

> "a new procedure applies to pending suits without breaking the 'rule of interpretation to the effect that statutes ought, if possible, to be interpreted so as to respect vested rights'. "[30]

> "There is a presumption that statutes do not operate with retrospective effect. 'Procedural' provisions, however, are not subject to the presumption. To the contrary, they are presumed to operate retrospectively."[31]

Unfortunately "The distinction between substantive and procedural provisions . . . is far from clear."[32] It has been held that "A provision is substantive or procedural for the purposes of retrospective application . . . according to whether or not it affects substantive rights."[33] The distinction between procedural provisions and provisions affecting vested rights is therefore vital, however difficult it may be to apply in practice: the presumptions applied by the courts in the case of these two very different types of provision are opposite.

> "The law is leery of retrospective legislation to begin with: the legislature will not lightly be presumed to have intended a provision to have retrospective effect when the provision substantially affects the vested rights of a party."[34]

---

[29] *Upper Canada College v. Smith* (1920), 61 S.C.R. 413, Duff J. (later Duff C.J.C.) at 423.

[30] *Wildman v. R.* (1984), 14 C.C.C. (3d) 321, unanimous decision at 337 (S.C.C.).

[31] *Sun Alliance Insurance Co. v. Angus*, [1988] 2 S.C.R. 256, unanimous decision at 262, reported under the name of *Angus v. Hart* in 52 D.L.R. (4th) 193.

[32] *Sun Alliance* at [S.C.R.] 262.

[33] *Sun Alliance* at [S.C.R.] 265.

[34] *Sun Alliance* at [S.C.R.] 266-267.

"Normally, rules of procedure do not affect the *content* or *existence* of an action or defence (or right, obligation, or whatever else is the subject of the legislation), but only the *manner* of its enforcement or use."[35]

The same principles apply to Acts relating to the rules of evidence — Acts which make something admissible in evidence that would not otherwise be admissible, or which give an effect to evidence which it would not otherwise have:

"The rule that an Act of Parliament is not to be given retrospective effect only applies to statutes which affect vested rights. It does not apply to statutes which only alter the form of procedure, or the admissibility of evidence, or the effect which the courts give to evidence."[36]

However, not all rules of evidence are purely procedural — it is possible for a rule of evidence to "create rights and not merely expectations" and if it does so it is treated as being "of a substantive nature".[37]

A useful summary of the applicable principles states that

"unless the language used plainly manifests in express terms or by clear implication a contrary intention — (a) A statute divesting vested rights is to be construed as prospective. (b) A statute, merely procedural, is to be construed as retrospective. (c). A statute which, while procedural in character, affects vested rights adversely is to be construed as prospective."[38]

---

[35] *Sun Alliance* at [S.C.R.] 265.

[36] *Blyth v. Blyth (No. 2)*, [1966] A.C. 643, Lord Denning (later Lord Denning M.R.) at 666.

[37] *Wildman v. R* (1984), 14 C.C.C. (3d) 321, unanimous decision at 337 (S.C.C.); *De Roussy v. Nesbitt* (1920), 53 D.L.R. 514, Harvey C.J. at 515 and 516 (Alta. C.A.).

[38] *Dixie v. Royal Columbian Hospital*, [1941] 2 D.L.R. 138, Sloan J. at 139 (B.C.C.A.).

41

THE AREA IN WHICH AN ACT OF PARLIAMENT OPERATES

AN ACT OPERATES WITHIN THE TERRITORY OF THE PARLIAMENT THAT MADE IT

For most practical purposes, a statute operates within the territorial limits of the Parliament that made it[1] and throughout the whole of that territory:

> "It will not be disputed that an Act of the legislature prima facie applies to the whole province."[2]

Lord Diplock expressed this principle by saying:

> "Because sovereignty is territorial, there is a presumption based on international comity that Parliament, when enacting a penal statute, unless it uses plain words to the contrary, does not intend to make it an offence in English law to do acts in places outside the territorial jurisdiction of the English courts — at any rate unless the act is one which necessarily has its harmful consequences in England."[3]

It must, however, be borne in mind that this is a principle of interpretation and not a restriction upon the power of Parliament to make laws. A Parliament can, if it chooses, express a statute to operate beyond the territorial limits of the area which it governs; and, in such a case, the courts would have to give that statute the full operation it is expressed to have.

Foreigners within the territory are required to comply with the legislation of the territory concerned. This applies not only to tourists moving from country to country, but to people who happen to be in a country or Province, or a local government area, other than that in which they ordinarily reside. For example, if a person living in Ottawa goes on holiday to Whistler in the Province of British Columbia, that person is required to obey the laws of the Province of British Columbia and the by-laws of Whistler Resort Municipality. The same would apply to an American visiting a Canadian city.

---

[1] *Alberta (Attorney General) v. Huggard Assets Ltd.*, [1953] A.C. 420 at 441.

[2] *Bradbury, Re* (1916), 30 D.L.R. 765, Harris J. at 767 (N.S.C.A.).

[3] *Lawson v. Fox*, [1974] A.C. 803 at 808.

APPLYING THE PRINCIPLE TO BODIES UNDER PARLIAMENT

A very similar principle is applied to laws made by bodies acting under parliamentary authority. Parliament has delegated the power to make law to a large and growing number of statutory bodies, such as government departments, commissions, boards and local government authorities. Those bodies make law in a wide variety of forms such as Orders in Council, regulations and bylaws. A body making law in that way is presumed to be empowered to make laws that operate only within its own territorial boundaries unless Parliament has expressly given it a wider law-making power.[4]

A local authority cannot validly make extraterritorial legislation without specific parliamentary authorisation, whereas Parliament can do it, but is presumed not to have done so unless the Act makes that intention plain.

PARLIAMENT CAN MAKE THE ACT OPERATE BEYOND ITS TERRITORY

Basically, there is nothing to prevent a Parliament expressing a law to operate beyond its territorial boundaries. It can, for example, make a law controlling the activities of its own citizens, irrespective of where they happen to be living. Thus, the Canadian Parliament could validly make a law controlling the activities of Canadian citizens, even though they happen to be living, for example, in England — provided, of course, that they have retained Canadian nationality.

Whether or not any particular statute does bind those nationals even although they are living outside the territorial boundaries, can only be decided by a proper interpretation of the Act itself. Some kinds of Acts are more likely than other kinds to be held to apply to nationals living in another country. For example, a statute controlling marriages, and prohibiting persons of close relationship marrying each other, may apply to those nationals irrespective of where they live,[5] but a statute that prescribes the particular weights and measures to be used when measuring goods for the purpose of sale will not operate outside the territory of the Parliament.[6]

If the Act of Parliament being interpreted creates an offence, there is "a presumption that an offence-creating section was not intended by Parliament to cover conduct outside the territorial jurisdiction of the Crown".[7] However, this is not a rigid rule. For instance, the English Court

---

[4] *R. v. Security Storage Co.* (1957), 22 W.W.R. 216.

[5] *Brook v. Brook* (1861), 9 H.L.C. 193 at 210, 11 E.R. 703 at 710.

[6] *Rosseter v. Cahlmann* (1853), 8 Ex. 361, 155 E.R. 1586.

[7] *Air-India v. Wiggins*, [1980] 1 W.L.R. 815, Lord Scarman at 820. See also *Cox v. Army Council*, [1963] A.C. 48.

of Appeal held it to be an offence to supply advertising material to be broadcast from outside the jurisdiction by a pirate radio station.[8]

APPLYING THE ACT TO FOREIGNERS BEYOND THE TERRITORY

The general rule is that a statute does not apply to things done by foreigners outside the territory governed by that Parliament:

> "Parliament has no proper authority to legislate for foreigners outside its jurisdiction, . . . no statute ought therefore to be held to apply to foreigners with respect to transactions out of British jurisdiction, unless the words of the statute are perfectly clear."[9]

However, if the foreigners living outside the territory have some sufficient connection with that territory, they can take advantage of the statute made by the Parliament of that territory.[10]

ACTIONS OUTSIDE THE TERRITORY AFFECTING PERSONS INSIDE IT

Even although a person is living outside the territory of the Parliament concerned, and is not a national of that territory, Parliament may still have power to govern his or her actions to some extent.[11] For example, there is a Federal law making it an offence for Canadian companies' subsidiaries to bribe officials in other countries.

---

[8] *R. v. Murray (Nicholas)*, [1990] 1 W.L.R. 1360 at 1368-1369.

[9] *"Amalia" The, Re* (1863), 1 Moore P.C. (N.S.) 471 at 474, 15 E.R. 778 at 779; *Air-India v. Wiggins*, [1980] 1 W.L.R. 815, Lord Scarman at 820.

[10] *Davidson v. Hill*, [1901] 2 K.B. 606; *Seale, Re*, [1961] Ch. 574.

[11] *United States v. Aluminium Co. of America*, 148 F.2d 416 at 443 (1945).

42

HOW ACTS OF PARLIAMENT AFFECT THE CROWN

THE MEANING OF "THE CROWN"

In this chapter the phrase "the Crown" is used as meaning what the ordinary man in the street would probably call "the government". "The Crown" is a phrase meaning the State as a body, by whatever name it is known in the particular country concerned. It does not mean the king or queen personally.

WHEN AN ACT OF PARLIAMENT BINDS THE CROWN

An Act of Parliament is made by the Crown. The rule, therefore, is that the Act of Parliament does not bind the Crown unless the Act expressly says it does. In the absence of express terms, the Crown is not bound[1] unless the necessary implication from the words used in the Act is that the Crown is to be bound.[2]

However, the law in this respect — as in many others — is broadening, and the Crown will be held to be bound by necessary implication much more readily today than it has been in the past.[3] It is not in itself sufficient to establish such a necessary implication that the Act was passed for the public benefit.[4] Further, a statute must "bind the Crown either generally or not at all." An Act cannot be held to bind the Crown "when the Crown is acting without any right to do so but not when the Crown does have such rights."[5]

Even although the Crown is not bound by the particular Act, it can

---

[1] *Theberge v. Laudry* (1876), 2 App. Cas. 102; *Cushing v. Lupuy* (1880), 5 App. Cas. 410 at 419.

[2] *Bombay Province v. Bombay Municipal Corp.*, [1974] A.C. 58; *Lord Advocate v. Dumbarton District Council*, [1989] 3 W.L.R. 1346, Lord Keith of Kinkel at 1360; *Friends of the Oldman River Society v. Canada (Minister of Transport)*, [1992] 1 S.C.R. 3, 7 C.E.L.R. (N.S.) 1 at 43.

[3] *Cronkhite Supply Ltd. v. British Columbia (Workers' Compensation Board)* (1978), 8 B.C.L.R. 54 (C.A.).

[4] *Lord Advocate v. Dumbarton District Council*, [1989] 3 W.L.R. 1346, Lord Keith of Kinkel at 1360.

[5] *Dumbarton District Council*, Lord Keith of Kinkel at 1362 and 1366.

still take advantage of it. Indeed, it "can take the benefit of any statute although not specifically named in it."[6]

THE EXTENT OF "THE CROWN"

It is not difficult to apply this rule when the question as to the meaning of the Act arises with respect to land owned and occupied[7] by the State itself. Difficulty does arise, however, in deciding whether the rule applies to some statutory authority that has been set up by Parliament.

---

[6] *Town Investments Ltd. v. Department of the Environment*, [1976] 1 W.L.R. 1126, Lawton L.J. at 1142.

[7] This means that the protection accorded to the State does not apply to tenants of Crown land.

43

HOW JUDICIAL DECISIONS AFFECT THE READING OF AN ACT

PRIOR JUDICIAL DECISIONS CAN BE TAKEN INTO CONSIDERATION

Although "sections must be considered . . . in light of the judicial interpretation of them"[1] it is not all judicial decisions that can be looked at for assistance in understanding an Act of Parliament. To be usable for this purpose, the decision must be a decision of a Supreme Court, or a court of similar status, or a higher court.

JUDICIAL DECISIONS ON PRINCIPLES OF THE COMMON LAW

Very important judicial decisions for use in understanding an Act of Parliament are those which expound or develop the principles of the common law. For example, the rules of natural justice (which require the giving of a fair hearing without bias on the part of the person conducting the hearing) have long been established as an important part of the common law.

JUDICIAL DECISIONS ON THE MEANING OF PARTICULAR WORDS AND PHRASES

It is not surprising that over the years a great body of judicial decisions has been built up on the meaning of particular words and phrases. These decisions are to be found in various judicial dictionaries. Care has to be taken in using them, because a word or phrase may derive its meaning from the context in which it occurs; but, subject to that qualification, resort to a judicial dictionary can assist the reader to understand the meaning of a word or phrase which would otherwise be ambiguous.

---

[1] *Three Bills Passed by the Legislative Assembly of the Province of Alberta, Re*, [1938] S.C.R. 100, Duff C.J.C. and Davis J. at 114.

EXISTING JUDICIAL INTERPRETATION OF A STATUTORY PROVISION

If a statutory provision has been interpreted in a particular way, and that interpretation has stood and been used over a substantial period of years, courts interpreting the provision will be expected to give the same interpretation unless and until it is either overruled or varied by a higher court.[2]

RE-ENACTMENT AFTER AN ACT HAS BEEN INTERPRETED BY THE COURTS

If, after a provision in an Act of Parliament has been interpreted by a superior court, Parliament enacts legislation which includes that same provision, there is a presumption that Parliament knew of the decision and intended the new legislation to have the meaning the courts had already placed on that provision. Thus it has been observed that

> "Had I been doubtful of the correctness of these decisions I would have thought that we should follow them in view of the circumstances that they have for many years been treated as stating the law of Saskatchewan on this matter and that since they were decided [the section] has been re-enacted without any material alteration".[3]

The presumption applies notwithstanding that there have been minor changes in the legislation when revising it.[4]

An interesting example of the application of this principle is that of a statutory provision which was held by judicial decision not to be wide enough to confer a right of appeal in certain circumstances. The legislature amended the statute and extended the right of appeal, but subsequently, in a re-enactment of the statute, the widening provisions were omitted, with the result that the re-enacted legislation was substantially in line with the original legislation which had been the subject of the judicial decisions. It was held that the re-enacted legislation was to be interpreted in the same way as the original interpretation.[5]

Of course, the situation may also occur in reverse: Parliament may deliberately legislate to change what the courts had decided was the effect

---

[2] *Laursen v. McKinnon* (1913), 9 D.L.R. 758 (B.C.C.A.); *Turner v. Insurance Corp. of British Columbia* (1982), 137 D.L.R. (3d) 188 (B.C.S.C.); *Canada Life Assurance Co. v. Rieb*, [1943] 1 W.W.R. 759 (Alta. T.D.).

[3] *Canadian Acceptance Corp. Ltd. v. Fisher*, [1958] S.C.R. 546, Cartwright J. at 553-554; *Street v. Ottawa Valley Power Corp.*, [1940] S.C.R. 40; *MacMillan v. Brownlee*, [1937] S.C.R. 318; *Fagnan v. Ure*, [1958] S.C.R. 377.

[4] *Reference re s. 189 of Railway Act, 1919, Canada*, [1926] S.C.R. 163, unanimous decision at 174-175; *Spruce Creek Power Co. v. Muirhead* (1904), 11 B.C.R. 68.

[5] *Halifax Pilot Commissioners v. Farquhar* (1894), 26 N.S.R. 333 (C.A.).

of the existing law. In that case, the judicial decision may assist in understanding the change that Parliament has made.

TECHNICAL LEGAL TERMS

There are many terms which have their own special meaning in law. Sometimes the meaning may be wider and sometimes narrower than the ordinary meaning of the word. When Parliament uses a word with a well-known legal meaning, the presumption is that it intended to use the word in its strict legal sense "unless a contrary intention appears."[6]

---

[6] *Income Tax Commissioners v. Pemsel*, [1891] A.C. 531 at 580.

44

SUBORDINATE LEGISLATION

SUBORDINATE LEGISLATION IS INTERPRETED SO AS TO BE WITHIN POWER

Subordinate legislation is legislation made by a person or body other than Parliament under authority granted by an Act of Parliament. Just as a statute must be constitutionally valid, so subordinate legislation, in order to have legal effect, must be within the powers granted by Parliament and must comply with any conditions laid down in the Act. It may happen that subordinate legislation is ambiguous, having two possible meanings, one of which would be within the power conferred by the Act, while the other would make the subordinate legislation invalid and ineffective as beyond the limits of the power conferred. In such a case the court will prefer that interpretation under which the subordinate legislation would be valid: "if the words used are capable of a reasonable construction that would keep the enactment within the limits of jurisdiction, they should be so construed."[1]

SUBORDINATE LEGISLATION CANNOT NORMALLY BE USED TO INTERPRET A STATUTE

By-laws or regulations or other subordinate legislation traditionally cannot be used to interpret a statute: "It is legitimate to use *the Act* as an aid to the construction of the regulations. To do the converse is to put the cart before the horse."[2] As Viscount Dilhorne has said: "I have no hesitation in rejecting the contention that rules made in the exercise of a statutory power can be relied on as an aid to the construction of a statute."[3] A distinction has to be drawn, however, between subordinate legislation of the ordinary type and subordinate legislation expressly authorised by Parliament to amend the Act. In the latter case, reference may be made to the subordinate legislation to interpret the Act in case of ambiguity. Lord Lowry has expressed the position in six propositions:

---

[1] *Friends of Oak Hammock Marsh Inc. v. Ducks Unlimited (Canada)* (1991), 9 C.E.L.R. (N.S.) 52 at 62 (Man. Q.B.).

[2] *Lawson v. Fox*, [1974] A.C. 803, Lord Diplock at 809.

[3] *Jackson v. Hall*, [1980] A.C. 854, [1980] 2 W.L.R. 118 at 125.

"(1) Subordinate legislation may be used in order to construe the parent Act, but only where power is given to amend the Act by regulations or where the meaning of the Act is ambiguous. (2) Regulations made under the Act provide a parliamentary or administrative contemporanea expositio of the Act but do not decide or control its meaning: to allow this would be to substitute the rule-making authority for the judges as interpreter and would disregard the possibility that the regulation relied on was misconceived or ultra vires. (3) Regulations which are consistent with a certain interpretation of the Act tend to confirm that interpretation. (4) Where the Act provides a framework built on by contemporaneously prepared regulations, the latter may be a reliable guide to the meaning of the former. (5) The regulations are a clear guide, and may be decisive, when they are made in pursuance of a power to modify the Act, particularly if they come into operation on the same day as the Act which they modify. (6) Clear guidance may also be obtained from regulations which are to have effect as if enacted in the parent Act."[4]

However, the normal rule is that, unless Parliament has conferred an express power to do so, subordinate legislation cannot be used to interpret the empowering Act.[5]

SUBORDINATE LEGISLATION IS INTERPRETED BY USING THE SAME RULES AS APPLY TO INTERPRETATION OF ACTS

Obviously, it would be very confusing if there were separate rules for the interpretation of Acts on the one hand and subordinate legislation on the other. So far as interpretation goes, therefore, the rules are the same.[6]

TERMS USED IN BOTH THE SUBORDINATE LEGISLATION AND THE EMPOWERING ACT

It is important to bear in mind that if a term used in the subordinate legislation is also used in the empowering Act, it must bear the same meaning as in that Act.[7]

SUBORDINATE LEGISLATION NEEDS AUTHORISATION TO BE RETROSPECTIVE

Subordinate legislation, even if stated to be retrospective, will not have that effect unless the statute under which it is made authorises retrospectivity.

---

[4] *Hanlon v. Law Society*, [1981] A.C. 124 at 193-194.
[5] *Geisha Garden Ltd., Re* (1960), 30 W.W.R. 617 (B.C.S.C.).
[6] *Martin v. Saskatchewan (Beef Stabilization Appeal Committee)* (1986), 48 Sask. R. 89 (Q.B.); *Creighton v. United Oils Ltd.*, [1927] 3 D.L.R. 804 (Alta. T.D.).
[7] *R. v. Westendorp* (1982), 17 M.P.L.R. 178, unanimous decision at 184 (Alta. Q.B.), reversed without affecting this aspect (1983), 20 M.P.L.R. 267 (S.C.C.). See also *Brittain Steel Fabricators v. New Westminster Bylaw 3869, Re* (1963), 39 D.L.R. (2d) 676 (B.C.C.A.).

45

THE CANADIAN CHARTER OF RIGHTS AND FREEDOMS

THE PURPOSE OF THIS CHAPTER

This chapter, like those preceding it, is designed to introduce the reader to the basic principles of interpretation, in this case those relevant to the subject-matter of the *Charter*. The number of judicial decisions in which interpretation of the *Charter* is involved is growing rapidly, and will continue to grow. Great care should be taken, therefore, to obtain skilled legal advice when reading the *Charter*.

THE NATURE OF THE CHARTER

The *Canadian Charter of Rights and Freedoms* has an unusual and important status. It stands higher than a statute but lower than the Constitution:

"This is not a statute . . . It was designed and adopted to perform a more fundamental role than ordinary statutes . . . It is, however, not a part of the Constitution of the country. It stands, perhaps, somewhere between a statute and a constitutional instrument."[1]

THE BASIS FOR INTERPRETING THE CHARTER

It has been held by the Supreme Court of Canada that

"The *Charter* is designed and adopted to guide and serve the Canadian community for a long time. Narrow and technical interpretation, if not modulated by a sense of the unknown of the future, can stunt the growth of the law and hence the community it serves".[2]

The task of interpretation of the *Charter* is not an easy one. It requires a balancing of certainty on the one hand and on the other hand the flexibility that is needed to meet the needs that will be generated inevitably

---

[1] *Skapinker v. Law Society of Upper Canada*, [1984] 1 S.C.R. 357, unanimous decision at 366, 9 D.L.R. (4th) 161 at 168.

[2] *Skapinker*, at [S.C.R.] 366, [D.L.R.] 168.

with changing social, economic and political conditions, and with changing moral standards:

> "The fine and constant adjustment process . . . is left by a tradition of necessity to the judicial branch. Flexibility must be balanced with certainty".[3]

Accordingly, the Supreme Court of Canada has applied "the principles of interpretation developed by the courts in the constitutional process of interpreting and applying the *Constitution* itself".[4]

THE WIDE APPROACH TO INTERPRETATION OF THE CHARTER

The impact of the *Charter* on many fields is clearly shown by its impact upon advertisement controls. A city was suffering from advertisements being pasted upon its structures, an unfortunate practice affecting the environment in a large and increasing number of cities. The city council made a by-law prohibiting the placing of advertisements on its public utility services poles, traffic control devices, and other structures owned by it. The by-law was held to be invalid as breaching the very wide scope given by the court to the provisions of the *Charter* which provides that "Everyone has the following fundamental freedoms: . . . freedom of thought, belief, opinion and expression, including freedom of the . . . media of communication".[5] That provision was interpreted on the basis of "a large and liberal interpretation":[6]

> "Turning to the interpretation of the *Charter,* the Supreme Court of Canada has stated on numerous occasions that the *Charter of Rights and Freedoms* must be given a large and liberal interpretation . . .
>
> The first step requires a determination whether the [poster pasting] activity fell within the sphere of conduct protected by freedom of expression . . .
>
> Stated in very general terms, it appears from [the judicial decisions on freedom of expression] that a person is entitled to use public property in the exercise of a right of freedom of expression unless that right seriously interferes with the use of the public property by the city or other individuals . . .
>
> . . . Posters are a well recognised form of communication of ideas which has been recognised for centuries."[7]

Another example of the wide approach adopted by the courts when interpreting the *Charter* is afforded by the cases on its prohibition of discrimination. That provision states that

---

[3] *Skapinker*, at [S.C.R.] 366, [D.L.R.] 168.
[4] *Skapinker*, at [S.C.R.] 366, [D.L.R.] 168.
[5] *Canadian Charter of Rights and Freedoms*, s. 2(b)
[6] *Edmonton (City) v. Forget* (1990), 74 D.L.R. (4th) 547 at 550, 1 M.P.L.R. (2d) 214 at 217 (Alta. Q.B.).
[7] *Edmonton (City) v. Forget* (1990), 1 M.P.L.R. (2d) 214 at 218, 219, and 226-227.

"Every individual is equal before and under the law and has the right to the equal protection and equal benefit of the law without discrimination and, in particular, without discrimination based on race, national or ethnic origin, colour, religion, sex, age or mental or physical disability".[8]

Considering the proper interpretation of that provision, the courts have gone beyond the dictionary definitions of discrimination and have held that term to include anything "which has the effect of imposing burdens, obligations or disadvantages on such individual or group not imposed upon others"[9] and "whether intentional or not".[10]

It should be noted, however, that having taken that wide approach to the interpretation of "discrimination," the Supreme Court of Canada has interpreted that term as limited to "personal characteristics"[11] and to personal characteristics limited to "race, national or ethnic origin, colour, religion, sex, age or mental or physical disability" or analogous personal characteristics.[12] On that basis of interpretation, membership of a profession, occupation or trade is not a personal characteristic and therefore is not protected by the *Charter*.[13] As Dickson J. (later Dickson C.J.C.) expressed it in another case, the interpretation of the *Charter* must not be such as "to overshoot the actual purpose of the right or freedom in question."[14]

The fact that there are those two different approaches in the one decision in respect of the one provision of the *Charter* may give flexibility,[15] but does not make it any easier for the reader trying to ascertain the proper meaning of the *Charter*. Generally, however, the approach adopted to interpret the *Charter* is a wide one. To take another example, in relation to a *Charter* affirmation that "Everyone has the right to . . security of the person"[16] it was held that that right "protects both the physical and psychological integrity of the individual".[17]

---

[8] *Charter*, s. 15(1).

[9] *Andrews v. British Columbia (Law Society)*, [1989] 1 S.C.R. 143 at 174.

[10] *Cosyns v. Canada (Attorney General)* (1992), 7 O.R. (3d) 641 at 656 (Div. Ct.).

[11] *Andrews* at 174.

[12] *Andrews* at 154.

[13] *Haddock v. Ontario (Attorney General)* (1990), 70 D.L.R. (4th) 644 (Ont. H.C.).

[14] *R. v. Big M Drug Mart Ltd.*, [1985] 1 S.C.R. 295 at 344.

[15] *Skapinker v. Law Society of Upper Canada*, [1984] 1 S.C.R. 357 at 366, 9 D.L.R. (4th) 161 at 168.

[16] *Charter* s. 7.

[17] *R. v. Morgentaler*, [1988] 1 S.C.R. 30, Wilson J. at 173.

APPLYING THE PURPOSIVE APPROACH TO INTERPRETING THE CHARTER

The purposive approach[18] has been applied to the task of interpreting the *Charter*. As an example, when the validity of a provincial statute was challenged on the ground of infringing the *Charter,* it was held that

"Before addressing the issue whether the . . . Act . . . violates the guarantee of freedom of conscience and religion . . . it is necessary to determine the legislative purpose of the statute being challenged."[19]

INTERPRETATION ACTS DO NOT APPLY TO THE CHARTER

For many years it has been the practise of the federal and provincial legislatures to enact *Interpretation Acts*. These Acts prescribe the elements of an Act and rules to be applied in construing statutes. Such Acts have no application to interpretation of the *Charter*.[20]

HEADINGS

Upon the basis that "These headings in Part I appear to be integral to the *Charter* provisions"[21] it has been held that

"At a minimum the heading must be examined and some attempt made to discern the intent of the makers of the document from the language of the heading . . . It is difficult to foresee a situation where the heading will be of controlling importance. It is, on the other hand, almost as difficult to contemplate a situation where the heading could be cursorily rejected, although, in some situations . . . the heading will likely be seen as being only an announcement of the obvious".[22]

BILINGUAL VERSIONS AFFECTING INTERPRETATION OF THE CHARTER

An English version of an amending Act had the effect of creating a change to previous provisions, whereas the French version did not. The English version was held to be in breach of s. 8 of the *Charter*.[23]

---

[18] See chapter 26.

[19] *Peel (Regional Municipality) v. Great Atlantic & Pacific Co. of Canada* (1991), 4 M.P.L.R. (2d) 113, Dubin C.J.O. at 119 (Ont. C.A.).

[20] *Skapinker v. Law Society of Upper Canada*, [1984] 1 S.C.R. 357 at 370, 9 D.L.R. (4th) 161 at 171.

[21] *Skapinker*, at [S.C.R.] 370, [D.L.R.] 171.

[22] *Skapinker*, at [S.C.R.] 377, [D.L.R.] 176.

[23] *Goguen v. Shannon* (1989), 50 C.C.C. (3d) 45 (N.B.C.A.).

USE OF AMERICAN COURT DECISIONS TO INTERPRET THE CHARTER

The view has been taken that caution must be observed in relying on American judicial decisions as an aid to interpreting the *Charter*. However, American decisions have been used and found to be "valuable" if there is the necessary caution.[24]

---

[24] *R. v. Rao* (1984), 9 D.L.R. (4th) 542 (Ont. C.A.).

46

BILINGUAL ACTS AND SUBORDINATE LEGISLATION

THE NATURE OF BILINGUAL ACTS AND BILINGUAL SUBORDINATE LEGISLATION

What is termed bilingual documentation is the printing of an English version and a French version of the same Act or piece of subordinate legislation. The copy of the document that is required to be bilingual is printed with the English version in one column, and side by side with it in a second column, is the French version.

THE FORM OF A BILINGUAL ACT OR BILINGUAL SUBORDINATE LEGISLATION

The following extract shows the way in which an Act is printed in bilingual form:

"Application vulnerable persons	3. — (1) The Act applies in respect of vulnerable persons who are sixteen years of age or older	3 (1) La présente loi s'applique aux personnes vulnérables âgées de seize ans et plus.	Application, personnes vulnérables
Same, other persons	(2) — This Act also applies in respect of other persons, whether or not they are vulnerable persons, but only for the purpose of providing rights advise and other advocacy services required by the *Consent and Capacity Statute Law Amendment Act, 1992,* the *Consent to Treatment Act, 1992,* the *Mental Health Act* and the *Substitute Decisions Act, 1992.*	(2) La présente loi s'applique aussi aux autres personnes, qu'elles soient des personnes vulnérables ou non, mais seulement s'il s'agit de leur fournir les conseils en matière de droits et les autres services d'intervention exigés par la *Loi de 1992 modifiant des lois en ce qui concerne le consentement et la capacité,* la *Loi de 1992 sur le consentement au traitement,* la *Loi sur la santé mentale* et la *Loi de 1992 sur la prise de décisions au nom d'autrui.*	Idem, autres personnes

Minister	4. The member of the Executive Council who is designated by the Lieutenant Governor in Council shall administer this Act.	4. L'application de la présente loi relève du membre du Conseil des ministres que désigne le lieutenant-gouverneur en conseil.	Ministre
	COMMISSION	COMMISSION	
Advocacy Commission	5. — (1) A commission to be known as the Advocacy Commission in English and as Commission d'intervention in French is hereby established	5. — (1) Est constituée une commission appelée Commission d'intervention en français et Advocacy Commission en anglais	Commission d'intervention
Composition	(2) The Commission shall consist of a chair and twelve other members, appointed by the Lieutenant Governor in Council on the Minister's recommendation.	(2) La Commission se compose d'un président et de douze autres membres, nommés par le lieutenant-gouverneur en conseil sur la recommandation du ministre.	Composition
Method of appointment	(3) The chair and eight of the other members shall be appointed from persons recommended to the Minister by the appointments advisory committee in accordance with section 16.	(3) Le président et huit des autres membres sont nommés parmi les personnes qui ont été recommandées au ministre par le comité consultatif de nomination conformément à l'article 16.	Méthode de nomination
Same	(4) The four remaining members shall be appointed from persons who, in the opinion of the Minister, have demonstrated a commitment to the purposes of this Act."[1]	(4) Les quatre autres membres sont nommés parmi les personnes qui, de l'avis du ministre, ont montré leur engagement envers les objets de la présente loi."[1]	Idem

THE WEIGHT TO BE ACCORDED TO THE ENGLISH AND TO THE FRENCH VERSIONS

The Federal Act dealing with the bilingual system provides that "In construing an enactment, both its versions in the official languages are equally authentic."[2] The Québec legislation provides differently, stating that "In the case of discrepancy between the French text and the English text, the French text prevails."[3]

---

[1] *Advocacy Act*, S.O. 1992.
[2] *Official Languages Act*, R.S.C. 1970, c. O-2, s. 9(1).
[3] *Interpretation Act (Québec)*, s. 40.1.

THE PARLIAMENTS WHICH USE THE BILINGUAL SYSTEM

The Federal Parliament of Canada is committed to use of the bilingual system and so are some, but not all, of the Provinces. The reader who does not know whether the bilingual system is operating in a particular Province should make enquiries to ascertain the position before attempting to read an Act or subordinate legislation.

THE STATUS OF A BILINGUAL ACT OR SUBORDINATE LEGISLATION

Under the bilingual system, both versions of an Act have the same official status and express the will of Parliament.[4] Federal subordinate legislation, and provincial subordinate legislation,[5] also operate on the basis that the two versions have official status.

EACH VERSION, WHETHER ENGLISH OR FRENCH, IS PART OF THE CONTEXT IN WHICH THE OTHER VERSION IS TO BE READ

It is not enough to read either the English version or the French version in the expectation of understanding the bilingual Act or the bilingual subordinate legislation: while it is an established principle that a provision must be read in its context,[6] the context under the bilingual system includes the other version,[7] and therefore both must be read to gain a proper understanding of the particular document being studied.

CONFLICTING VERSIONS — THE IMPORTANCE OF GRAMMAR

If either the English or the French version is grammatically correct and the other is not, the grammatically correct version should be adopted.[8]

---

[4] *Québec (Attorney General) v. Blaikie*, [1979] 2 S.C.R. 1016; *Manitoba v. Forest*, [1979] 2 S.C.R. 1032.

[5] *Québec (Attorney General) v. Blaikie*, [1981] 1 S.C.R. 312.

[6] See chapter 29.

[7] *Aeric Inc. v. Canada Post Corp.* (1985), 16 D.L.R. (4th) 686 at 707 (Fed. C.A.); *Blouin c. Dumoulin*, [1958] Qué. Q.B. 581 (C.A.).

[8] *Composers, Authors and Publishers Assoc. of Canada v. Western Fair Assoc.*, [1951] S.C.R. 596.

CONFLICTING VERSIONS — THE ADVANTAGE OF CLARITY

If one of the versions (French or English) is ambiguous and the other version is not, the unambiguous version should be adopted.[9] Similarly, if one of the versions is clearer than the other, the clearer version should be used.[10]

CONFLICTING VERSIONS — OBJECTIONABLE AND UNOBJECTIONABLE PROVISIONS

It may happen that the relevant provision in the French or the English version is unobjectionable, but the same provision in the other is in an objectionable form. In such a situation "that which is free from objection according to the recognised canons of construction should be adopted".[11]

CONFLICTING VERSIONS — BRINGING THE TWO INTO ACCORD

It may happen that one of the two versions has words which could be given two different meanings. If that occurs, and the other version only has one meaning, the construction to be adopted is that which brings the two versions into accord.[12]

CONFLICTING VERSIONS — CHOOSING THE WIDER RATHER THAN THE NARROWER VERSION

Unfortunately, the two versions are not necessarily correct translations. Both may be clear to the reader, but the wording may vary from one to the other. Even the name of a committee may appear differently in the two versions. For example, what was referred to in the English version of an Act as the "appointments *advisory* committee" appears in the French version as "le comité *consultatif* de nomination" which, being translated into English reads "the consultative nomination committee".[13] There is an important difference between an "advisory" committee on the one hand and a "consultative" committee on the other hand.

---

[9] *Cardinal v. R.* (1979), 97 D.L.R. (3d) 402 at 405 and 406.

[10] *Greene v. D.R. Sutherland Ltd.* (1982), 40 N.B.R. (2d) 27 (Q.B.).

[11] *Food Machinery Corp. v. Registrar of Trade Marks,* [1946] 2 D.L.R. 258, Thorson P. at 263 (Ex. Ct.). See also *R. v. O'Donnel,* [1979] 1 W.W.R. 385, Bull J.A. at 389, *Cardinal v. R.* (1979), 97 D.L.R. (3d) 402.

[12] *Canada (Deputy Minister of National Revenue) v. Film Technique Ltd.,* [1973] F.C. 75 (T.D.).

[13] *Advocacy Act,* S.O. 1992, s. 5(3).

In another instance, both versions were clear in their wording, but the French version used the word "could" and the English version the word "would". The court interpreting the provision preferred the wider term "could".[14]

CONFLICTING VERSIONS — THE USEFUL VERSION WILL BE PREFERRED TO ONE LACKING IN UTILITY

If one version of an Act is so worded that the Act makes no change to the existing law, while the other version makes a change, the version making the change is to be preferred.[15]

THE PURPOSIVE APPROACH

What is known as the purposive approach to interpretation requires the reader to consider what is the purpose or intention of the Parliament enacting the statute or of the person or body making the subordinate legislation, then to seek an interpretation which accords with that purpose or intention.[16] That purposive approach has been adopted as a means of resolving upon a meaning which will be equally acceptable for the English and French versions.[17]

PENAL ACTS

If the English and French versions of a penal Act differ, that version most favourable to the accused will be adopted.[18] This accords with the interpretative principle discussed in chapter 39. However, it should be noted that a different court used the purposive approach to obtain an interpretation which sustained the higher penalty prescribed in one version and not in the other.[19]

THE DIFFICULTIES CREATED BY THE BILINGUAL SYSTEM

It must be obvious that the bilingual system cannot avoid breeding problems and difficulties. Divergences between the English and the French

---

[14] *R. v. Collins*, [1987] 1 S.C.R. 265.
[15] *Klippert v. R.*, [1967] S.C.R. 822.
[16] See chapter 26.
[17] *Black and Decker Manufacturing Co. v. R.*, [1975] 1 S.C.R. 411, Dickson J. (later Dickson C.J.C.) at 420; *R. v. Popovic*, [1976] 2 S.C.R. 308; *R. v. Cie Immobilière BCN Ltée*, [1979] 1 S.C.R. 865.
[18] *R. v. Cohen* (1984), 15 C.C.C. (3d) 231 (Qué. C.A.).
[19] *R. v. Voisine* (1984), 57 N.B.R. (2d) 38 (Q.B.).

versions have been said to be "frequent, creating problems of interpretation."[20] If the drafting of an Act or an instrument of subordinate legislation is difficult and gives rise to problems (as it does in many instances), how much greater is the risk of such problems arising when the provision has to appear simultaneously in two different languages? Even if a word in one language generally corresponds with the word used in the other language, there are likely to be subtle differences which can be seized upon by litigants. Côté lists other difficulties, saying "for example, how can terms from civil law be translated into English when they have no common law equivalent: e.g. the pledge (nantissement) and the hypothec? . . . the same problem arises translating common law terms into French . . . in addition there are the standard problems common to all translation."[21]

---

[20] Côté, P-E, *The Interpretation of Legislation in Canada* (Les Éditions Yvon Blais Inc., Cowansville, 1984) p. 252.
[21] Côté, p. 252.

47

NOW READ ON

HIGHLIGHTS AND HISTORY

The Act of Parliament has a history extending back over more than 700 years. As should only be expected, that history has its highlights and its humour. The reader who finds pleasure in the curiosities of the law can gain pleasure from reading such long titles as that of

> "An Act to repeal the Act of Parliament of Ireland, of the Sixth Year of Anne, Chapter Eleven, for explaining and amending the several Acts against Tories, Robbers, and Raparees",[1]

or

> "An Act for Improving the Dublin Police",[2]

or from the Act which provided for the appointment of a local government officer to be known as a "garbler". That interesting Act provided that a garbler

> "at the request of any person or persons owner or owners of any spices drugs or other wares of merchandise garbleable and not otherwise shall garble the same".[3]

These and many other curiosities of the law are set out in interesting fashion in Sir Edward Megarry's book, *Miscellany-at-Law.*

FURTHER READING ON THE RULES FOR FINDING THE MEANING OF ACTS OF PARLIAMENT

The object of the present book has been to set out as simply as possible the basic rules that the courts have laid down for the reading of Acts of Parliament. The footnotes in this book have given references to the decisions of the courts in which the reader can find the judges' statements of the rules set out in the text of the book. Those references have been designed to help the reader who wants to take the study of these rules fur-

---

[1] *The British Act* 28 & 29 Vict c. 33, quoted in Megarry, *Miscellany-at-Law* (3rd imp., Stevens & Sons, 1958), p. 339.
[2] Referred to in Megarry, p. 365.
the intricacies of what is known to the lawyer as statutory interpretation.
[3] 6 Anne c. 68, 3, quoted in Megarry, p. 337.

ther, but it has not been the intention to provide a full scale textbook on
The reader who desires to pursue those intricacies in their full technical
detail should turn to the following books:

CANADIAN TEXTBOOKS

Côté, P-E, *The Interpretation of Legislation in Canada* (Les Éditions Yvon
Blais Inc., Cowansville, 1984)
Dreidger, Professor EA, *Construction of Statutes* (Butterworths, Toronto,
1983).

ENGLISH TEXTBOOKS

Craies on Statute Law (7th ed., Sweet & Maxwell, 1971).
Maxwell, *The Interpretation of Statutes* (N.M. Tripathi Private Ltd., Bombay, 12th ed., Langan P. St. J., 1976).
Odgers, *The Construction of Deeds and Statutes* (5th ed., Sweet & Maxwell, 1967).

GLOSSARY

Act: a law which has been made by Parliament—an Act of Parliament

Amending Act: an Act passed by Parliament to alter another existing Act or to alter an enactment.

Assent: the approval given to an Act of Parliament by the reigning King or queen or the Sovereign's representative.

Bill: the draft of a proposed Act of Parliament (the term "Bill" is used to describe the draft before Parliament has passed it as an Act).

Code: a law passed by Parliament with the intention of giving a comprehensive coverage of the law on a particular subject matter and replacing the previous law relating to that subject matter.

Consolidating Act: an Act passed to bring into one Act of Parliament an original Act together with all the amendments that have been made to the original Act by various amending Acts of Parliament, or an Act passed to bring into one Act of Parliament provisions which have previously been scattered in various Acts which it repeals.

Delegated legislation: law which is made by some person or body other than the Parliament and acting under the authority of an Act of Parliament.

Division: if an Act of Parliament is divided into parts those parts which may themselves be subdivided into divisions each of which is likely to contain a number of sections.

Enactment: an Act

Expropriation : the process by which a landowner's land is taken by a government (whether Federal, Provincial, Territorial, or local government) or by some other statutory authority.

Hansard: the publication in which are recorded the speeches made in Parliament.

Heading: words appearing at the top of a part or division of an Act of Parliament, they approximate to the chapter headings in a book.

Legislation: law made by a body which has power to make law—the term is often used to refer to the Acts of Parliament, but it can also be used to refer to law made by persons or bodies whose law-making powers are given to them by Act of Parliament.

Long title: if an Act of Parliament has two titles, the longer of those two is known as the long title. It give some indication of the scope of the Act. See also Short Title in this glossary

Marginal note: a note set in the margin of the Act, it sets out (not always accurately) an indication of the matters dealt with in the section or subsection.

Paragraph: a portion of a subsection.

Part: for an Act of Parliament the part corresponds to the chapter of a book.

Precedent: a decision by the Supreme Court or by some other court of the same status or superior to it.

Pt: an abbreviation for "part".

s.: an abbreviation for "section".

Schedule: a provision of an Act of Parliament appearing at the end of the Act, it is most commonly used to prescribe a form that is to be used in administering the Act or to prescribe rules for carrying some provision of the Act into effect. It corresponds to an appendix in a book.

Section: every Act of Parliament is divided into sections which are numbered consecutively and which approximate to the verses of a book of the Bible.

Short title: the name of the particular Act of Parliament.

Sidenote: another name for marginal note.

ss: an abbreviation for "sections".

Statute: another name for an Act of Parliament.

Subordinate legislation: a law which is made by some person or body other than the Parliament and acting under the authority of an Act of Parliament.

Subsection: a section may itself be subdivided into provisions which are known as "subsections" and which are themselves numbered numerically within the section.

Title: each Act of Parliament may have two titles. See **Long title** and **Short title** in this glossary.

INDEX

A

Absurdity
avoidance 89-92

Act of Parliament
ambiguous 9, 25, 31, 39, 42, 88-89,
 154, 160-161
amending Act 153
analysis 45-47
area in which operates 177-179
bilingual 195-200
business community initiating 3
cabinet initiating 3
codes 153-154
commencement date 6-7, 33-36
commission initiating 3-4
community pressure altering 6
community pressure initiating 3
conflicting provisions 51
consideration by Parliament 5-6
contents, statement of 45-47
continues in force indefinitely 6, 36
Crown affected by 181-182
date on 33
declaratory Act 154
definitions 63-69
decisions 53-54
drafting 4-5
elements of 15
enabling Act 154-155
enacting words 27
explanatory Act 155
extraterritorial operation 177-179
first Act 1
fraud inducing enactment,
 irrelevant 7
government department initiating 4
headings 55-58
implied repeal 150-151
judicial interpretation 68
local government body initiating 3
long title 23-25
misprint 9
mistake in 9, 125-130
nature 1
number increasing 9
number of Act 19-21
omissions from 121-124
origin 2-3
paragraphs 49-51
parts 53-54
penal Act 160-161
political party initiating 3
preamble 37-39
provisos 75-76
punctuation 77-78
purposes sections 41-43
purposive approach to
 interpretation 97-104, 175,
 192, 199
read together with other Act 68-69
recent Act prevails over older
 Act 150-151
recitals 37-39
referential 11-13
regnal year 17
remedial Act 155-156
repeal, implied 150-151
revised Acts 156-157
royal assent 33
schedules 71-74
sections 49-51
short title 29-32
subsections 49-51
table of contents 45-47
tax Act 161-162
validating Act 158

Amending Act
alteration of words from those in
 principal Act 153
difficulties in finding 153
"principal Act", meaning 153

Analysis
effect 47
names, alternative 45
nature 45-46
use 47

Arrest
ambiguous provision 161
narrow interpretation of power 161

B

Bilingual Acts
both languages to be considered 197

Bilingual Acts — *continued*
clarity, importance 198
conflicting versions 197-199
difficulties 199-200
English version, weight 196
form 195-196
French version superior in
    Quebec 196
grammar important 197
nature 195
Parliaments which use 197
penal Act 199
purposive approach 199
subordinate legislation 197
useful version preferred 199

Bill
amendment 5-6
committee, parliamentary,
    considering 4
consideration 4-6
history of in Parliament
    irrelevant 107
managers, parliamentary,
    considering 6
meaning 5
Parliament considering 5-6
Private Member's Bill 3, 100
readings 5
rejection 5

Bylaws — *see* **Subordinate legislation**

C

**Canadian Charter of Rights and
    Freedoms**
American judicial decisions used to
    interpret 193
bilingual, effect 192
headings 192
interpretation Acts inapplicable 192
interpretation, basis 189-190
interpretation, wide 190-191
nature 189
purposive approach 192
wide interpretation 190-191

Charter of Rights and Freedoms — *see*
    **Canadian Charter of Rights and
    Freedoms**

Class rule
applicability 134-135

general word essential 133
general word must follow after class
    of specific words 133-134
nature 131-132
specific words, class of, must
    precede general word 133-134
specific words, meaning of not
    ascertainable by 135
specific words, two minimum 134

Code
ambiguous 154
nature 153-154
prior Acts not used to interpret 154
uncertainty in, effect 154

Commencement date
commences at beginning of day on
    which comes into force 33
date on Act 33
date to be proclaimed 35
deferred commencement 34-35
deferred commencement, prosecution
    during invalid 35
different dates for different
    provisions 34
midnight commencement 34
retrospective 36, 154
revision not changing 36, 157
royal assent day, commencement
    before or after 34-35
royal assent day, commencement
    on 34

Common law, Act affecting
literal interpretation 167
narrow interpretation 166-167
privacy, right to 166
self-incrimination 167

Consolidating Act
caution needed in interpreting 116
difficulties 116

Context
whole of Act to be consid-
    ered 98-99, 113-116

Crown
Act binding on 181-182
extent of 182
meaning 181

D

Declaratory Act
example of 154
nature 154
retrospective 154

Definitions
Acts read together 68
context, contrary, affecting 66
definitions in other Acts 68-69
drafting difficult 63
effect 65-66
"includes" 66-68
"means" 66-68
"means and includes" 68
need for 63-64
repetition avoided by 64
section containing 64-65
section containing, dangers 64-65
use of 63-64

Delegated legislation — *see* **Subordinate legislation**

Dictionaries
Black's Law Dictionary 81
Canadian Legal Dictionary 81
judicial dictionaries 68-69
Oxford English Dictionary 81
phrase, meanings of individual
words not to be used 81
use 68-69
Webster's Dictionary 81

Divisions of Act
effect 54
form 53-54
interpretation of Act assisted by 54

Drafting
Act of Parliament 4-5
criticised 9-11, 155
definitions 63
difficulties 4-5, 63
mistake 9
oversight 9
pressures on 9
referential 11-13
remedial Act 155
subordinate legislation 4

E

Ejusdem generis — *see* **Class rule**

Enabling Act
example of 154
literal interpretation, when 154-155
purpose of 154
strict interpretation, when 154

Enacting words
effect 27
form 27

Environmental Controls
balancing exercise 98
concern for protection of
environment relevant 98

Explanatory statements
departmental 111-112
governmental leaflet 112
inadmissible 111-112
mischief rule may be assisted by 112

Express inclusions
caution in use of 142-143
definitions, use of rule in relation
to 142
effect 141

Expressio unius exclusio est — *see*
Express Inclusions

Expropriation Act
narrow interpretation 164
procedural Act 165-166
purposive approach 165

Extrinsic materials
board of inquiry report 110
circumstances, surrounding,
relevant 109
drafter's report 111
law reform commission
report 109-110
parliamentary committee report 111
royal commission report 110
use 109-110

F

Foreigners
extraterritorial, Act applying to 179

Forms
schedule containing, use 74

G

General and specific provisions
special provisions prevail over
general ones 51, 83, 149-150

Golden rule 91

Grammatical rule — *see* **Plain
measuring rule**

H

Hansard
aid to interpretation 107
common law use limited 105-106
common law use limited,
why 106-107
mischief rule application assisted
by 105
nature 105-108

Headings
ambiguity essential for interpretation
by 57-58
Canadian Charter of Rights and
Freedoms 192
effect 57
form 55
interpretation, Act, assisted by 56-57
nature 55
only one section under 58
plain meaning not to be altered
by 57
preamble effect of 57
use of 55-56

I

Implied terms 123-124

"Includes"
effect 66-68

Injustice
avoidance 89-92
plain meaning rule not affected
by 90
warning as to interpretation to
avoid 91-92

J

Judicial decisions
American 193
common law determined by 183
existing decision 184
inferior court, decision
irrelevant 183
legal terms, meaning determined
by 185
phrases, meaning determined by 183
re-enacted after 184-185
superior court decision relevant 183
words, meaning determined by 183

Judicial dictionaries
useful 69

L

Legislation
Act — *see* **Act of Parliament**
bylaws — *see* **Subordinate legislation**
delegated legislation — *see*
Subordinate legislation
impact on every walk of life iii
regulations — *see* **Subordinate
legislation**

Long title
ambiguity resolved by 25
clear words not to be altered
by 23-25
form 23
interpretation, Act, assisted by 24-25
meaning of Act ascertainable
from 23
part of Act, whether 24
plain meaning rule not affected
by 25
preamble compared 38
scope of Act wider than long title,
effect 24
use to interpret Act 24-25

Literal rule — *see* **Plain meaning rule**

M

Marginal notes
alternative system 61
dangers to use of 60
form 59-60
interpretation Act, assisted by,
whether 60-61

Marginal notes — *continued*
misleading 60
nature 59
Parliament not altering 60
part of Act 59
value 61-62

Meaning of particular words and phrases
Act 203
amending Act 203
assent 203
bill 203
building 63, 121
changed meaning 81
circumstances changed since Act
    enacted 80-81
code 203
consolidating Act 203
constant meaning 79-80
Crown 181
date at which Act enacted, meaning
    then used 80-81
delegated legislation 203
dictionary definitions 68-69, 81
different meanings of same word 80,
    98
difficulty 79-81
division (of Act) 203
enactment 203
expropriation 203
forthwith 143
Hansard 203
heading 203
includes 66-68
intention 99-100, 103
judicial dictionaries 68-69
legal terms 185
legislation 203
long title 205
marginal note 204
means 66-68
means and includes 68
ordinary meaning 80
or 101
orphan 63
paragraph (of an Act) 204
part (of an Act) 204
phrase, meaning difference to
    meaning of individual
    words 81
precedent 204
principal Act 153
s. 204

schedule 204
sections 204
short title 204
side note 204
ss. 204
statute 204
subordinate legislation 204
technical terms 80-82
title 204

"Means"
effect 66-68

"Means and includes"
effect 68

Mischief rule
applying the rule 93, 96
ascertaining the mischief or
    defect 95
board of inquiry assisting 110
commission reports assisting 110
explanatory statement, departmental,
    assisting 112
Hansard assisting 105
law reform commission report
    assisting 109-110
nature 93-94
plain meaning rule not affected
    by 96
questions to be asked when using 93
reason for remedy 95
remedy adapted by Parliament 95
state of law before Act passed 93-94
use 93, 96, 110

Misprints 128-129

Mistakes
common causes of 125
correction by court 129-130
drafter's oversight 127-128
factual, effect 125-126
law, effect 126-127
misprints 128-129
occurrence 9, 125-130
oversight, drafter 127-128
policy, mistake, effect 126

N

Noscitur a sociis — *see* **Similar meaning
words**

O

Omissions from Act
clerical 122
court cannot remedy 121-122
implied terms 122-125
intention of Act relevant 123

Ordinary meaning rule — *see* **Plain meaning rule**

P

Paragraphs
conflict between 50-51
form 50
interpretation, Act, assisted by 50
part of Act 50

Parliament
backbenchers 3
managers 6
members 3

Parts of Act
effect 54
form 53-54
interpretation, Act, assisted by 54

Penal Act
ambiguous 160-161
bilingual 199
narrow interpretation 59
retrospective 172
whole Act to be read 160

Plain meaning rule
absurdity, effect 86, 88
difficulties irrelevant 85
effect 85-86
grammatical rule another name for 86
headings not to alter 57
importance 87
inconsistency with other provisions of Act, effect 55
injustice not precluding 90
literal rule another name for 86
long title not to alter 24
mischief rule not to alter 96
opinion, reader's, not to affect 86
ordinary meaning rule other name for 86
plain words necessary for rule to apply 87
preamble not to alter 38-39

punctuation not to alter 38-39
purposive approach overriding 99, 101
unjust, effect 86
unreasonable, effect 85-86
vested rights 163-164

Power conferred by two sections
conditions fettering one, unfettered power prevails 51

Preamble
ambiguity resolved by 39
form 37-38
long title compared 38
name 37
nature 37
part of Act 38
plain meaning not affected by 38
schedule conflicting 73, 74
subordinate legislation 38

Private Member's Bill
nature 3
rarity 3, 100

Procedural Act
narrow interpretation 174

Proviso
effect 75-76
form 75
nature 75
read in light of its section 75
strict interpretation 75-76
unnecessary 76

Punctuation
early Acts lack 77
interpretation, Act, assisted by 77-78
plain meaning rule not to be altered by 77-78
use of 77-78

Purposes sections
ambiguity resolved by 42
difficulties 42-43
finding the purposes section 92
form 41
interpretation by use of 41
part of Act 41
place within Act 42
purposive approach — *see also* **Purposive approach**
traps to use of 42-43
use to interpret Act 41

Purposive approach to interpretation
bilingual 199
Canadian Charter of Rights and Freedoms 192
caution to be adopted in using 103-104
dangers 104
difficulty 100, 103-104
expropriation Act affected by 165
importance 97, 101
intention, difficulty to ascertaining 98
"intention", meaning 99-100
intention to be effectuated 97-99
necessary implication 102-103
object of Act 97
plain meaning rule overriding 100-101, 103-104
plain meaning rule overridden by 99, 101
purposes section — *see* **Purposes section**
subject matter of Act relevant 98
unambiguous provision, plain meaning rule applied 100
unavailable, when 100-102
unlikely that Members would be aware of complexities 100
usefulness disputed 101-102
whole Act to be considered 98-99

R

Regulations — *see* **Subordinate legislation**

Repeal of Act
implied 150-151

Remedial Act
drafting inept, effect 155
exclusive remedy 156
purpose of 155
wide interpretation 155

Reports
board of inquiry 110
drafter's report 111
law reform commission report 108-109
miscellaneous reports 111
parliamentary committee report 111
royal commission 110

Retroactive — *see* **Retrospective**

Retrospective
clear words needed 171
declaratory Act 154, 174
evidentiary provision 174
intention 171
penal provision 172-173
power to enact 36, 170
presumption against 170
procedural provision 174
subordinate legislation 188
validating Act 158

Revised Act
altering existing law, presumption against 156
amendments made by 36, 157
commencement date 157
consolidation by 156
dangers 157
object 156
words changed, irrelevant 157

Rights and freedoms — *see* **Canadian Charter of Rights and Freedoms**

Rules of interpretation
absurdity, avoidance 89-92
advantages from use of iv
arrest, Act providing for 161
change imposed 161-162
class rule 131-135
ejusdem generis rule 131-135
error caused by failure to use iii
express inclusions 141-143
expressio unius exclusio alterius est 141-143
expropriation Act 164
extrinsic materials 109-112
general, specific, provisions conflicting 51, 183, 149-151
golden rule 93-96
inconsistent Acts 149-151
injustice, avoidance 89-92
mischief rule 93-96
narrow interpretation 159-167
need for iii, 9, 13
noscitur a sosiis rule 137-139
omissions from Act 121-124
other Acts used to interpret 145, 148
pecuniary obligation imposed 163
penal Act 159-161
plain meaning rule 24, 38-39, 57, 77-78, 85-87, 90, 96, 99, 101, 172

Rules of interpretation — *continued*
procedural Act 165
purposive approach to interpretation
of 97-104, 165, 192, 199
recent Act prevails over older
Act 150-151
recitals 37-39
referential Act 11-13
retrospective Act 36, 154
rewording of Act not
interpretation 119
sense to be made if possible 117-118
similar meaning words 137-139
specific, general, rules
conflicting 51, 83, 149-151
surplussage avoided 117-118
tax imposed 161-162
use of rules, importance iii
validating Act 158
vested rights affected 163-164
words not to be discarded 117-118
whole Act to be considered 98-99,
113-116
words of similar meaning 137-139

S

Schedules
conflict with preamble 73-74
conflict with section 73
forms 72-74
nature 71-73
part of Act, whether 73
preamble conflicting with 73-74
section conflicting with 73-74
status 73

Sections
conflict between 50-51
form 49
interpretation, Act, assisted by 50
part of Act 50
schedule conflicting 73
whole Act to be considered 114-116
whole section to be con-
sidered 113-114

Short Title
ambiguity resolved by 31
interpretation, Act, assisted by 29-32
legal effect 29-32
long title incompatible with 32
nature 29
place where short title is found 29

use to interpret Act 29-32

Sidenotes — *see* **Marginal notes**

Similar meaning words
associated with each other 137-138
caution in use of rule 138-139
nature of rule 137

Special and general provisions
special provision prevails over
general provision 51

Statute — *see* **Act of Parliament**

Subordinate legislation
bilingual 197
extraterritorial operation 178
interpretation to keep within
power 187
maze iv
preamble 38
retrospective 188
rules of interpretation applicable 188
statute not interpreted by 187
words used in empowering Act 188

Subsections
conflict between 50-51
form 49
interpretation, Act, assisted by 50
part of Act 50

T

Table of contents — *see* **Analysis**

Tax Act
exemption, wide interpretation
against taxpayer 162
narrow interpretation 161-162

U

Unreasonableness
plain meaning not affected by 85

V

Validity Act
example of 158
power to enact 158
purpose of 158
retrospective 158

Vested rights
  Act affecting 163-164, 172
  narrow interpetation of Act
      affecting 163-164
  onus 163
  plain meaning rule applied 163-164,
      172
  power to affect 172

W

Words and phrases — *see* **Meaning of
  particular words and phrases**